Sound and Sign

Childhood Deafness and Mental Health

Sound and Sign

Childhood Deafness and Mental Health

Hilde S. Schlesinger and
Kathryn P. Meadow

University of California Press
BERKELEY · LOS ANGELES · LONDON

University of California Press
Berkeley and Los Angeles, California
University of California Press, Ltd.
London, England

ISBN: 0–520–02137–1
Library of Congress Catalog Card Number: 77–174455
Printed in the United States of America

5 6 7 8 9 0

Contents

Tables

Figures

Preface

The research and clinical work described in the following pages has been a true adventure, made possible by innumerable individuals who have shared the vicissitudes—both the joys and the disappointments—of our work over the past five years.

The clinical work had a serendipitous beginning when one of us (H.S.S.) signed a casual but soothing "H-I" to a disturbed deaf patient in a hospital psychiatric ward. Within a week it seemed the entire deaf community knew of the psychiatrist who had some proficiency in manual communication. The requests for help that came streaming in illustrated both the absence of mental health services and the need that existed for them in the deaf community. With the help of a small planning grant from the Vocational Rehabilitation Administration a very modest clinical program and planning operation began at the Langley Porter Neuropsychiatric Institute in San Francisco.

Meanwhile, across the bay in Berkeley at the California School for the Deaf, the other member of our team (K.P.M.) was engaged in sociological research designed to illuminate the relation between family patterns and social-intellectual-linguistic development in deaf children. A fortuitous meeting of psychiatrist and sociologist revealed we shared a number of "hypotheses" about the social and emotional consequences of deafness, derived independently from our differing disciplines and our clinical/research interviews and observations. From this meeting grew a rewarding collaboration resulting in the present volume.

We have been truly fortunate in working with a talented, creative, and dedicated group of people. All of the contributors to this book have worked with us as members of the project staff. The specific nature of their contributions is acknowledged in footnotes to the various chapters. Responsibility for Chapters 2, 3, 4, 8, and 9 was undertaken by H.S.S. A major part of both the data analysis and the writing of Chapter 8 was completed by two members of the clinical staff, Winifred DeVos, A.C.S.W., and Holly Elliott, M.S. Responsibility for Chapters 5, 6, and 7 was undertaken by K.P.M. with assistance in the collection and analysis of data from H.S.S. and from Constance B. Holstein, Ph.D., for Chapter 5. Carole Geballe was particularly helpful in the collection and analysis of data presented in Chapter 4. Arline Cottrell and Katherine A. Leland, M.A., contributed to the collection and analysis of data presented in Chapters 4, 5, and 6.

In addition, Kerry Hemmeter, Carolyn Huff, Elvi Lannon, and Paula Mathieson have assisted in preparing the many revisions of the manuscript. David and Christine Day helped with the data analysis, and the editorial skills of Dr. Ellen Y. Siegelman greatly improved the format. Sabine Jaspe prepared the index. Adrienne Morgan was the technical illustrator. We acknowledge with thanks the substantive suggestions for revision of earlier versions of the manuscript by the following persons: Dr. Ursula Bellugi, Dr. Lloyd Meadow, Dr. Peter F. Ostwald, Dr. William C. Stokoe, Jr., Mr. Peyton Todd, and Dr. McCay Vernon.

Erik Erikson kindly consented to the use of the material in Figure 1. Permission for reproduction of Figure 2 was granted by The Macmillan Company. The support of Grant Barnes and Susan Peters of the University of California Press during the final stages of manuscript preparation was much appreciated.

The initiation of mental health services for the deaf, with associated research, can be traced almost directly to a number of persons associated with Social and Rehabilitation Services of the Department of Health, Education and Welfare: the creative foresight of the late Miss Mary Switzer, then Commissioner of the Vocational Rehabilitation Administration; Dr. L. Deno Reed, Executive Secretary of the Sensory Disabilities Research Study Section; Dr. Boyce Williams, Chief, Communications Disorders Branch; Mr. Dale Williamson, Social and Rehabilitation Service, Region IX; and the late Mrs. Beatrice Lamb, Vocational Rehabilitation Counselor for the Deaf, San Francisco Department of Vocational Rehabilitation. We would like to acknowledge Mr. John Darby, Executive Director of the San Francisco Bay Area Hearing Society, who acted as catalyst in the preliminary planning stages. We appreciate the help of many persons at the Langley Porter Neuropsychiatric Institute, particularly Dr. Alexander Simon, Medical Director; Dr. Leon J. Epstein, Associate Medical Director; and Dr. S. A. Szurek, Director of Children's Service. The support of the State of California Department of Mental Hygiene has also been a necessary and welcome ingredient of our work. Our sometime mentors and informal consultants loom large in the formulation of many of the ideas expressed in these pages. They are Dr. Irving N. Berlin, Dr. John A. Clausen, and Dr. Portia Bell Hume. We are grateful to the members of the Bay Area deaf community for the enthusiasm with which they have supported our efforts. The deaf children and their parents who participated in the research have been more than cooperative, as have teachers and administrators in every school program we have approached.

Our major financial support was from the Social and Rehabilitation Service (Grants RD-2408 and 14-P-55270/9-03). We are grateful for this support and for the financial assistance provided by Maternal and Child Health and Crippled Children's Services (HEW) Grant No. H-331, The San Francisco Foundation, The Rosenberg Foundation, the Langley Porter Neuropsychiatric Institute (General Research Support Grants), National Institute of Mental Health Grant No. MH 8659-07 to the Langley Porter Neuropsychiatric Institute's Children's Service, and the University of California, San Francisco (Research Evaluation and Allocation Committee).

To these many friends and colleagues, agencies, and enabling institutions, we wish to say, many thanks.

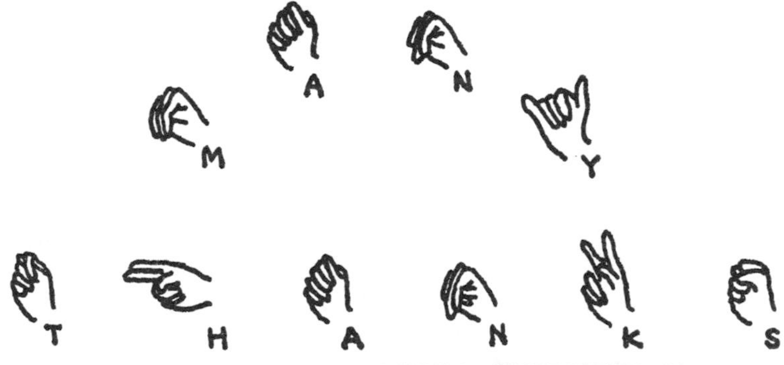

HILDE S. SCHLESINGER, M.D.
KATHRYN P. MEADOW, PH.D.

1

Introduction

Profound childhood deafness is more than a medical diagnosis: it is a cultural phenomenon in which social, emotional, linguistic, and intellectual patterns and problems are inextricably bound together. The diagnosis immediately plunges parents and children into a potential conflict between the exclusive use of muffled or non-existent *sounds* and the exclusive or auxiliary use of visual gestural *signs*. From our vantage point, parents and professionals must consider the optimal growth patterns of the deaf infant from diagnosis to adulthood if they are to provide him with the key ingredient in the developmental process: communication with significant others. For the infant who is profoundly deaf from birth or shortly thereafter, the development of meaningful and joyful communication usually does not evolve naturally and without conflict as it does for most hearing infants. If the deaf child's parents have normal hearing they may find his handicap difficult to accept. Their efforts to mold their child in their own image may precipitate a paralysis of negativism that focuses on the very skills the parents are most anxious to encourage: speech, lipreading, and (native) language development. The parents themselves may become enmeshed in a conflict between educational philosophies that often seems impossible to resolve. Their anxieties are passed on to the child in spite of their best attempts at avoiding this danger.

With modern advances in audiology and hearing aids, most if not all deaf children can utilize some sounds from their environment. Some can be trained to utilize their residual hearing even to help them comprehend speech, depending on the pattern and severity of their hearing loss. In spite of these modern innovations, however, cognitive retardation and psychological maladaptation remain frequent among deaf children and adults. The core of these difficulties may lie in the absence of gratifying reciprocal communication within the family during the deaf child's early years. As the deaf child grows and develops, problems related to this diminution of communication show a cumulative increase. Many authors have pointed out that deaf people possess certain cognitive lags and a psychological uniqueness. Studies of educational achievement almost universally indicate a three- to four-year lag: the average deaf person reads at fifth grade level or below; only 12 percent are said to achieve true linguistic competence; only 4 percent are proficient speechreaders or speakers (Furth, 1966). A lack of meaningful language input in the early years may contribute to the low school achievement of deaf students, if we accept the theory of a "critical period" for language learning and cognitive development (McNeill, 1966).

Psychologically, the most frequently stated generalization about deaf individuals is that they seem to reflect a high degree of "emotional immaturity." Levine (1956) describes this complex in terms of egocentricity, easy irritability, impulsiveness, and suggestibility. Myklebust (1960) finds the deaf are immature in "caring for others." Altshuler (1964) characterizes the deaf as showing egocentricity, a lack of empathy, gross coercive dependency, impulsivity, and an absence of thoughtful introspection. The consistency of these observations by independent investigators working with populations of varying ages and backgrounds, both normal and maladjusted, lends added credence to their validity.

Given this consensus, understanding the source of those characteristics becomes even more important. That is, does the absence of early auditory stimulation, feedback, and communication in itself create a propensity toward a particular adaptive pattern? Or, alternatively, does early profound deafness elicit particular responses from parents, teachers, siblings, and peers that contribute to developmental problems leading to the patterns described above? These are questions that are difficult to resolve in an either/or way, since the concomitants of organic deafness and the social expectations it arouses in others are intertwined from the very beginning. Rather than belaboring the nature/nurture controversy, it is more fruitful to look instead at the entire life cycle, examining instances of optimal and minimal adjustment and seeking out the antecedents, correlates, and consequences of these patterns. Another related strategy is to look at the early environment of the deaf child to see how it can be made more conducive to learning. Recent evidence from developmental psychologists stresses the importance of the first few years of life for cognitive development. (For excellent summaries of theory and research on early environmental enrichment see Caldwell, 1967, and Hunt, 1964.)

Such a focus on the developmental approach and eventually on environmental enrichment could, we believe, lead to advances in the area that Rainer and his colleagues (1963) consider the "most urgent" for the average deaf person: preventive mental health planning. This is defined by Caplan (1964:68) as the identification of the "commonly occurring hazardous circumstances in a community (and their modification) . . . so that their impact on the population is less severe." This means that "people will have a chance to find healthy . . . means of handling" the environmental stress to which they are exposed.

Lack of professional support at the time of diagnosis, parental reaction to the diagnosis, parental distortion of normal childrearing practices, are only part of the stress inherent in the development of the deaf child. However, the main area of stress remains the use or non-use of sign language in any of its several versions.

Sign language is the hallmark of the adult deaf community. In a reaction against the stigma placed upon their language, many deaf adults depreciate the value or even the usefulness of hearing aids, speech, or lipreading skills.

In addition to the American Sign Language, there are a number of features that reflect the cohesiveness of large numbers of deaf adults and enable us to think in terms of a "deaf community."

The group definition is strengthened with the knowledge that deaf persons are characterized by intermarriage. In the survey of the deaf population of New York State, for example, it was found that only 5 percent of women born deaf, and about 9 percent of women who became deaf at an early age, were married to hearing men (Rainer et al., 1963:17). Voluntary associations include a National Association of the Deaf with many thousands of members and a semi-monthly publication, *The Deaf American.* In addition most states have subsidiary associations with publications of their own. State residential schools for the deaf form a nationwide network that supports the cohesiveness of the subculture. Also in existence is a national deaf sports organization that sends delegates to the World Deaf Olympics, a deaf fraternal order with the primary purpose of offering special insurance for members, and innumerable local deaf social and sports clubs. Thus, there is much evidence of the activities of a deaf community. However, the feature of overriding importance is the means of communication by the members of the community: a manual language of signs.

An understanding of the deaf community in which a majority of deaf adults elect to participate is of some importance for an appreciation of the parameters of the conflict about educational philosophies, the viewpoint of deaf adults, and the kinds of alternatives that will eventually be open to deaf children whether their parents are deaf or hearing.

Most deaf children are born to hearing parents, most of whom have no prior knowledge about or contact with profound congenital deafness. Although deaf children are usually surrounded by hearing persons in their homes and in their neighborhoods, most of their schoolmates are also deaf. The common human need for identification with others like one's self is apparent among deaf children, first in their recognition of others who also wear hearing aids, later in their recognition of others who also use the language of signs. The language of signs, although it is known by most if not all deaf adults, is usually prohibited to deaf children. It is learned surreptitiously from peers and must remain hidden from hearing adults. The reason for this ban against a potentially helpful means of communication is a pervasive fear that the use of signs will inhibit the development of speech and lipreading skills. These skills are defined as the most important for deaf children. Oral skills are seen by hearing parents as the badge of entry into their world —the world of the hearing. The absence of speech skills makes deafness "visible" (or rather, audible) and emphasizes the differences between parents and child. These are some of the emotional reasons for the tremendous emphasis placed on the learning of oral skills. There are, of course, any number of practical, coping reasons for hoping that deaf children may learn to communicate in ways most readily understood in the larger community. But the unwillingness of hearing parents and teachers to accept a second, different communicative mode is often so strong as to reflect feelings of stigma regarding differences. Only by understanding the environmental exigencies experienced by the deaf individual at every stage of the life cycle can we hope to understand the consequences of severe auditory deprivation. For a variety of reasons, research about and services for the deaf community have been fragmented and diffuse. Too often, professionals responsible for the early diagnosis and treatment of the preschool deaf child have relatively little contact with others who work with older children, adolescents, and adults. They do not foresee the long-range consequences of early stresses and interventions; professionals as well as parents often make an unwarranted optimistic projection for the future development of deaf children. Conversely, workers concerned with the education, rehabilitation, or treatment of deaf adults have little experience with and little appreciation for the problems with which educators, parents, and therapists of very young deaf children must deal. They do not easily come to an understanding of how they got this way. Out of this fragmentation, this strict division of labor by age-graded segments, have grown myriad misunderstandings, rivalries, and seemingly conflicting philosophies about the treatment of deaf children and adults. All these confusions work to the detriment of the deaf individual, who is caught in the midst of his well-meaning but conflicted helpers.

The studies to be described in the following pages attempt to apply a developmental approach to the study and treatment of deafness. Thus, the clinical treatment of disturbed deaf persons at all ages has been augmented by research involving deaf children and adolescents whose growth and development has *not* resulted in severe behavioral and cognitive problems. This research, in turn, has been informed by the experiences of therapists working regularly with deaf patients who might be described as casualties of their environment, or as being unable to cope with the demands made upon them by a hearing world. Therapists working with very young deaf children and their families on our project also have the opportunity to work with deaf adolescents and with deaf adults. The variety of clients in such a case load enables them to evaluate the developmental processes associated with deafness from several differing viewpoints.

The perspective on deafness reflected in the needs of a parent who has just learned his child is deaf is much different from the perspective on deafness reflected in the therapeutic process evident in working with a deaf adult. The parent may be filled either with anguish or with inflated hopes for the deaf child's future. The deaf adult may be lacking in sympathy for his own parents' anguish and embittered because his parents were never able to relinquish their inflated expectations for his achievement. Both these perspectives certainly reflect the reality of the individuals involved. Both are deserving of sympathy and understanding. Both, however, are limited and incomplete. The developmental problems of deafness differ at each age level and often hinge on communicative competence. The several facets of our work, each with a slightly different focus, provide numerous opportunities for complementary feedback among and between professionals, yielding opportunities for increased understanding.

In the following pages, each chapter reflects a different aspect of our attempt to illuminate the relationship of deafness and mental health. Chapters 2 and 3 present a theoretical framework for viewing the development of deaf individuals through the life cycle. Chapters 4 through 6 present the results of research studies related to developmental aspects of deafness. These include a study of the linguistic development of four young deaf children exposed to both oral and manual communication within their families; a study of mother-child interaction in families with deaf and with hearing children; and a study comparing the functioning of deaf children with deaf parents and with hearing parents in residential and day schools. Finally, chapters 7 through 9 assess some evidence of the increased incidence of behavioral problems in a deaf school population and discuss direct and indirect treatment of mental health problems in a deaf population through therapy or consultation. The final chapter describes a suggested model for a comprehensive program of community psychiatry for a deaf community.

2

A Developmental Model Applied to Problems of Deafness

> Our subjects want to be whole and the clinicians must have some theories and methods which offer the patient a whole world to be whole in.
>
> ERIKSON, 1964:136

Our impulse for synthesis, for finding unities, has been expressed in Chapter 1 of this volume and in several publications (Schlesinger, 1970, 1970*a*; Meadow, 1968*c*). We seek to bridge the gulf between the deaf and the hearing, between research and services for the deaf, between professionals for the deaf child and the deaf adult. We also seek a unifying theory that would explain the persistent discrepancy between the normal potential and the depressed achievement of the deaf. We have therefore sought to understand the interaction between the environment and the deaf individual by building a developmental framework that might help to explain the gulfs and the discrepancies.

A review of the literature dealing with psychiatric services to adult deaf populations tends to corroborate the findings reported by behavioral scientists regarding the psychological uniqueness and the cognitive retardation of many deaf individuals (Rainer et al., 1963; Rainer and Altshuler, 1966, 1970).

Chapter 2 is by Hilde S. Schlesinger.

Rainer and Altshuler have described (1966:84) a typical cluster of symptoms found in deaf patients:

> a lack of understanding and regard for the feelings of others (empathy), coupled with limited awareness of the impact of their own behavior on others, an egocentric view of the world, and gross coercive demands to have their needs and wishes satisfied; a reaction to frustrations, tensions or anxiety typified by a kind of primitive riddance through action, rather than through internal conflicts with self-imposed controls and constraints.

The literature also reveals that the incidence of schizophrenia is no higher among the deaf than among the hearing population, but the incidence of increased problems of living, of "immature personality," and of "impulsive disorders" appear inordinately higher (Rainer and Altshuler, 1966). We have drawn on this knowledge in our attempt to provide mental health services to a deaf population and their family members.

Certain shared themata began to emerge from our earliest days of clinical work. We met patients whose lives were riddled by the consequences of unbridled impulsivity. We encountered innumerable patients whose controls remained externalized and vaguely perceived, and who lived as if by a rule book of etiquette (Levine, 1956) rather than by internalized controls. We met many parents who complained about the arduous task of communicating with their deaf children. And we met their counterparts—children grown to adulthood, bitter about their parents. They derided and despaired of the parental insistence on "being normal" (as represented by normal speech); the universal pressure to get them to belong to "the hearing world"; the false hopes and the frequent failures, and the pressure to adjust rather than to grow.

We began to wonder whether we could trace the impact of auditory deficit back through the developmental steps, the "critical moments" that Erikson has so eloquently defined. It is difficult and may not be productive to delineate the effects of the deficit itself (as separate from its interplay with significant others), but as researchers and clinicians we have come increasingly to see how human growth—anatomical, neurological, and psychological—depends on environmental factors. We began to wonder whether the environmental factors affecting the resolutions of the critical moments throughout the development of the deaf individual were significant; and what is more important, whether these factors might be alterable through specific interventions.

In order to make our theoretical position clear to the reader, we would like to trace the development of the deaf individual in an Eriksonian epigenetic scheme. Erikson maintains that the whole life cycle, the eight stages of man, can be seen as an integrated psychosocial development in a sequence of critical phases. A critical phase can be described as a biologically motivated process of maturation which requires psychological adaptation to achieve a new level of development. Each phase is characterized by a phase-specific task which must be solved although the *Anlage* (the precursor) for the solution is prepared in the previous ones and is worked out further in the subsequent ones.

> Each successive step then is a potential crisis . . . used in a developmental sense to connote . . . a turning point, a crucial period of increased vulnerability and heightened potential, and therefore, the ontogenetic source of generational strength and maladjustment. (Erikson, 1968:96)

Each crisis can be described in terms of extremes of successful and unsuccessful solutions, although the usual outcome is a balance between these two extremes: (1) Basic Trust versus Mistrust; (2) Autonomy versus Shame and Doubt; (3) Initiative versus Guilt; (4) Industry versus Inferiority; (5) Identity versus Identity Diffusion; (6) Intimacy versus Isolation; (7) Generativity versus Stagnation; (8) Integrity versus Despair. The successful solution of any crisis depends on its difficulty and the resources (individual, parental, and societal) immediately available. Erikson has stated in several places that "we are gradually learning what exactly not to do to what children at what age, but then we must still learn what to do spontaneously and joyfully." We hope that our analyses will help lessen the inimical influences on the deaf child's development and will give some clues about what society and parents can do spontaneously and joyfully.

BASIC TRUST VERSUS MISTRUST—INFANCY

The basic task of infancy, which spans the period from birth to twelve or eighteen months, is to establish a sense of trust in the world, which will become a feeling of hope about oneself and the world. The successful resolution of this critical moment depends on the mutual regulation between mother and child. This is a period during which the infant (by active participation) conveys the message—exultant or despairing—"I am what I am given." It is a time when ideally the infant finds that the physical environment and the people that inhabit it are trustworthy, that they respond to his needs in largely positive and predictable ways.

The present literature on the early stages of child development is vast and often confusing, but there does seem to be some consensus on the optimal learning environment for the young child as one in which the young child is cared for (a) in his own home, (b) in the context of a warm, nurturant emotional relation, (c) with his mother (or a reasonable facsimile thereof) (d) under conditions of varied sensory and cognitive input (Caldwell, 1967).[1] We shall touch upon these assumptions throughout our discussion.

What about the context of a warm, nurturant relation with the child's mother? The ability to provide this depends on the mother's successful resolution of the normative crisis of pregnancy and parenthood, which depends on the maturity of the mother, influenced in turn by her self-esteem as a person and a mate, and her readiness and her willingness to have a child. Furthermore, it depends on her ability and willingness to have a particular child of a particular sex and temperament (Thomas et al., 1968) at a specific moment of her life. The successful resolution of the crisis of motherhood also depends on the familial and cultural support to the new mother.

The concern with the varied sensory input is of more recent origin than the focus on the nurturant quality of the maternal person. Psychoanalysis has frequently referred to the incorporative modes of early infancy and to the development of an early sense of identification as a precursor to the adult identity. Erikson (1968) does briefly discuss the fact that the "senses take

1. Caldwell questions, however, our "overly vigorous support of (a) when (b), (c) or (d) might not obtain."

in what feels good"; but for our major understanding of the crucial importance of early cognitive experience we must turn to Piaget, Hebb, and others. Hunt (1964) has summarized this body of cognitive theory and research and generally emphasized the importance of the environment in early perceptual and cognitive experience. We learn that at gradually increasing ages the perceptual and cognitive input must be varied (the infant must see and hear a variety of environmental stimuli); these stimuli must become familiar to the infant; and they must become reproducible by him.

The Impact of Deafness on Basic Trust

Literature on the birth of defective children (reviewed in Ross, 1964; Wright, 1960) clearly indicates that their normal mothers go through stages of guilt, sorrow, mourning, and anger, which may well interfere with stable, warm relations with their infants. Our clinical work confirms findings (Fellendorf and Harrow, 1970; Meadow, 1968*b*) that the new parents of a deaf child are frequently "let down" by the experts at the time of diagnosis. A large majority of these parents do not receive adequate support from the professionals they have sought out for diagnostic certainty, therapeutic guidance, and prognostic formulations. The medical expert is hampered by ubiquitous ignorance about deafness, an equally ubiquitous repugnance to give out "bad news," a frequent reluctance to deal with so-called irreversible defects, and a vast array of conflicting ideologies surrounding deafness in the young child. The often maligned "anxious parents" who go "shopping for experts" must indeed shop around arduously before finding experts who can guide them in rearing a deaf child successfully. Finding helpful experts, meeting other parents, working out varieties of compensatory solutions for the deficit—all these partial resolutions free the parent to be more effective.

Interestingly, deaf parents of deaf children appear to expect the diagnosis and to accept it at a much earlier age. There is also some experimental and clinical evidence (Meadow, 1967) that indicates deaf parents of deaf children cope with the crisis of diagnosis easily and quickly, while their hearing counterparts prolong and intensify it. Once the initial diagnosis is made, deaf parents are less likely to seek confirmatory diagnosis or a miraculous cure.

Turning to the cognitive environment of the deaf infant, our tentative data do suggest that deaf infants may be "more quiet" and slightly more passive. If this be true, they may not actively seek out the environment, and their parents in turn may permit them to rest more quietly without providing them with the variety of stimuli so necessary for ongoing cognitive development. What steps might be taken to help a deaf child to approximate the oft-quoted Piagetian aphorism (Hunt, 1964) "the more a child has seen and heard, the more he wants to see and hear"? The literature on audiology more and more demonstrates that sophisticated hearing aids can successfully be worn by the very young infant so that he may *hear more*.

As for seeing, deaf children may need a greater variety of visual stimuli to compensate for the lack of diminution of auditory stimuli. Burlingham (1967) refers to the overwhelming importance of sound in the lives of blind children. A number of studies (Meadow, 1967; Brill, 1960; Stuckless and Birch, 1966) indicate that the reason deaf children of deaf parents do better cognitively may be that such deaf infants *see* language at an earlier stage of development; this frequent exposure to "seen language" may enable the infant *to see more,* thus cumulatively fostering the sensorimotor schemata (Hunt, 1964). There may be "critical periods" at which different kinds of behavior are most effectively learned and incorporated. If such learning does not take place at the appropriate times, it may be less completely learned and may break down in times of stress.

We have briefly discussed the caretaking and the external sensory environment, but what about the deaf infant himself? How does the lack of auditory contact with the environment affect his cognitive and affective being in the sensorimotor infancy stage? We do not know because, unfortunately, few observational studies of deaf infants have been performed. Downs (1968), Lenneberg (1967), and other workers have noted the deaf infant goes through the usual developmental steps in the sequence of vocalizations, and presumably other developmental milestones. We remain to wonder on two accounts. For the hearing infant the warmth and nurturance is perceived almost immediately when he hears the bustle announcing the arrival of the caretaker; this immediacy must be delayed for the deaf infant, who must wait to see or touch the maternal person before obtaining gratification. Furthermore, the hearing infant's responsiveness to the perceptual input implies that audition plays a major role in the perceptual organization. For as Hunt says (1964:88) "something heard becomes something to look at, something to look at becomes something to grasp, and sometimes something to grasp becomes something to suck." We do not know if the absence of audition changes the deaf infant's organization of perceptual inputs or his abilities to actively retain or regain certain patterns of stimulus change.

Thus during this early stage the parents and experts who make up the external environment clearly suffer from the auditory deficit of the infant; it is unclear how much the infant suffers, directly and indirectly, but the impact of the deficit becomes clearer in the stages that follow.

AUTONOMY VERSUS SHAME AND DOUBT—EARLY CHILDHOOD

The basic task of early childhood, the period from eighteen months to three years, is to develop a sense of autonomy, the sense of being a separate human entity who has control over his body and can influence the environment. This autonomy is accompanied by a feeling of good will toward self and environment. The successful resolution of this critical moment depends on "mutual regulation" between parent and child, so that the child may develop a feeling of "I am what I will." Bitter power struggles often develop between the parents and the child, who is "Making rapid gains in muscular maturation, verbalization and in discrimination and the consequent ability—and doubly felt inability—to coordinate a number of highly conflicting action patterns characterized by the tendencies of holding on and letting go" (Erikson, 1968:107).

This developing will to retain or release at will affects the entire being of the young child. Behaviorally the child is frequently described as stubborn, as alternately clinging to mother or violently pushing her away, alternately accepting and refusing the power struggle of toilet training. It appears as if the child were saying "I want to do with my muscles, my words, and my sphincters (which all have recently and laboriously come to be under my control) what feels good to *me*." If the parents have some sense of dignity as autonomous human beings, they will be able to help the child form a benevolent conscience during this willful period. They will gently help him to "stand on his own feet while at the same time protecting him from meaningless and arbitrary experiences of shame and of early doubt" (Erikson, 1968:110). But if the outer controls are not firmly reassuring, if the child is denied the gradual and guided experience of the autonomy of free choice, he may develop a precocious conscience. He will turn against himself all his urge to discriminate and to manipulate. He may become obsessed with his need to control the environment and will do so stubbornly and repetitively. Such attempts are the infantile source of later efforts in adult life to govern by the letter rather than by the spirit of the law. Outer controls applied with too much shaming, however, may produce in the child a secret determination to get away with things, may indeed lead to defiant shamelessness (Erikson, 1963).

The Impact of Deafness on Autonomy

We speculate that *words,* like people or products, also can be held onto or let go at will. Fully aware that speech learning is an arduous cognitive task, we are accumulating clinical and research evidence that noncognitive, psychological forces also play their role in the mutism of many deaf individuals. As the mother can precipitate battles over toilet training, she can precipitate similar battles over "word training," and in both battles the child can self-destructively win. There is evidence from the clinical literature of nondeaf but mute children that delayed talking can be a specific syndrome (Filippi and Rousey, 1968), or that elective mutism (Levy, 1955) can have an interpersonal origin. These nondeaf, mute youngsters interestingly enough demonstrate signs of negativism, impulsive aggressiveness, fearfulness of adult disapproval, and provocation of adult nurturance and overprotection, all of which can be seen as sequelae of an unresolved crisis of autonomy.

Deaf youngsters show delayed resolutions of the crisis of autonomy in many areas other than the verbal. Accounts of delayed toilet training, feeding problems, impositions of stringent safety measures abound in our clinical and research material. It appears clear that an optimal imposition of restraints on the young child is hampered by the lack of meaningful reciprocal communication at this age. The parents fear to let their deaf child stand on his own feet, despite numerous professional exhortations to do so. This is less true of deaf parents of deaf children, who appear to be more comfortable with their children, admit to fewer eating and toilet training problems, and permit earlier independence and autonomy.

There is some indication that by being gentle and warm in areas of behavior that are extremely important to her, the mother will secure willing acquiescence; being punitive and cold, on the other hand, may bring temporary conformity but ultimately will spur rebellion and resentment (McCandless, 1961). Speech seems to be *the* area of importance to most parents of deaf children, and therefore research into the effectiveness of parental insistence on the production of the spoken word could have theoretical and practical relevance. It may be that many children perceive such insistence as punitive and react by rebellious muteness. Our own work so far indicates that a reduction in the anxious demand for oral communications by parents, teachers, or therapist has enabled many deaf youngsters to delight in their usage of speech for the first time. We shall comment further on interpersonal aspects of language and speech acquisition in the chapter on linguistics.

As a result of the added arenas in which power struggles can be waged with their parents, many deaf children go through this stage with an intensity of negativism that interferes with normal maturation. Levy (1955) postulates that oppositional (or negative) behavior originally serves many useful purposes, primarily that of resistance to external influences and formation of a more powerful self-concept. The capacity to resist external influences thus enables the child to use and develop inner controls and to develop feelings of separateness and independence. But when an obstacle occurs in the way of this maturational process, when the child habitually loses in the struggle for autonomy, then these resistant feelings take on a hostile quality.

INITIATIVE VERSUS GUILT—CHILDHOOD AND THE ANTICIPATION OF ROLES

The task of childhood—three to six years—is to develop a sense of initiative with a feeling of the purposefulness of life and of one's own self. With optimal resolution of the previous stages, the child has reached a more advanced kind of identification; he is by now convinced that he is a person on his own and must now find out the kind of person he may become (Erikson, 1968). The chant of this age could be "I am what

I can imagine I will be." Children at this stage frequently attach themselves to people with occupations they can grasp: firemen and policemen, gardeners and plumbers. Erikson feels that such superficial identification with adults who are removed from the child may be safer than identification with the unequal, superior parent. Ideally, however, he feels that children can develop a more realistic identification with parents as people "who feel equal in worth although different in kind or function or age. [This identification] permits a peaceful cultivation of initiative, a truly free sense of enterprise" (Erikson, 1959:82).

The normal child moves intrusively into a larger society: he does so by vigorous locomotion, occasional aggressiveness, expression of so-called infantile sexuality, and insatiable curiosity manifested by unceasing questions. As in all stages of development, the environment must present certain minimum nutriments to further the growth of the child. Earlier, a variety and abundance of meaningful sensory input were of prime importance; now the responsiveness of the environment to the child's activities assumes primary importance. The parents need to be able both to let the child pursue his locomotor and manipulative intentions and to provide answers to his endless questions. Without these supports during the second, third, and fourth years of life, a child cannot continue to profit no matter how favorable his circumstances during the first year (Hunt, 1964).

Ideally, the parents at this stage must show the child by example and by simple precept the ethos and morality of the society within which they live. The child in turn must begin to experiment with his initiative and to test the world about him: "May I do such-and-such, or will those powerful adults stop me, or disown me?" As Erikson says (1968:119), "The great governor of initiative is conscience. . . . It is the ontogenetic cornerstone of morality." Conscience at this age has a tendency to be more intransigent than the parents had desired and requires an obedience more literal than the parents had intended. The indispensable contribution of this stage to later identity development is that of freeing the child's initiative and sense of purpose for adult tasks which promise but cannot guarantee a fulfillment of one's range of capacities. The sense of purpose is the courage to envisage and pursue valued goals uninhibited by guilt and by fear of unreasoning punishment (Erikson, 1964).

THE IMPACT OF DEAFNESS ON INITIATIVE

The childhood stage is characterized in the normal youngster by marked verbal and motor exuberance. In the deaf child, this exuberance is doubly inhibited—the verbal exuberance is almost invariably diminished by a paucity of symbols, but the feelings remain exuberant, and it is not surprising that youngsters "deprived of the ability or opportunity to express powerful feelings in words . . . usually erupt in actions" (Katan, 1961). The motor exuberance is thus *potentially increased* for the deaf youngster; but in practice this increase is inhibited by the innumerable safety limits parents place on their deaf youngsters, reducing their intrusive meanderings into the outside world. School settings (most deaf children attend schools at early ages) frequently place a premium on immobility. Very young children are expected to sit still for long periods in order to observe the teacher vigilantly. This forced inactivity appears to place a stress on many children, a stress that may preclude learning, especially for the large-muscled young boys.

Unfortunately, the optimal teaching situation for motorically exuberant youngsters with inadequate auditory contact with the environment is hard to define and harder to achieve. Furthermore, in the poignant search for normal speech, parents and educators disregard research findings from child development and learning theory and behave as if reciprocal communication by gestures or by American Sign Language will in some magical way interfere with speech development. Thus the child's verbal and motor exuberance remains inhibited by his own deficit and by the restrictive environment.

The environment places an additional deprivation on the development of the deaf youngster. Although identifications at this age still remain primarily familial, there is increasing evidence from research on ethnic minority group children that self-esteem is already developing, that a youngster at this age "knows" if his person is seen as good or bad by the overall society (Coles, 1964; Goodman, 1964; Pettigrew, 1964). The deaf child of hearing parents is characteristically deprived of contact with successful deaf adults, a fact that may deeply influence his self concept. For if he only sees deaf children and never meets deaf adults, he may develop distorted expectations of what happens to deaf children grown up: Do they become like the hearing? Do they go into hiding? Do they disappear? Do they die? The deaf child of deaf parents clearly has higher self-esteem at the early ages (Meadow, 1967). Research on disadvantaged youngsters has shown that their self-esteem and school achievement rise dramatically when successful adults of their own color or linguistic competence are introduced into their social and learning environments (Ervin-Tripp, 1966).

Another characteristic of this age is the torrent of questions children release. These questions are not forthcoming from the deaf child at this age, and if they were, the parent would have an impossible task to explain complicated events to a linguistically impoverished child. The analogue with the culturally deprived child is striking. Researchers on disadvantaged children from minority ethnic groups tell us that "the verbal patterns provided by the parents are important not only in terms of information-processing, but also in terms of establishing reasons for external events and reasons for behavior" (Kessler, 1970).

As Hess and Shipman (1968) noted in contrasting middle-class and lower-class black children, the deprivation among the lower-class children appeared to be a *deprivation of meaning* in the early cognitive relation between mother and child. This environment produces a child who relates to authority rather than to rationale, who may often be compliant but is not reflective in his behavior, and who thinks of the consequences of an act largely in terms of immediate punishment or reward rather than in terms of future effects and long range goals. All this sounds hauntingly like the description of the deaf patients given at the beginning of this chapter. The parallel between children who are linguistically deprived by virtue of deafness and those who are deprived because of race and social class deserves to be investigated further (Schlesinger, 1970*a*).

INDUSTRY VERSUS INFERIORITY—SCHOOL AGE

The basic task of the school years—from ages six to eleven—is to develop a sense of industry, with an accompanying feeling of competency. Having mastered a basic trust in the environment and the people that inhabit it, the child becomes a relatively autonomous human being who feels he can be what he imagines he will be. Now during the school years, he can proclaim, "I am what I can learn." This necessitates a feeling of competence which is "a free exercise of dexterity and intelligence in the completion of tasks, unimpaired by infantile inferiority" (Erikson, 1964:124). A successful resolution of this critical period depends on the child's weathering of the previous crises and his interaction with a society, a family, and a learning environment which expects success from *that* particular child, in *that* particular period of history in *his* particular way.

The Impact of Deafness on Competency

We have discussed the unsuccessful resolutions of the prior crises for the deaf child, and now let us emphasize the potentially noxious contributors to a false or distorted crisis resolution on the part of the social *environment* that surrounds him.

Society has not always been kind to its "different," exceptional members. It has condemned them, excluded them, and refused them succor and education (Schlesinger, 1970*a*). Some vestiges of these earlier patterns can still be seen in these more humanitarian times. There is still a pervasive disapproval of one of the most potentially useful coping mechanisms of deafness—the American Sign Language. People are uncomfortable with those who are different, and deafness more than other disabilities appears to frighten the uninitiated into a "shock-withdrawal-paralysis" reaction on their first exposure. To function optimally under these circumstances can be a Herculean task. Adding to the sense of provincialism and despair felt by many teachers for the deaf, almost yearly publications lament the "failure of deaf education," and thus provoke expectations of further failures on the part of the teachers.

Teachers who feel estranged from society, or who feel estranged from the children they teach naturally have difficulty convincing their young students that learning has a pay-off. Teachers who have become convinced that a particular group of children are nonachievers or lowachievers can approach the learning environment with negative expectations, which in turn can reinforce underachievement (Rosenthal and Jacobson, 1968; Gozali, 1969). Teachers who do not have insight into the positive values of culturally different learners and understanding of their learning style, language and modes of behavior (Daniel,

1967), or teachers who evoke fear and hostility (Sarason et al., 1960) are ineffective in motivating their pupils to learn.

Many teachers of the deaf have consciously and conscientiously struggled with these challenges. But even with the most dedicated teachers, the deaf child will demonstrate a delayed solution of the crisis of competency and achievement as defined by the majority culture. Although Furth (1970) finds less retardation in symbolic manipulation or in the performance of Piagetian tasks than other authors do, he does not dispute the "verbal inferiority" of most deaf subjects. It must be remembered, however, that no tests of "verbal competency" have generally been given in the language of signs, known by most deaf adolescents and used by 80 percent of deaf adults with their deaf friends (Crammatte, 1968).

IDENTITY VERSUS IDENTITY DIFFUSION—ADOLESCENCE

Adolescence, the period from approximately eleven to eighteen, can be seen as a "way of life" different from childhood and adulthood. Problems of emancipation, independence, and freedom from the family occupy the early stage, while problems of social role and personal purpose within the wider world occupy the later stage. Over the whole span of adolescence, the developmental task is to integrate earlier elements into a true sense of identity as a separate individual, no longer taking a partial or external view of the self.

Although adolescence is traditionally considered a time of great stress and difficulty for the youth, his parents, and the adults who deal with him, some recent studies question this assumption. While the period may be *disturbing* for all the participants in the identity struggle of the adolescent, it need not be *disturbed*. One can at least imagine an optimal solution of the adolescent crisis in which the adolescent is ready for the encounter, parents who for many reasons need not and therefore do not fear the encounter, and a society that is flexible enough to absorb the oncoming generation with all its differences.

The *adolescent* ready for the encounter, he who may travel through a gloriously vital phase, will be one who is able to approach it with those crises of trust, will, imagination, and competency relatively resolved.

The *parents* who do not fear the encounter will generally be parents who have resolved their own adult crises of generativity and care; whose personal, occupational, marital, and parental roles are relatively satisfactory; and who are able to look at the product of their care and generativity—their child—in a positive way. Thus they need not see the adolescent primarily in terms of an object to be lost, or an object of envy, or an intruder on the adult scene, or an unsatisfactory product of their labors.

A *society* that will promote an optimal resolution of the adolescent crisis is one that, despite its rapid shifts and rapid ideological changes, has the latitude and flexibility to absorb individuals who vary in their strengths and weaknesses, their conformity and rebelliousness, their similarities and differences. Society thus must have prepared the budding citizen for work, and the work market must be adaptive to individual differences and special needs. For if society gives certain so-called disadvantaged youths only the prospect of failure, the disadvantaged young person may have only "two choices: to accept social rejection and educational or occupational failure in a pattern of fatalism and passivity, or to lash out violently against the society which condemns him to inferiority, deprivation, and humiliation" (Joint Commission, 1970:358).

The Impact of Deafness on Identity

The typical deaf adolescent approaches the crisis with a delayed or incomplete resolution of the previous crises. Thus even if optimally established in the earliest stage, his trust receives innumerable jolts, as he repeatedly meets others who do not accept his deficit, who appear fearful in joint human endeavors, who idolize a normalcy he cannot achieve instead of cultivating his unique areas of competency. The next three childhood stages of autonomy, initiative, and competency are probably directly affected by the linguistic deprivation of most deaf individuals, as language assumes paramount importance for academic learning and for the "learning" of interpersonal relationships.

Thus the deaf youngster approaches adolescence with varying degrees of unresolved crises. What of the parents of the deaf adolescent? All too often they have crises of their own that tend to interfere with the optimal resolution of the adolescent crisis. Frequently the parents are no longer able to deny the encompassing effect of deafness on some of their cherished goals. Many parents successfully maintain the myth that their deaf infant or child will one day appear normal, will speak normally, will mate with a hearing spouse, will show none of the "stigmata of deafness," will not talk with his hands, will perform academically at the level of his hearing peers. The period of latency, with its relative calm, permits the parents to maintain this ideal untarnished. In adolescence, with the oncoming resolutions of vocational and marital choice, the parents, to their dismay, may note that their youngster relates more easily with other deaf peers, frequently ignoring his own family. Many adolescents will reverse roles and keep from their parents the knowledge of their "ignoble" competencies in sign language, in order to protect the allegedly fragile self-esteem of their parents. Many others will fervently herald their negativism toward the parents and their identification with the peer group by using sign language to the utter exclusion of speech.

The parents may realize for the first time that the vocational choices of their deaf children are strictly limited both by academic underachievement and by the linguistic retardation and the nonoccurrence of the miracle of normal speech. Having placed themselves in the position of providing prolonged, arduous, intensive help in the tasks of early child rearing, many parents hope that deferred gratification will finally come to them during their child's adolescence—a hope often bitterly unfulfilled. Their reactions vary. Sometimes they will try futilely to bind the adolescent more closely to the family, in the expectation of a delayed miracle; sometimes their parenting may turn into overt rejection as if to say, "You have not lived up to my expectations, and both of us are doomed."

The identity road of deaf adolescents takes many paths. Some adolescents militantly enter the "deaf world" and exclude at least temporarily any contact with the "hearing world." Others avoid the deaf world; refusing any association with deafness, they may pursue an isolated "as if" identification with the hearing world. In an analogy with Negro identification patterns, "they pass." The consequences of "passing" are often pathological. Thus, Parker and Kleiner (1965) note a large body of research documenting the unhealthiness in aspiring to be white: "Almost every clinical study of psychopathology among Negroes indicates that the Negro who is not identified with other members of his group, or who aspires to 'be white,' is relatively more prone to manifest various forms of mental ill health" (p. 157). As in the case of blacks, or immigrants, the most successful identifications may occur in those individuals who accept the differences imposed by color, language, or minority group mores. The successful individual may thus live in many worlds; the alienated individual may be a stranger in all.

The generation gap may become an insurmountable chasm if the adolescent rejects the hearing world of his parents, and if the parents reject the deaf world of the child.

INTIMACY VERSUS ISOLATION—YOUNG ADULTHOOD

The young adult has become a free, self-governing being. However, "when one has become an individual, one stands alone and faces the world in all its perilous and overpowering aspects" (Fromm, 1941:29). The developmental task of this period is to restore not the old primary tie with the world and its inhabitants, but a more mature relation with man and nature. This period reflects the oft-quoted, somewhat laconic, statement by Freud that *Lieben und Arbeiten* (love and work) are the hallmarks of a healthy individual. The successful attainment of these characteristics entails a successful resolution of the adolescent identity crisis. Those who are not sure of their identity dare not commit themselves to work for fear of being submerged by the world and its institutions. Those who are not sure of their identity dare not submit to interpersonal intimacy for fear of losing their fragile sense of self. Love is a deceptively simple, yet difficult word. Its most mature form

> is a very specific feeling; and while every human being has a capacity for love, its realization is one of the most difficult achievements. Genuine love is rooted in productiveness and may properly be called, therefore, "productive love." Its essence is the same whether it is the mother's love for the child, our love for man, or the erotic love between two individuals. . . . (Fromm, 1947:98)

It is a love that involves knowledge, responsibility, care, and a genuine interest in furthering the growth and development of the other person.

And yet love so defined presupposes the ability to fuse identity with the mate. This act of fusion is frightening to those who fear a loss of identity. The young person who is not sure "will shy away from intimacy or throw himself into acts of intimacy which are promiscuous without true intimacy." These youths may "frequently settle for highly stereotyped interpersonal relations and come to regain a deep sense of isolation" (Erikson, 1968:136).

Work is a deceptively simple, yet complex word. Although the meaning of work has changed through the ages, it has always denoted sustained energy expended for a goal. But the value of the work and its goals has changed. An early positive reference to work is found in the rabbinical literature:

> In the thought of the Rabbis, work—not only intellectual but manual—reacquires dignity and value. 'Love work' is the maxim of Samea. To work is to cooperate with God in the great purpose of the world's salvation. Man's labor tends to approach somewhat to that of God, for in the Cabalistic doctrines, the labor of man continues and prolongs the divine energy which overflowed in the act of creation. . . . (Tilgher, 1962:13)

Tilgher shows how through the ages work has variously been viewed as degrading, as necessary, and at times even as divine. The version most congruent with modern psychiatric theories is that any kind of work, even sports "gives a man the joy of victorious force, bestows on him the harsh pleasure of feeling his personality triumphant" (Tilgher, 1962:23).

The Impact of Deafness on the Ability to Love and Work

Many of our young adult deaf patients give evidence of identity diffusion. In this period they have become separated from the rather protective settings of most school situations, and they find the world quite different. Their former identity in school proves inadequate for an identity in the world. Some young adults have previously achieved competency in the school setting, measured in terms of grades and achievement test scores and the ability to live by the rules of the school. But they find that the world outside does not measure with grades, and its rules are less tangible. Those who have not achieved internalized controls for behavior nor internalized motivations for exercise of skills tend to have a traumatic period in young adulthood; this trauma often surprises their parents and teachers who judged from their success in the world of school that they were equipped to face the larger world. In this traumatic relocation, they frequently take refuge in previously abandoned stances of dependence.

Others among our patients had not achieved competence or identity even within the school setting. The more stressful requirements of the world intensified their styles of defending against stress: some showed an intensification of impulsiveness, others an increase of dependence, and still others showed an automatonlike conformity in which each became "exactly as all others are and as they expect him to be" (Fromm, 1941).

For those who are successful, love and work can become the satisfying and exhilarating companions of young adulthood. For those who have not reached the required level of maturity, love and work will retain infantile characteristics. Intimacy will be replaced by isolation, or by frantic, superficial relationships. Work may take the form of a repetitive frenetic change of jobs or be replaced by total avoidance of exercise of skills, all of which will be unaccompanied by any sense of gratifying commitment. Work paralysis is seen by Erikson (1959:144) as

> the logical sequence of a deep sense of inadequacy . . . of one's general equipment. Such a sense of inadequacy . . . may convey the unrealistic demands made by an ego ideal . . . may express the fact that the immediate social environment does not have a niche for the individual's true gifts; or it may reflect the paradoxical fact that an individual in early school life was seduced into a specialized precocity which early outdistanced his identity development.

These three pathways are often seen in the development of deaf patients. Their parents often make unrealistic demands. And when hearing parents have objected vociferously to having deaf teachers for their deaf children, their growing deaf youngster may wonder if the niches available to him may not be unnecessarily restricted. Furthermore, many deaf youngsters and their admiring parents are seduced into a belief in the "specialized precocity" of the deaf child. Sometimes the truly outstanding oral skills of the youth produce expectations of equally outstanding (but not necessarily accompanying) language and social skills.

GENERATIVITY VERSUS STAGNATION—PARENTHOOD

The task of parenthood is the constructive concern with the guidance of the next generation, either through biological offspring or through other altruistic endeavors of care and creation. The mere fact of having children, however, does not automatically guarantee generativity. Both ethological studies and research on child development, as beautifully integrated by Bowlby (1969), show that young animals and children alike require early "maternal attachment" for later healthy development.

More specifically, there is a direct relation between receiving early adequate mothering and being able later in life to become an adequate, nurturant mother. Several animal experiments (Bowlby, 1969) indicate that animal infants deprived of maternal attachment at a critical age may be unable to mate or to bear young at a later period of life. Human mothers (the paternal role and its development is not as yet so clearly defined) who have done well in their psychosocial development will be able to bear their children and care for them confidently, competently, and selflessly. They will be able to introduce the young into the continuing cycle of generations.

The Impact of Deafness on Generativity and Care[2]

Individuals who still demand coercive gratification of their own needs will have difficulty in receiving a child in trust and postponing some narcissistic needs in favor of the biological, emotional, and cognitive needs of the new infant.

We have met immature deaf parents with their children who were unable to see their infant as a feeling being. Their

2. We have attempted to trace carefully the difficulties inherent in being the parent of a deaf infant, child, and adolescent. Being the parent of an adult deaf person presents further difficulties, for those deaf individuals who have not reached maturity continue to demand and expect "gifts" from their parents and others in their environment. They may indeed not be able to provide gifts to their own newborn infants.

infants remained nameless for prolonged periods of time, they were "mascoted," and treated like dolls or objects. Some immature deaf parents have felt so incompetent in the task of child-rearing that their infants were cared for by maternal grandmothers.

On the other hand, many competent and mature deaf parents have developed a false sense of inadequacy—a feeling possibly promoted and provoked by society.[3] Several of our deaf mother-patients developed a symbiotic relation with their hearing children, expecting the child to be a protector, a guide through the mazes of the hearing world, a source of unrealistic gratifications.

Another area of interest is the comparison of deaf mothers with their deaf and hearing children. Rainer et al. have indicated in their different works that deaf mothers "do better with their deaf than with their hearing children." On the other hand, they feel that deaf parents express a preference for hearing children as noted in a questionnaire and by the trend of a larger family size in deaf families with a deaf child (1963).

Our clinical experience indicates that this "preference" may be a fruitful area of research. Generally speaking, our deaf patients have had less difficulty with their deaf than with their hearing children. Many of the deaf parents have complained more bitterly about the hearing than the deaf child. We occasionally have heard the seemingly paradoxical statement "I do not know how to communicate with my child because he hears." Some deaf parents clearly told us they preferred a deaf offspring. It might be that these deaf parents had incorporated their own hearing parents' stance toward child-rearing. Because the hearing parents had made it abundantly clear that being different from one's parents was not desirable, it became difficult in turn for their deaf offspring to accept a hearing child. A few of the deaf parents have shown an interesting phenomenon—a temporary paralysis of parental competency and nurturance for their chil-

3. It has been of marked interest (and sadness) to us that society repeatedly expects incompetency on the part of deaf mothers. The project frequently has received phone calls from welfare workers anxious to remove a healthy infant from parents known to us as competent—solely on the grounds of parental deafness. Deaf parental competency was recently questioned, but received judicial approval in a case where a deaf couple had originally been denied the adoption of a child (251 Cal. App. 2nd, 221).

dren who were reaching school age. Historically these deaf parents told of their own removal from the familial home with attendance at a residential school. It was as if these deaf parents had incorporated the belief held by their own hearing parents: "I am not able or competent to rear my child after the age of six, nor do I want to."

It has become clear to us that generativity and care can be seriously distorted through unresolved early developmental crises. It has also become clear that a sense of generativity and care may be difficult to maintain—even when present—in the face of society's stigma toward the deaf and toward deafness.

INTEGRITY VERSUS DESPAIR—OLD AGE

The aging person, having adapted himself to the triumphs and disappointments of the stages of man, will experience the culminating sense of integrity at the eighth stage (Erikson, 1968). Integrity entails the ability to envisage human problems in their entirety, a detached concern with life itself in the face of approaching death. The "autonomous" among the elderly continue to renew themselves, continue to grow. Others are merely "adjusted" or well preserved in old age. "If responsibility accompanies maturity for the autonomous and takes the place of maturity for the adjusted, the anomic find their way to neither" (Riesman, 1954:383). The ability to remain productive, or to adjust and accept decreased productivity, enables the old to continue seeing themselves as an integral part of society and to view their own life cycle benevolently. Those enmeshed in despair have the heavy sense "that time is short, too short for the attempt to start another life and to try out alternate roads of integrity" (Erikson, 1959:98).

THE IMPACT OF DEAFNESS ON THE INTEGRITY OF OLD AGE

The fact that deaf individuals can develop to the level of integrity and wisdom has been shown to us again and again, if not by most of our patients, then by our deaf colleagues. A beautiful tribute to ego development in the face of adversity, based on experience of and with the deaf, is Joanne Greenberg's moving novel, *In This Sign* (1970). And although the book remains a tribute, it fails to encompass a description of deaf individuals known to us who have reached yet higher levels of achievement and growth.

All we can say is that both literature about, and our direct experience with, the aged deaf is extremely scanty. We simply do not know the effect that deafness has on the crisis of old age. It could be that the impact of deafness on old age is even more devastating or alternatively the deaf might be better equipped by a life of deprivation to adjust to the added handicap. It may be that many aged deaf become more "autonomous" as the hearing world no longer pushes for impossible achievements; it may be that many remain merely "adjusted" because of the numerous delays in their ego development; it may be that many remain "anomic" because their identity was never clarified. We feel that these outcomes for the aged deaf pose interesting questions for future research.

AFTERWORD

It must be obvious that we have described the impact of deafness on the eight stages of man in its most noxious and nefarious form. We are fully aware from our contact with deaf individuals that the eight stages can be traversed more productively, more joyfully, and with a more adequate resolution of each developmental crisis. This more successful passage through the life cycle we have found most often (although not exclusively) in the deaf children of deaf parents. We hope that our account has helped to explain this higher achievement. We also hope that it will help hearing parents to ponder, to increase the acceptance of deafness in their children, and with this acceptance help their children to meet and master the challenges of each life crisis.

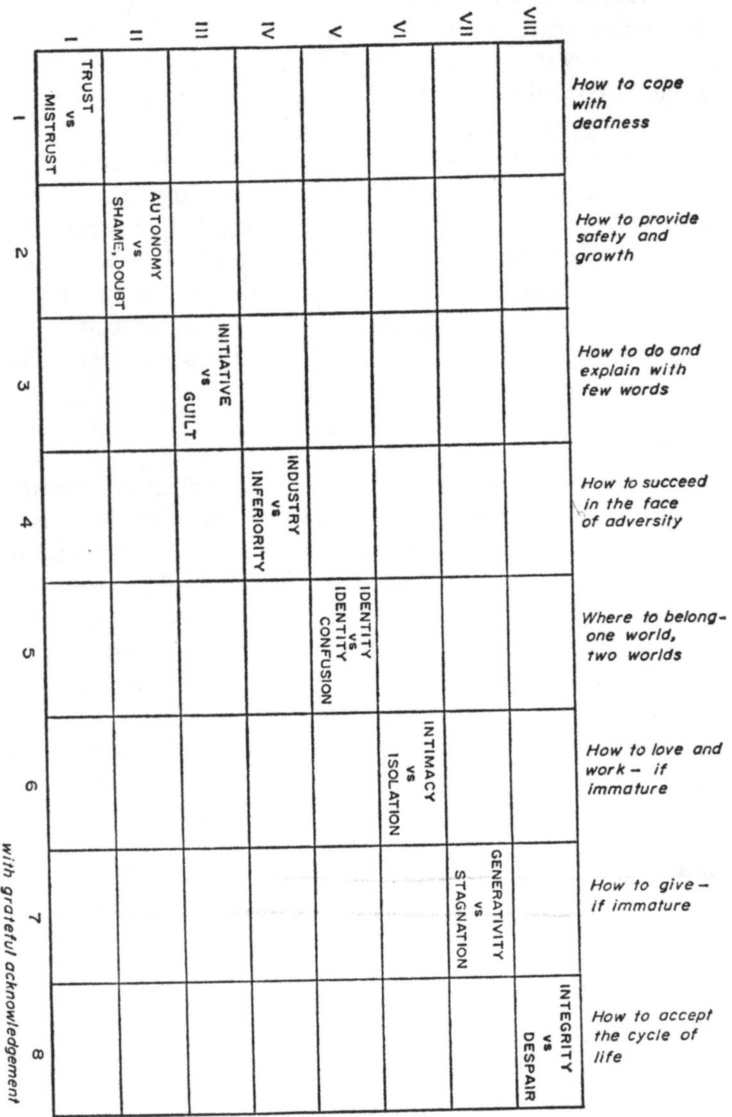

Figure 1 A DEVELOPMENTAL MODEL APPLIED TO PROBLEMS OF DEAFNESS

3

New Perspectives on Manual Communication

Manual communication is used in varied forms by most deaf individuals; the American Sign Language is probably used by most deaf adults in the United States today. Children, however, usually are assiduously kept from its usage, and tend to learn it surreptitiously and from peers rather than authoritative adults. It has always had vociferous opponents, who consider it anathema, and joyful proponents, who consider it a miracle. Our new perspectives may place the reality between these two extremes.

In oral languages a message consists of sounds intricately interwoven, produced by the organs of speech and received by the ear. In American Sign Language a message consists of intricate visual patterns, produced by gestures and received by the eye. Each gesture is made by one or both hands, held in a specific configuration and at a particular portion of the message-sender's body; the hand or hands are either still or traverse a certain motion for a particular meaning. The configuration of the hand, its placement in front of the body, or the motion itself may be varied in such a way as to produce signs that are related in meaning. For example, male signs are characteristically made on or near the forehead, female signs on or near the lower cheek. *Mother* and *father* are made in precisely the same way except for the difference in location (*mother* is signed with open hand at the cheek, *father* is signed with open hand at the forehead);

Chapter 3 is by Hilde S. Schlesinger.

female cousin and *male cousin* are also differentiated solely on the basis of location. "Disagreeable" signs are made with the "V" hand,[1] (although index and middle fingers are slightly flexed); signs like *steal, difficult, problem,* and *selfish* are all made with the same hand configuration but in different locations and with different accompanying motions. The action itself has grammatical correlates. Thus *improve* is made with the ulnar surface of one hand placed on the dorsum of the other hand and moving rhythmically upwards towards the elbow, while *dis-improve* or getting worse is made in the reverse order (starting near the elbow). Similarly, future time is indicated with a movement from the face forward, while past time is the same movement done backwards.

Sign languages used by the deaf in different countries bear some similarities to each other. Deaf participants at world congresses seem to have fewer difficulties understanding each other than do the hearing participants. Nevertheless, enough differences exist that it cannot be said that a truly international sign language exists, despite efforts in that direction.

The American Sign Language of the deaf is probably a direct descendant of the *signes méthodiques* described by Charles Michel de L'Épée in 1776. Reference to manual communication can be found as far back as Latin Bibles of the tenth century. Apparently many countries have had philosophers, educators, or religious people who became interested in providing the deaf with a manual system of language. However, no direct studies have attempted to test the real effectiveness of sign language in diminishing the chasm between the potential and the achievement of the deaf.[2] But as we shall indicate below, related findings in various fields suggest that manual communication can enhance the growth of the deaf child to mature adulthood. We shall sum-

1. The examples given represent one sign for which one word (Stokoe's gloss or English equivalent is given) and are underscored. Another system of manual communication is fingerspelling a one-for-one representation of alphabetical symbols. This system can be used by itself to represent each English word via its alphabetical components, or it can be used to supplement sign language for words not presently available in signs. Furthermore, numerous signs use one of the alphabetical hand configurations, although the movement of the hand and the placement in front of the body differ for specific meanings.

2. Quigley's study (1968) is the most direct attempt. However, his study focused on the classroom rather than the family setting and utilized the Rochester method rather than sign language.

marize briefly some of the relevant findings and hypotheses from studies of deafness, neurology, ethnocentrism and bilingualism, cultural disadvantage, and child development.

DEAFNESS

We have previously indicated that deaf children of deaf parents have been found to perform at a higher level than do deaf children of hearing parents. Brill (1960, 1969) noted that children of deaf parents showed "better adjustment." Indeed, the deaf children of deaf parents consistently have higher language scores than do deaf children of hearing parents. They have a "better command of language" (Stevenson, 1964) and higher scores in reading, vocabulary and fingerspelling (Quigley and Frisina, 1961; Stuckless and Birch, 1966). Meadow's work (1967) is extensively described in Chapter 6 together with the current extension of the earlier findings. In the present context, however, it is important to note that the small number of children with deaf parents who had received extensive early oral-aural training concomitantly with early manual language tended to have higher ratings for speech and lipreading ability.

Throughout our research and clinical observations we have noted two variables that may account for the overall functioning of deaf children with deaf parents: (1) the greater acceptance of deafness with its concomitant greater ease of child-rearing, and (2) the early parental input of manual communication with the earlier onset of receptive and expressive communication for the child.

Some observers believe that "acceptance" alone accounts for the difference. However, a definition or analysis of the word/feeling "acceptance" is difficult indeed. We have met hearing parents of deaf children, as we have met hearing parents of hearing children, who for reasons of their own found it difficult to accept any child born to them. We have met others who have accepted the child but continue to reject all aspects of deafness (i.e., denying the impact of deafness, refusing hearing aids). Others accept the child with the deafness, but refuse to accept what they consider a stigma of deafness—the American Sign Language. Finally, a few hearing parents do not consider sign language a stigma, but rather a bridge to their youngster.

As suggested before, it appears that both a warm, nurturant emotional relation and a varied sensory and cognitive input are necessary ingredients for an optimal learning environment. Most of the mothers we observe seem to provide the warm, nurturant relation, but what about the varied sensory and cognitive input?

Wyatt (1969:1–21) sensitively describes optimal maternal linguistic input, which she feels represents an interweaving of speech and nonverbal communications. Optimally, maternal speech is described as short, simple, clearly articulated, grammatically correct and matched to the child's level of language acquisition. Wyatt, however, places at least equal weight on maternal actions such as mutual delight in each linguistic event, a conjoining of speech and physical activities, and the provision of immediate, specific, appropriate and rewarding feedback to the child's verbal and nonverbal messages.

> The interaction between mother and child was as much nonverbal as it was verbal. The mother followed Ricky with her eyes almost continuously; she played with him; she cuddled him, carried him, directed and protected him. Mother and child obviously were close to each other, both physically and emotionally. This young mother, from her appearance a lower-middle-class woman, was an excellent speech model for her small son. She spoke to him in short simple sentences, using a limited vocabulary that most probably he was able to comprehend. Her short phrases and sentences were grammatically correct, and she articulated clearly. Watching her play with Ricky, one could sense her delight in the child. (Wyatt, 1969:6–7)

The point to be made here is that without a viable communicative system, available to both mother and child, there is no possibility of the kind of optimal combination of warmth and linguistic input described above. For most deaf mothers and a few hearing mothers, sign language is the means through which the necessary linguistic competence becomes available.

Another frequently cited criticism of studies involving the superior functioning of deaf children of deaf parents has been the somewhat greater expectation of brain damage and related learning disabilities in cases of exogenous (as opposed to hereditary) deafness. But Vernon and Koh (1970) report an interesting study that suggests that early manual communication input rather than an absence of neurological involvement underlies the superior functioning of deaf children of deaf parents. Two groups of thirty-two children were matched for age, sex, and IQ. Both groups had family pedigrees clearly indicating hereditary deafness—one group had deaf parents (the "early manual group"); the other (the "early oral group") had hearing parents but other deaf relatives. Vernon and Koh found that the early manual group demonstrated better overall educational achievement including superiority in reading skills and written language. Comparison of speech intelligibility and speech reading indicated no differences. The authors found the linguistic superiority particularly striking since the linguistic level of the deaf parents was on the average grossly *below* that of the parents of the oral sample.

NEUROLOGY

The author has often been struck by the lack of attention paid to a comparison between the effector (motor) mechanism for speech and the effector (motor) mechanism for sign language. Although neurology has not yet achieved complete understanding of the process of speech, some interesting findings emerge. The organs for hearing (the cochlea) and for speaking (larynx) are separate and distinct. There are minimal internal neuro-anatomical pathways between the centers of the brain for speaking and hearing, and those which do exist are not unique to man (Orr and Cappannari, 1967). The neurological representations of the speech area are as yet incompletely known. What seems to be generally accepted as a result of many experiments is that cortical stimulation can produce vocalizations, but cannot in the course of many experiments produce a word or speech. On the contrary, cortical stimulation has been known to produce speech arrest. Thus it is felt that speech is probably produced by inhibitory actions. The close anatomical proximity in the brain between the motor area for speech and the motor area for the hand has been of marked interest to some neurologists (Penfield and Rasmussen, 1950; Penfield and Roberts, 1959), to psychiatrists (Arieti, 1967) and to others (Bruner, Olver, Greenfield et al., 1966; Orr and Cappannari, 1967). The highly similar neuronal type in both these areas has also been pointed out (Ransom and Clark, 1959).

Developmentally, the relation between motor control of the hand and motor control of the muscles of speech production is

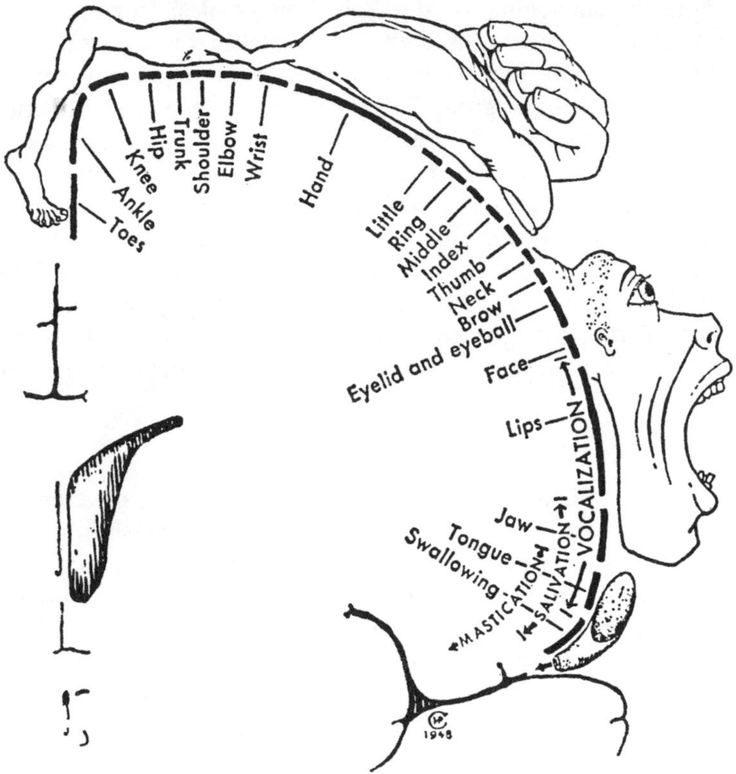

Figure 2 The localization pattern on the human motor cortex. (Figure 115 from Penfield and Rasmussen, 1950, *The Cerebral Cortex of Man.* Used with the permission of the Macmillan Co.)

also of interest, since the child's ability to speak has been observed to coincide with his ability to inhibit the grasp reflex. Arieti (1967) points to the fact that hand and mouth share activities other than word or language formations (e.g., eating); he feels that these collective actions probably "were accompanied by vocal sounds which became words."

Many have indicated parallels between motor, especially upper motor, development and language development. As Orr and Cappannari put it:

> It is this fact—the hand with its precise, complex highly integrated faculties evolved concomitantly with

> the marked expansion of the cerebral cortex in size and complexity and both of these apparently parallel development of language—that is so challenging. (Orr and Cappannari, 1967:66)

An additional example of possible hand-speech associations is the "go bye-bye" ontogenesis described by Penfield and Roberts (1959). Not once do they mention a motion accompanying the phrase. And yet virtually no child, hearing or deaf, learns this phrase without accompanying motoric expression.

Kinesics appear to be a necessary prerequisite for certain speakers. Mayor LaGuardia is said to have used two sets of gestures: one for English, and one for Italian. Neapolitan speakers whose hands are held are said to be unable to speak fluently.

Professor Sapon,[3] in a demonstration of verbal operant conditioning, gave the following example: A youngster had been conditioned to "know" and say the words "red, green, blue" and the experimenter wanted to condition the word "and." The youngster was unable to produce the word orally until the experimenter invented a motoric sign (index and third finger crossed —as in *r* in the sign language—pulled horizontally from left to right). After seeing the gesture, the child was able to say "and."

Another interesting possibility comes from a combination of findings from two separate sources: Myklebust (1960) has reported that of all language units, prepositions alone do not show the usual lag in language acquisition in deaf children; and McNeill (1970*a*) describes a study by Clark for evidence that prepositions are at first expressive of movement.

In view of these hints and puzzles it is remarkable that so little attention has been paid to the motor-speech relation in studying the development of expressive language in either hearing or deaf children. These clues suggest many possibilities for new research in language acquisition and associative learnings.

ETHNOCENTRISM AND BILINGUALISM

We have previously indicated that deaf individuals have been found to use sign language primarily with their deaf friends (Crammatte, 1968). Many deaf persons can thus be described

3. Stanley M. Sapon is Professor of Psycholinguistics and Psychology and Director of the Verbal Behavior Laboratory, The University of Rochester, New York.

as living in a bilingual environment in which parents, teachers, and society generally stress spoken English, while peers stress sign language. As in many bilingual situations, one of the languages is frequently devaluated and stigmatized.

Traditionally, although Europeans have valued multiple language acquisition, Americans have tended to feel that bilingualism is "bad"—that it may have deleterious effects on personal and intellectual development (Lambert and Peal, 1962). This view, however, is more and more being treated as an unfounded ethnocentric bias. So, for example, Diebold (1966) found that cases of genuine bilingual pathology were related to a crisis in personal and social identity symbolized by negative attitudes toward the language. These attitudes usually occurred in a monolingual society where there were antagonistic pressures for linguistic acculturation, and where the minority language was stigmatized as socially inferior. Yamamoto (1964:476) agrees and states that "a truly bilingual situation where two languages are on equal footing is rarely encountered."

Lambert and Peal (1962) found their bilingual research subjects to be far superior to monolinguals on both verbal and nonverbal tests of intelligence. They attributed these findings to the possibility of greater "conceptual flexibility" on the part of the bilinguals. Ervin-Tripp (1966) indicated that the learning of both English and Spanish may be enhanced in a school that provides Spanish-speaking teachers for its Spanish-speaking pupils. Schlesinger (1970) notes a similar occurrence in the acquisition of English by youngsters speaking foreign languages. Labov (1964) has suggested that antagonistic attitudes toward a second communicative system create major obstacles to successful dialect switching. Bernstein (1961) has suggested that a "public language" must be freely accepted if the "formal language" is to be successfully learned. Thus, all these authors stress the possible cognitive advantages of bilingualism given an atmosphere of acceptance and opportunity for utilization. Such benevolence toward different languages is not frequently found in Anglo-Saxon countries—particularly if one of the languages uses body motion in the elaboration of its symbols.

On the other hand, an ethnocentric bias also exists within the population primarily using sign language. The author has frequently suspected a stigma towards the spoken language among deaf adults, possibly created by the onerous years of arduous language learning. Among adolescents it may even be responsible for the frequent occurrence of stigmatization of speech when, after years of sign language taboo, they suddenly discover its potentialities. This we postulate would not occur if both speech and sign language were on equal footing from early childhood onwards.

Penfield, the renowned neurologist, has the following to say about bilingualism in English-speaking countries:

> It has been said that an Anglo-Saxon cannot learn other languages well. This is only because, as he grows up, he becomes a stiff and resistant individualist, like a tree—a sort of oak that cannot be bent in any graceful manner. But the Anglo-Saxon, if caught young enough, is as plastic and as good a linguist as the child of any other race. (Penfield and Roberts, 1959: 235–236)

What does the ethnocentric bias allege about the American Sign Language? It has been accused of not possessing syntactic rules. Stokoe (1970*a*, 1970*b*) refutes this. He states that there are varieties of American Sign Language ranging from one that more or less faithfully represents English in signs and finger-spelled words to one that has a syntax quite different from that of English. But all varieties have elements that contrast with each other: places or *tabs* where signs start, act, or end; designators (*dez*), the appearance of the hand or hands; and *sigs,* the action itself (Stokoe, 1970*a*:4). Signs made of these elements combine in certain ways and not in others, i.e., following syntactic rules. As a result some sign phrases closely parallel English phrases, but other sign phrases do not. These when *translated word-for-sign* look like ungrammatical English. The same can be said for any other translation into a foreign language. Even when the same word exists, it may have a different meaning when translated word-for-word. A good example is that of the old Jewish refugee couple in the movie *Casablanca,* who appeared anxious to disassociate themselves from Nazi Germany and incidentally the German language. Their dialogue, if remembered correctly, goes like this: Husband: "What clock is it?" Woman: "Eight clock." Husband: "Such clock already?" This "nonsense" sentence makes perfect sense if retranslated word-for-word into the German language. Sign language has also been accused of not possessing meaning, because signs are not always isomorphic with English words. The English word "stress," the German "Alpenstock," the French "savoir faire," the Yiddish "chutzpah," the Spanish "simpatico" have never had accurate, concise translations into another language.

Furthermore sign language has been said to have a paucity of vocabulary. Nida (1958:283) suggests that "subcultures have proportionately more extensive vocabularies in the area of their distinctness." Eskimos have more words for snow, some African languages have more words for cattle than we possess in English (Ervin-Tripp, 1966). Sign language remains to be investigated in this regard. Furthermore, there is evidence that languages which exist in a state of subjugation or stigmatization may not blossom like other living languages. Thus, the very complaint about sign language, that it possesses a paucity of vocabulary, may be responsible for that paucity. The author has witnessed a spurt of new signs among certain intellectual deaf populations that may well resemble the spurt in Hebrew since Israel became a state.

CULTURAL DISADVANTAGE

The literature on ghetto minority group children bears some curious similarities to research findings in the area of deafness. Most researchers postulate that minority group children and deaf children have the potential for normal development and achievement. The focus has been on identifying those factors amenable to positive programs of intervention in order to increase achievement. Patterns of psychological adaptation and cognitive achievement described above for the deaf population are similar to those found among the culturally disadvantaged (Deutsch, 1963; Hunt, 1961; Riessman, 1962). There is a growing feeling among those concerned with the disadvantaged child that the provision of a richer, more meaningful environment at a critical, early age can help to change potentially "disadvantaged" youngsters into more productive ones. Here is increasing evidence that the term "enrichment" does not refer to a haphazard increase of stimuli, but to a careful match between the circumstance encountered by the child and the schemata he has already assimilated into his repertoire (Hunt, 1961). Many feel that excessive but meaningless stimuli in the environment have the effect of inducing habitual inattention and "tuning out"

(Deutsch, 1963), or of developing a negative valence for all cognitive learning situations (Hess and Shipman, 1968), or that exposure to a more complicated model may not be optimal for acquisition of the simplest concepts (Entwisle, 1969).

These findings are of great importance for an approach to the environmental enrichment of deaf youngsters who are frequently subjected to an intensive barrage of barely meaningful or meaningless acoustic stimuli (Schlesinger, 1970*a*). The evidence indicates that the stimuli must be varied, enriched, and matched to the child's existing schemata. Furthermore, he must be permitted to respond to the stimuli. Receptively, the stimuli for the deaf child have a strange intermittent quality: during didactic sessions stimuli may frequently represent a barrage; during ordinary family events they may drop to a minimum, as the deaf child is left out of the family rituals. Expressively, the deaf child has fewer opportunities to respond to his incoming stimuli; the barrage itself may leave him floundering and he is frequently not "listened to" because of the prolonged delay in the development of speech, the frequent unintelligibility of his speech and his parents' reluctance to accept and understand his gestural language.

Furthermore, Goodman (1964) and Deutsch (1964) have shown that children are beginning to develop a sense of self-awareness and of ethnic and racial differences as early as ages three or four. Deaf children may also at this early age perceive that others feel they have a low probability of success. We believe that this awareness of self-worth and social stigma plays an important role in the child's ability to profit from an enriched environment. For the child may need to feel that he is worthy of enrichment for his own sake, and not for the sake of becoming like others who are hearing. Thus a tragic and self-fulfilling circle of prejudice-self-devaluation-low achievement may operate similarly in the deaf and the disadvantaged groups.

CHILD DEVELOPMENT

Psychiatrists and psychologists have frequent encounters with children who are mute or have a distorted speech pattern despite normal auditory and speech mechanisms. Delayed onset of speech can have a psychological origin in otherwise normal children (Filippi and Rousey, 1968; Lenneberg, 1967; Levy, 1955). Despite the controversial nature of childhood autism, many authors (e.g., Bettelheim, 1967; Despert, 1968) feel that language development in autism has an interpersonal basis in which the children hide their thoughts behind esoteric language symbols or bury them completely in mutism.

Montaigne has written that, "The word is half his that speaks and half his that hears it." Clinical observations of highly verbal parents with their young hearing children frequently reveal that the parents behave as if the word belonged primarily to them and not to the child who "hears it." The child may remain mute despite indications that his linguistic competence is normal. Insistence on verbal production on the part of these children only accomplishes the opposite of the desired behavior.

We have noted in our clinical cases that insistence on verbal behavior from young deaf children can result in a spurt of vocabulary not used with communicative intent. The parents who are able to convince the child that the word is indeed half his are more likely to have a child with a communicative personality rather than a parroting personality. In our experience this task is facilitated for parents who choose to use manual communication with their very young children.

With the above in mind, a linguistic study by Cazden can be viewed in psychiatric terms. Cazden (1968) reports on her earlier work (1965) in which two groups of children aged two-and-a-half years were subjected to experimental linguistic intervention. One group of children (called the expansion children) received 100 percent "expansion" of their speech by the experimenter during the three-month experimental period (one hour a day for five days a week while looking at picture books). For example, if the child said, "Doggie bite," the experimenter would say, "Yes, the doggie is biting." The second experimental group received what Cazden called modeling (deliberately not expansions). An example of modeling to the above "doggie bite" might be, "Yes, he's very mad." The results, as based on a language competency test, were clear cut: the modeling children gained more than the expansion children, and both did better than an untreated control group.

We postulate that 100 percent expansion can be seen by the children as unceasing correction—an interminable improvement of their cherished utterances without any dialogue with an accepting adult. What Cazden calls modeling can well be seen by the children as true dialogue wherein their message was accepted as it was, while the experimenter returned with a message—itself given in expanded version—thus creating a human communication. This interpretation is of great interest in what happens to deaf children as they learn spoken language; correction rather than dialogue is the typical adult response.

Our psychiatric experience has shown that if the child's manipulation of the environment is delayed until he is able to cope by purely spoken, verbal means, other areas of development may also be thwarted. Most investigators feel that children with learning disorders may need learning techniques that stress action and physical involvement (Rioux, 1967). The insistence on motor inhibition does not take into consideration that children appear to have differing preferred modalities for learning: visual, auditory, motor, or mixed. Some authorities hold that acceptance of the preferred modality will ensure optimal use of other, more neglected modalities through association pathways (Berlin, personal communication). This approach is the direct antithesis of that usually presented to the parents of deaf children. Thus, not only are the children prevented from achieving reciprocal communication, but also they are prevented from using all possible avenues to the development of language.

One more item of particular interest must be mentioned—the usual frustration involved in reciprocal communication when one of the partners is not understood or cannot understand the other. Such frustration has been reported almost universally in interchange between adult deaf and hearing individuals and is reported ubiquitously in our clinical work. Our research data involving forty preschool deaf children indicate that more than half of the parents complain about frustration involving "understanding"; 15 percent complain they cannot understand the child, whereas 38 percent complain of their own inability to be understood by the child. (These percentages appear to increase as the child grows older, as evidenced by our clinical observations of the parents of deaf children.) We have hypothesized that the level of frustration inherent in deaf child-mother communications is considerably decreased when sign language and fingerspelling are introduced at the earliest possible age.

SUMMARY

In the preceding pages, an attempt has been made to review the literature in five different areas, and to suggest how research findings and clinical observations may provide new perspectives on the American Sign Language as used by the deaf. The five areas of knowledge reviewed were language and education of the deaf; neurological functioning; ethnocentrism and bilingualism; cultural disadvantage; and psychiatry and child development.

It was suggested that evidence from these fields helps to explain why sign language has been held in disrepute for so long. Furthermore, it has led us to an increased conviction that sign language, especially under certain circumstances, may be beneficial for deaf children. These optimal conditions would include an early input of manual communication, associated with excellent oral/aural training wherein both signs and speech are equally valued by parent (and subsequently, by child), and wherein their combined use is free of conflict. At the very least, these studies should provide the basis and the impetus for additional research.

4

Language Acquisition in Four Deaf Children[1]

> There was language . . .
> in their very gestures.
>
> SHAKESPEARE, *The Winter's Tale,* V.ii

This chapter describes the language acquisition of young deaf children whose parents through necessity or choice have all used American Sign Language with them. The children are thus learning to describe the world, ask questions, and declare their desires (affirmatively, negatively, or imperatively) via an intricate system of gestures. We have postulated that these youngsters would traverse stages similar to those children traverse learning English or other spoken languages. The prolonged theoretical portion that follows is considered necessary for several reasons: the study of sign language as a *language* is relatively new; studies on the acquisition of sign language are virtually unknown; and the reasons for this dearth of information are considered important to the present study.

Chapter 4 is by Hilde S. Schlesinger, with the assistance of Carole Geballe, Arline Cottrell, and Katherine Leland.

1. We gratefully acknowledge the most helpful suggestions of Dr. Ursula Bellugi and Dr. William C. Stokoe, Jr. The combination of their expertise in psycholinguistics and their knowledge and sensitivity to the problems of deafness made these comments particularly welcome and useful.

BRIEF REVIEW OF PSYCHOLINGUISTICS

There appears to be universal agreement that children acquire specific aspects of the language of their culture at certain definite ages and in certain sequences. The how of the acquisition is subject to much debate. Clearly both maturation and learning are necessary conditions, but neither is sufficient (McNeill, 1970*a*). It is important to note that language exists simultaneously in an intricately interrelated manner, on the three levels of sound, shape, and sense characterized as phonology, syntax, and semantics respectively (Moores, 1970).

> Recent studies look upon a young child as a fluent speaker of an exotic language. The psycholinguist's problem, therefore, is analogous to the problem faced by a field linguist. Both the students of Urdu, say, and the student of child language want to characterize a speaker's grammar, and neither supposes he will profit much in imposing the grammar of well-formed English onto the corpus. (McNeill, 1966:16)

The development of phonology has been described by Ervin-Tripp (1966), McNeill (1970*a*), and Lenneberg (1967), among others. Irwin and Chen (1946) have established norms for phonological development between zero and thirty months. A useful, concise description of phonologic stages can be found in Lillywhite (1958), who states that most sounds are mastered by age four although some (*s, z, sh, ch* and *j*) may continue distorted until seven-and-a-half years of age. We learn from Ervin-Tripp (1966) that for *hearing* preschool children the sound of words rather than their meaning is salient; this attention to the phonetic aspect decreases with age. The shape of language refers to grammar: syntax and morphology. Again there is general agreement that the child passes through certain sequences in dealing with the shape of words and sentences. When he has acquired a corpus of words (see "sense" below), the child begins some time between eighteen and twenty-four months to combine these words into "sentences." These early sentences are called telegraphic by Brown and Fraser (1964) since the sentences are reduced, almost the way that adults reduce sentences for telegraphic transmissions. However, the children are not abbreviating well informed, grammatically complete sentences; the children possess a simple grammar, the output of which is telegraphic speech (McNeill, 1965).

The early grammars of children emerge when two elements (words or signs) are combined into utterances. These combinations have been described by Braine (1963), and we shall refer to them more fully in describing the language of one of our four subjects (Karen). It is important to realize that many utterances, while entirely consistent within the child's system are not simple imitations of adult utterances. Many of the productions have never been heard or seen before by the child and are generated by the child's own internally consistent rules.

The child eventually formulates grammatical rules (see McNeill, 1970*a*) for longer, more complex sentences. Children develop negatives in a series of sequences described by Brown, Cazden, and Bellugi (1968). Thus, for example, children first negate by saying "no me want," then "I not want," then "I don't want." Children's questions have been similarly described and classified (Klima and Bellugi, 1966). Syntactical competence can be studied by observing the spontaneous occurrences of particular grammatical features or by eliciting performance by means of a number of tests, including those recently devised for plurals (Ervin, 1964), for negatives (Bellugi, 1967), or for a grammatical array that includes plurals, tense markings, and comparative markings for adjectives (the "wug" test, Berko, 1958).

It is important to note for our future discussion that Ervin (1964) found that grammatical organizations of *imitations* are identical to grammatical organizations of *spontaneous speech.* McNeill (1966) provides the following dialogue, which illustrates this finding:

Child: Nobody don't like me.
Mother: No, say "nobody likes me."
Child: Nobody don't like me.

(eight repetitions of this dialogue)

Mother: No, now listen carefully; say "nobody likes me."
Child: Oh! Nobody don't likes me.

This reflects the fact that children cannot imitate those linguistic forms they have not yet internalized.

The sense of language (semantics) is the most difficult to define, and the most important to the field of psychiatry. The birth of meaning—that is, symbol formation, in the child is the subject of many different theories. What is generally agreed upon by psychoanalytic theory and the developmental theories of Piaget and others is that the very young infant does not differentiate between himself and his environment. During the sensorimotor stage of development the infant learns to differentiate self from non-self without linguistic symbols. Somewhat later, the child learns that objects have names. In order to achieve this feat, a child must add to the discrimination between himself and objects the further distinction between himself and words, and between words and objects (Werner and Kaplan, 1963).

The child's first words are considered by most trained observers to be "holophrastic"—that is, each word has a much broader and more diffuse meaning for the child than it does for adults.

> In effect holophrastic words stand for sentences. The utterance "milk" can mean for a one-year-old "I want some milk," "The milk is on the floor," "Don't give me any more milk," "I want Pablum," etc. . . . it is conceivable that the child is trying to construct a sentence dictionary in which each word corresponds to a sentence interpretation. (McNeill, 1966:63)

Vetter (1970) describes initial vocabulary growth as a slow process. Following the utterance of his first word, the child may still know a very small number of words even after several months. At some point, however, the child reaches the naming stage, at which the acquisition of vocabulary accelerates rapidly, as shown in this table compiled by Smith in 1926 (reproduced in Vetter, 1970:49).

Year level	*Mean number of words that child can produce and respond to*
1	3
2	272
3	896
4	1540

A more recent study of average vocabulary size (Lenneberg, 1966) tends to corroborate the above means.

Our semantic emphasis in the case material will be on vocabulary and holophrasis; we shall not deal with the more complex semantic effects such as negation and reversibility except in passing.

THE IMPACT OF DEAFNESS

While there is a deplorable lack of research on the phonology of the deaf (Rosenstein, 1965) we do know that speech intelligibility among the deaf is generally considered to be poor. The quality of their voices is said to be strained, possessing an abnormal pitch with dramatically different intonation patterns and a decreased control for intensity of sounds compared to hearing peoples' voices (Lenneberg, Rebelsky, and Nichols, 1965). The McGill group (Lach et al., 1970) indicates that all their deaf subjects—aged eleven to thirty-two months—were functioning at a level far below the Irwin and Chen (1946) phonological norms. They state that it took twelve months of specific training to accomplish as much as twelve months of untutored living does for the hearing infant.

Lenneberg, Rebelsky, and Nichols (1965) indicate that crying and cooing are regulated by physical maturation and initially at least are not contingent upon specific acoustic stimuli. Thus, deaf children are usually described as developing normal patterns of vocalizations until about six to nine months of age. At nine months a decrease of vocalizations is noted in the absense of corrective hearing aids.

There is very little literature on the language achievement of deaf children between the ages of nine months and six to seven years. Clinical and anecdotal materials, however, reveal that these children are showing the beginnings of the cumulative deficit in language that is invariably reported among deaf school children and adults. Our own findings comparing Mecham scores of the deaf and hearing subjects in our study of deaf preschoolers (Chapter 5) can be seen in table 1.

Studies of school-age deaf children uniformly suggest that the underlying area in which a deaf child is weakest is in language ability (Moores, 1970). On academic achievement tests, deaf children score lowest on word meaning and paragraph

TABLE 1
Mecham Scores of Deaf and Hearing Children

Language Age in Months *(quartiles)*	*Deaf*		*Hearing*	
	%	(*N*)	%	(*N*)
5–16	35	(14)	—	(0)
17–28	40	(16)	—	(0)
29–52	23	(9)	25	(5)
53–69	3	(1)	75	(15)
Totals	101	(40)	100	(20)
Average Age	43.8		43.7	

meaning subtests. Furth (1966) indicates that only 12 percent of deaf adults achieve true linguistic competence and only 4 percent are proficient speech readers or speakers. In summary, by the time they have reached adulthood, most deaf adults have not mastered the shape, sound, and sense of the primary language of America—oral English.

This does not mean, however, that deaf adults are languageless; most of them use the American Sign Language competently (Best, 1943; Rainer, Altshuler, and Kallman, 1963; Kohl, 1966). Although there is some controversy in the field, there is strong support for the belief that the American Sign Language of the deaf (Stokoe et al., 1965) fulfills the requirements of a genuine language: "any symbolic system which is learned, which consists of conventional basic units and rules for their arrangement, and which includes a conventional set of arbitrary signs for meanings and referents" (Ervin-Tripp, 1966). Despite the frequent usage of the American Sign Language among the deaf, its linguistic structure has not been analyzed except in a few recent studies by Stokoe (1965, 1970*a*, in press); Tervoort (1968); McCall (1965).

RATIONALE AND METHODOLOGY

We have received impetus for the following study from the research and clinical data summarized in this chapter and from the related evidence summarized in the previous chapter. In outline, deaf children of deaf parents have been found to have a distinct advantage in many areas of cognitive and psychological functioning, compared to deaf children of hearing parents. We have hypothesized that one of the reasons for these differences is the early possibility of parent-child communication by means of manual language.[2] It is doubly difficult to find young deaf children whose parents are using sign language early. First, the overall incidence of deafness is low, and less than 10 percent of deaf children have deaf parents (Rainer, Altshuler, and Kallman, 1963:237). Second, until very recently it was almost impossible to find hearing parents who used sign language with their deaf infants and children. We were most fortunate to find four children who met certain criteria (see below) over the course of the last three years.

The children differed in terms of their parents' hearing status and the time of initiation of sign language input. However, they all had a severe hearing loss (at least 80 decibel loss in the better ear). Copies of the audiograms appear on the following page. All had parents who used sign language and spoken English simultaneously even though the pattern of input was variable. Each family—two deaf, two hearing—will be described individually, but baseline data can be found in tables 2 and 3.

TABLE 2
Available Data for Language Acquisition

Age (First Contact)		*Age Feb. 1971*	*Number of Months in Study*	*Hours of Videotape*	*Number of Visits*
0;8,1	Ann	2;1	15	10½	23
2;7	Karen	5;5	31	6¼	23
2;8	Ruth	3;5	9	16	9
3;4	Marie	5;3	21	10½	16

Each child was seen monthly for varying periods of time in sessions lasting from one to four hours. The parent-child sessions were videotaped at home, on outings, in school or in the project office, and were generally spontaneous, with occasional structured test situations.

2. Personal communication from Dr. Rosslyn Gaines—unusually frequent hand movements were also noted in a hearing infant of deaf parents—a paper is in process by Gaines, Hardyck, and Petrinovich.

TABLE 3

Characteristics of Families Participating in Linguistic Study

Parents	*The "B" Family*	*The "A" Family*	*The "S" Family*	*The "C" Family*
Hearing status	deaf, of deaf parents	deaf, hearing parents	hearing	hearing
Age	late 20s	late 30s	mid-30s	early 40s
Socio-economic	M-housewife F-skilled trades	both professionals	M-housewife F-military officer	M-housewife F-professional
Education	M-high school graduate F-State resident school for deaf graduate	both college graduates	M-2 yrs college F-4 yrs college	M-jr. college graduate F-BA, 2 yrs post-graduate
Manual communication	since birth	since high school	$1\frac{1}{2}$ yrs	$1\frac{1}{2}$ yrs
Communicative style	both use signs and voice	both use "SEE," fingerspelling, and voice simultaneously	both use signs, fingerspelling, and voice	both use "SEE," fingerspelling, and voice simultaneously
Relation to deaf community	visit clubs and athletic events of the deaf	leader in deaf organizations	new to area, but making contacts with deaf adults	leader in parental organizations for the deaf
Number of other children	none	none	3 hearing children	4 hearing children

TABLE 3 (cont.)

*Child**	*Ann*	*Karen*	*Ruth*	*Marie*
Birth Date	*12/20/68*	*8/19/65*	*9/4/67*	*10/18/65*
Etiology of deafness	heredity	probably rubella	rubella	possible rubella
Age at diagnosis	3 months	before 17 months	9 months	before 12 months
Amount of hearing loss (better ear)	85 decibels	80 decibels	85 decibels	82 decibels
Hearing aid use	rarely used	at school, home	used consistently	always at school, intermittent at home
Age at adoption	not adopted	17 months	not adopted	6½ months
Age at introduction to manual communication	birth	17 months	15 months	3 yrs 1 month
Age at beginning of study	8 months	2 yrs 7 months	2 yrs 8 months	3 yrs 4 months
Age: Feb. 1971	2 yrs 1 month	5 yrs 5 months	3 yrs 5 months	5 yrs 3 months

* Names of all research subjects and patients have been changed throughout the book to insure anonymity.

ANN: THE BIRTH OF MEANING

Our youngest subject was observed during a critical period (from age 8 months to 22 months), and therefore her data will be used more extensively than those from the older subjects. We use this case to demonstrate parental linguistic beliefs and style; a record of her motoric and linguistic development; acquisition of individual signs; and deviations from standard usage and/or meaning. Ann's linguistic development is compared with

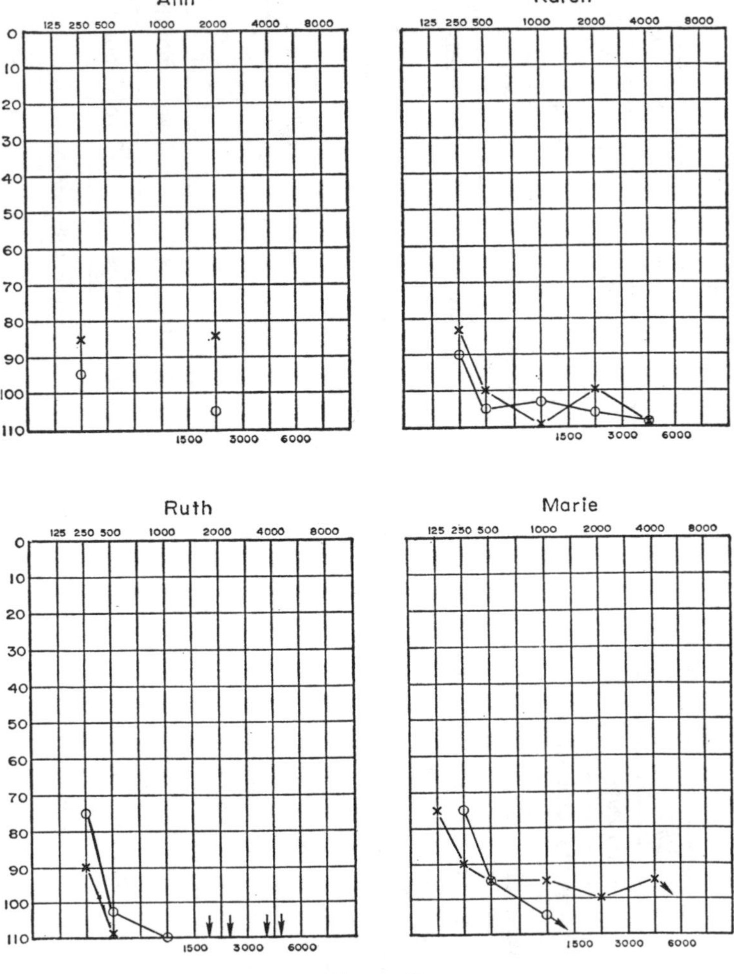

Figure 3

that of two hearing children who learned sign language through a deaf grandmother residing in the home.

BIOGRAPHICAL

Ann B. is the only child of a young deaf couple in their twenties. Both parents are themselves the children of deaf parents and learned sign language at an early age. Both parents

---

Legend for Figure 3

ANN This audiogram for Ann at eight months of age represents fragmentary responses to pure tone stimuli in both ears strongly suggestive of a severe to profound bilateral impairment of hearing. The lack of bone conduction responses precludes any statement concerning the nature of this hearing loss.

KAREN Karen's responses at age five years to Conditioned Orientation Reflex (COR) audiometric techniques indicate a profound impairment of hearing in both ears. The etiology is said to have been maternal rubella. This child appears to have residual hearing extending into the upper speech frequency range.

RUTH These findings for Ruth at about two years of age indicate a profound bilateral impairment of hearing. Bone conduction testing could not be accomplished. Speech detection thresholds are in agreement with the pure tone results: Right ear, 85 dB; Left ear, 100 dB. This degree of impairment is consistent with the history of maternal rubella.

MARIE Audiometric testing for this child at age five years reveals a bilateral hearing impairment of profound degree. Pure tone thresholds for the left ear appear to reflect residual hearing extending across a broad range. Speech detection levels are consistent with the tonal thresholds: Right ear, 82 dB; Left ear, 85 dB.

The audiograms of these four children, and their responses to sound in everyday life, reflect the fact that there are still many things to be learned about the use of residual hearing. We feel that parental attitudes toward hearing aids, and toward speech training are very important. Other important elements are the age at which training begins, skill of teachers involved, and patterns of hearing loss.

We would like to acknowledge, with thanks, the help of Jacqueline E. Hynes and Ray V. Lage in the interpretation of the four audiograms. Both Miss Hynes and Mr. Lage are clinical audiologists at the Franklin Medical Center's Hearing, Speech, and Language Center, Mrs. Wilda Flower, Director. (All four audiograms are ISO 1964.)

are high school graduates, have worked at skilled trades, and are active members in organizations and clubs for the deaf.

Ann's deafness was diagnosed at three months of age. Since almost all of her maternal relatives are deaf, her parents were not surprised at the time of diagnosis. The parents accepted the recommendations of a hearing aid and auditory training sessions for a few months, but soon declared that Ann was rejecting the hearing aid. Neither parent presently uses a hearing aid. Mrs. B. said she had been "forced to wear one in school, but that it was more irritating than helpful in understanding speech." [3] Mrs. B. was herself raised in a home where both manual and oral modes of communication were valued, and she attempts to provide both sets of cues to her infant daughter. She is also teaching Ann to lipread, a skill which she considers more important than speech "since most deaf people's speech isn't understood well." Mrs. B. uses English syntax in her written English, while alternating between English and sign language syntax in her signed/spoken communications. She switches modes—signs, spoken words, and written words—easily and without self-consciousness. Mr. B. uses writing less frequently but has been very patient in the repetition of a spoken, signed, or fingerspelled message that was not immediately understood by the researchers.

Motoric-Linguistic Development

It is widely hypothesized that language has a biological time table: an interlocking motoric and linguistic developmental schedule. Table 4 indicates the milestones which Ann passed from eight to twenty-two months. The milestones are recorded either in researchers' observation notes or on videotape.

Table 4 clearly shows not only that Ann is motorically at or somewhat beyond her age level, but also that her language development is accelerated. Thus, for example, Ann at age nineteen months had a vocabulary of 117 signs compared to the repertoire of "more than three, but less than fifty" words mentioned by Lenneberg (1967) as within the typical range in hearing children.

Some readers may question the extent of Ann's symbolic use of language under the assumption that sign language is an

3. Some of our clinical data indicate that when parents do not feel comfortable with or about a hearing aid, they are hampered in their ability to help the child use it successfully.

TABLE 4
Interrelated Patterns in Ann's
Motoric and Linguistic Development

Age	*Motor Development*	*Language Development*
8 months/ 1 day	Stands holding on; thumb opposition when grasping plastic beads	Blinking in response to sound with hearing aid. "Vocalizations and gestures convey emphasis and emotions." (S8)
9 months	Playing "peek-a-boo"	
10 months/ 5 days	Claps hands; pulls to standing position; creeps efficiently (S10)	"Beginning to differentiate words by making differential adjustment"; waves "bye-bye." Hits side of head with heel of open hand (like *father*). Hits side of head with fist (like *stupid*). (S10)
10½ months		Hand in loose fist to mouth (like *eat*).
11 months	Secures toy from under cup (C10) Four teeth	Vocalizes negatively after mother gives a mock scolding with "*no.*"
12 months	Hits cup with spoon (C10) Marks with pencil (C12) Squeezes doll (C11) Stands alone	Covers face with both hands to avoid mother. Turns to see who is recipient of sign language. SIGNS: *pretty; wrong.* Understands "come here." (S12)
13 months	Takes first steps alone	
14 months		SIGNS: *cat, sleep, bye sleep.*
14½ months	Unwraps toy (C14) Inserts peg (C14) Holds three cubes (C14)	SIGNS: *hat, eat, no;* imitates mother.

TABLE 4 (cont.)

Age	*Motor Development*	*Language Development*
15 months	Drinks from straw	SIGNS: letter *r*, *smell, dirty, no smart, mommy, daddy, kitty, dog, pretty, wrong, sleep, eat, milk, bye-bye, good, car, no,* Ann (with letter *a*). SIGN VOCABULARY TOTAL: 19 SAYS: "mama" and "hi" Points to nose and ear upon oral request. (S12)
16 months	Drinks from cup and glass	SIGN: *cow.*
17 months	Sits in regular chair	Joins two words (C22; G21): *bird wait bird* *water milk* *good finished* *eat cracker* *cookies more* *home car* *girl funny* *sleep up* *dirty dog*
18 months/ 10 days	Throws ball with both hands, gait semi-stiff (S18)	SIGN VOCABULARY TOTAL: 106 LETTER TOTAL: 3
19 months	Scribbles spontaneously (C18) Build tower 5 blocks (C20 with 3) Walks upstairs with help (B20.3) Walks downstairs with help (B20.5) Twelve teeth	Points to 3 parts of doll (C20). Attempts to follow directions (C20). Pulls person to show (G21). Echos by gestures or words (G21). Identifies 2 pictures from name (C22). SIGN VOCABULARY TOTAL: 117 LETTER TOTAL: 5 (fingerspelling)

TABLE 4 (cont.)

Age	*Motor Development*	*Language Development*
$19\frac{1}{2}$ months		SIGN VOCABULARY TOTAL: 142 LETTER TOTAL: 14 (fingerspelling)
22 months/ 10 days	Runs (S24) Alternates between sitting up and standing (S24)	*Boy girl play* *Me girl* *Hello thank you food* Language creation and interest (S24)

KEY: C = Cattell Score (in months) G = Gesell Score (in months)
B = Bayley Score (in months) S = Slobin Score (in months) from Lenneberg, 1967

ideographic language in which the signs for many words physically resemble the object or action described. While this is true in some cases it is far from true in all. Many signs bear no obvious relation to their origin even for adults, i.e., *American* is represented by both hands with fingers interlaced moving in small circles—allegedly because such a hand construction resembles Lincoln's log house. Certainly when we study Ann's total sign vocabulary at age eighteen months it is difficult to imagine that even with her intelligence she was able to pursue the etymology of such signs as *milk* (hand as in movement of milking cow), *girl* (thumb stroking cheek as for tying little girl's bonnet), *water* (with index, middle, and ring fingers stretched out, as for the letter "W," and held to chin), *smart* (index finger to forehead moving upwards and out), or *funny* (index and middle fingers touching tip of nose and moving outward). She might, however, have had enough experience with life to reason out the signs such as *dog* (palm of hand tapping knee), *ice cream* (hand held to mouth with slight licking protrusion of tongue), or *rain* (both hands held above head with fingers moving individually and downwards). Even giving Ann great credit for remarkable etymological talent at eighteen months, at least half of her sign repertoire can have no ideographic meaning to her at that tender age. Thus, Ann still has a sign vocabulary that compares very favorably with the spoken vocabulary of hearing children.

We have now indicated that parallels exist between speech acquisition and sign language acquisition in terms of onset, sequence and numbers. Other parallels present themselves: the acquisition of the shape and sense of language can be described identically for children using speech or signs. However, the "sound" of spoken language is replaced by the "sight" or "appearance" of sign language: what Stokoe calls the "vocal-visual" differences.

We shall now concentrate on the acquisition, use and meaning of Ann's first individual signs—the one-word utterances of hearing children. These can be described in terms of meaning and development.

ONE-WORD UTTERANCE-MEANING

One-word utterances of hearing and deaf children represent both the birth of meaning and the birth of grammar. One-word/sign can express a feeling, label or name an object and/or fuse the label with the feeling about the object. The word/sign can also be classified according to a single feature. Thus, for example, Ann used the sign *dog* appropriately for pictures of dogs, real dogs and the Doggie Diner Restaurant; the sign *dog* may also have referred to all animals, or even to all animate objects that do not resemble parents. Thus:[4]

Age 16 months: In front of the television set.

> Ann, her parents and the researchers were watching the astronauts land safely after their abortive moon venture. Mrs. B. clapped when the helicopter touched down on the ship. As the astronauts emerged from the helicopter, Ann signed *dog* and pointed to the television. The mother indicated *"wrong, man"* and continued watching. Later the same day Ann signed *dog* for the picture of a child.

Age 16 months, 6 days: At the lion grotto at the zoo.

> Mother: *"lion"*
> Ann: *dog*

4. Italics refer to signs, italics and quotes refer to signs and words, quotes alone refer to spoken words: e.g., *Signs; "Signs and Words"*; "Words."

Mother: "*No,* it's a *yellow kitty.*"
Ann: *dog* (pointing to the lions as they are leaving)
Dog was also used for the elephants, goats, monkeys (both lemurs and great apes), and dolphins. However, on the same day *kitty* was also used for a bird, goat, baby lions, and baby hippo. At the dolphin tank Ann looked through a glass porthole and saw the dolphin swimming underwater and signed *bird.* Ann often added a voiceless "woofing" to her sign of *dog.* Her mother frequently tried to interfere with the global usage by holding on to Ann's hand when the sign was used inappropriately or imprecisely.

Age 17 months: *Dog* in response to girl picture card.

On the other hand a single-word utterance, as in the phenomenon of holophrastic speech, can even have the conceptual content of a full sentence. A one-word child utterance can have an adult sentence equivalent. Thus for Ann:

Smell at age 15 months had at least three adult equivalents:
"I want to go to the bathroom"
and "I am soiled please change me"
and "I want the pretty smelling flower."

Wrong at age 12 months had the following adult equivalent:
"I don't like it when mama pays more attention to the doll than to me."

At age 16 months, Mrs. B. referred to Ann with an *a* hand. Then she changed to a *b* hand. Ann signed *a* then took the *a* to her chin: *wrong.* English equivalent "You made a mistake."

At age 16 months Mother asked, "How *old* are *you?*" Ann signed *old wrong.*
adult equivalent: "I want to tease you and not answer the question again"

Water at age 17 months. Ann signed *water milk.*
adult equivalent: "I want something to drink."

At age 17½ months Ann signed *water*.
adult equivalent: "Mother, I don't want the milk you gave me, water is better."

At age 19 months *water* (while in playyard).
adult equivalent: "Let's go and get some water."

Eventually one-word utterances used holophrastically no longer suffice to express complicated ideas and two- and three-word/sign utterances appear in children's languages. So it is with Ann (see table 4), and in her case, as in others, they represent early grammar and can be analyzed. We have, however, concentrated on such an analysis for another youngster, Karen, subsequently described.

ONE-WORD UTTERANCES-DEVELOPMENT

Hearing children acquiring spoken languages go through a series of steps in the acquisition of a word. A joint behavioral and linguistic longitudinal study of normal first-language acquisition describes one child's acquisition of the word "shoe" (Bullowa et al., 1964). We were able to follow several signs through comparable stages of achievement and we can offer examples of different signs at each of Bullowa's stages:

Stage 1: "Mother produces word in association with object." At 12 months, Mrs. B. said and signed *"mama"* and pointed to herself on several occasions. Mr. B. also signed *mama* and pointed to his wife.

Stage 2: "Child attempts imitation which mother rejects." A gesture of the index finger poking repeatedly on the neck at the jawline was felt by the researchers (at 12 months) to be an attempted imitation of *mother,* but was not recognized as such by Mrs. B., who maintained that Ann merely pointed to herself in many different places.

Stage 3: "Child's imitation accepted by mother." The standard sign *mother* was accepted by Ann's mother at 15 months. Also at 12 months Ann signed *pretty* and her mother immediately recognized it, and said "pretty" to the researchers and made the sign on Ann's face while also saying *"pretty."*

Stage 4: "Child uses word spontaneously in association

with object and is understood by mother." At 14½ months, Ann picked up a hat and signed *hat* and was understood by mother

Stage 5: "Child uses word spontaneously when object is not present." At 17 months Ann and her family had come to the project office for videotaping. While waiting for lunch in a nearby restaurant, Ann asked *home, car?* Her mother explained they would *eat first* and *go home* in the *car later.*

Stage 6: "Child achieves adult standard production of word." At 19 months, Ann tells her mother *come cookie* and leads her into the house to get one. Both signs were standard.

Since the study of early sign language acquisition is in its infancy we would like to comment further about some interesting stages in Ann's usage of three basic signs: *no, bye,* and *wrong.*

no:

At 14½ months, Ann used head shaking, negative vocalizations, and direct action to register her unhappiness with a situation. Until this time she had not used the sign *no* although her parents had been signing it to her for several months. On the day of our visit, we observed the mother signing *no* repeatedly to Ann. The lilting movement, the closeness of the sign to Ann's face, and her mother's facial expression assured us this was a playful message rather than one registering disapproval. Although the sign was made very close to her face, Ann did not blink, but began to imitate the motion. She began by opening and closing her right hand in rather gross movements; the gesture rapidly became more refined with the thumb meeting the index and second fingers; and then the hand turned inward so that she was making the movement right in front of and toward her nose.

bye:

From the age of 8 months to about 16 months, Ann used a waving motion to signal both approaching and departing objects and people—her doll, animals at the zoo, the camera, and mother.

The waving was also performed while holding an object (e.g., a spoon) in her hand.

Once (at 10½ months) she was observed to turn the waving inwards toward herself.[5]

By 16 months Ann had differentiated "coming" and "going," using waving for parting and using *hello* signed with cupped hand to forehead and then outward, for greeting people (even when they were not looking her way or reciprocating); she also signed *hello* for greeting her family on home movies, and for objects in her presence (the camera and flowers).

wrong:

In the American manual alphabet, the letter "y" is with a closed fist with the thumb and little finger outward. When this hand configuration is used tapping the chin, it means *wrong* or *mistake*. The parental input was the standard sign. At 12 months Ann was using the sign appropriately at least some of the time (e.g., complaining that mother was giving attention to a doll rather than to her). Her hand configuration was incomplete; the little finger (which is hard to control) did not move outward, so that the letter resembled the letter *a*; the fist was very loose and the placement was often further under the chin than the adult sign. At 16 months the little finger occasionally completed its motion making the correct *y* configuration. At 17 months, Ann was shown a picture card with the letter "y" for yarn. Ann took the card, ran to the sink, pointed to the sink and signed *drink* (letter "y" with thumb to mouth). Ann then ran back to the living room arms extended in "y" formation and making airplane sounds, appearing to use language in a deliberately ludic (playful) way. At 22 months Ann was

5. The *no* and the *bye* (and also the *bird*) signs were inverted from the standard adult sign, that is the signs pointed *toward* her, as she had seen them made. We have noted similar incidents in other young children acquiring sign language, and we feel it may represent an egocentric bias—namely, that the child is unable to reverse the perception because his perception is the only one that exists in the early sensorimotor stage. On the other hand the child may be reversing the direction of the sign for practice purposes, i.e., so he can compare it with the signs he has seen.

> observed to sign *play* (hand held in "y" formation), and *yellow* (hand held in "y" configuration vertically and with a quick wrist-twisting motion). In the short space of fourteen months, Ann learned to discriminate between signs that are very close in configurations—*wrong, "y," play, drink, yellow,* and *airplane.*

Just as hearing children must mature in order to reproduce the sound of language in its more adult forms, the child acquiring sign language does not use all aspects of a sign (Stokoe's *tabs, dez,* and *sigs*) in their adult forms. We have witnessed a number of interesting childlike or immature variations in addition to standard production of signs. Sometimes Ann's hand configuration was standard, but her placement was not. Signs were made in the mouth rather than at the chin (*dirty,* 19 months), (*pig,* 17 months); in the mouth rather than at the nose (*flower,* 17 months). At 16½ months, Ann made *kitty* on the lips instead of at her cheek, and at 19 months *who* also occurred on the lips rather than on the chin (parental input includes one finger to chin). *Fish* at 18½ months was not only in front of the chest (standard), but also in front of and at the side of the face. *Funny* was signed with a great range of movement, beginning as expected in front of the nose, then below the face, then above the head (17 months). *More* (18 months) was signed above head level rather than chest level. At various ages *bye* was waved at shoulder height, at the side, in front of the abdomen. At 18½ months Ann signed *train* correctly, but on the floor (where the toy train did, in fact, run). Finally Ann signed *dog* on both her mother and father, rather than on her own knee (18½ months).

Some signs varied in hand configuration. *Girl* was made as expected with the thumb stroking the cheek, but also with cupped, loose "c" hand—brushing jaw near chin (17 months) and with the index finger rather than the thumb at 12 months. This substitution of thumb-index finger is interesting and was also noted in the early signing of *mother* with the index finger rather than the thumb touching the side of the neck.

More rarely the configuration and placement were standard, but the movement was altered. *Car* (17 months) was signed with both arms up, but with no steering motion. *Kitty* was given a downward stroke rather than a horizontal one at 16 months.

And there were times when Ann used both hands although one-hand signing is standard. For example, *bird* was signed appropriately with one hand, while *milk* was produced with both hands. And finally it was noted that Ann substituted an object for her finger when she signed *key* by placing an actual key as if it were the correct finger placement against the open palm (19½ months).

PARENT-CHILD COMMUNICATION

In addition to an analysis of Ann's utterances, we have been vitally interested in the reciprocal communicative events between parents (primarily mother) and child. We find that these interchanges are characterized by early reciprocal understanding, and are permeated with genuine enjoyment. Understanding or early meaning and enjoyment in mother-child communicative events may well represent one of the necessary features of normal language development. Thus the following meaningful communicative events:

14½ months: Ann went to steps leading upstairs. Mother asked, *"sleep you?"* Ann nodded, waved bye and climbed upstairs. Ann was left with hearing babysitters. Before her mother left she said, *"Don't cry, Mommy Daddy going out, will come back."* Ann appeared to understand and the tears did not flow.

15 months: Ann was offered a blade of grass by one of the researchers. She took it, but placed it into the researcher's mouth, and turning to her father she signed *dirty*.

16 months: Ann's mother asked *Where cow? Look.* Ann signed *cow* and went to fetch a picture card with a cow on one side and a kitten on the other. Ann held the correct side up.

16½ months: Ann's mother pointed to a large dog statue advertising a Doggie Diner and said *"What?"* Ann signed *dog*.
Ann found a clean diaper in her mother's purse after an outing. She pulled it out, grinned, turned

to her mother and signed *smell.* Mother changed her.

19 months: Ann signed *come cookie* and headed for the kitchen door. Ann and her mother came out with a cookie, but Ann then signed *water* and mother dutifully returned to the kitchen. Ann looked for mother who had left temporarily and asked *mother?* She appeared satisfied with the answer *Mother will come back.*
Showing off a dangerous athletic feat, Ann was warned *Fall, hurt, cry.* She observed the admonition and got down.

19½ months: Ann reminded mother with the sign *toothbrush* that her teeth had to be brushed.

These human interchanges may appear to be very elementary to some readers. Yet parents of deaf four- and five-year-olds often report repeated inability to differentiate between their child's desire for food or drink, food or toileting, etc. In this light, these interchanges appear quite accomplished.

Hearing parents use differing communicative styles with their hearing infants. Ann was our first infant with sign language input and we were careful to observe the parental communicative style. From the beginning it was noted that the mother introduced an abundance of tactile stimuli—running toys and her fingers over Ann's face and head, tickling, gently tapping to get her attention. Signs were frequently made on the child herself, including the following:

stupid (10 months), *love* (11 months), *you* (gently poking Ann's abdomen at 12 months), *good* (rubbing abdomen at 12 months), *father, good-bye* and *pretty* all three reaching around from behind as Ann sat in her lap (10 months), *sorry* (17 months), *monkey* and *lion* (16½ months), *horse* and *bear* (at 17 months), and *elephant* at 18 months. As noted above, Ann herself signed *dog* on both her mother and father around 18½ months. She also signed *good* on her mother (12 months), but displaced it upward—rubbing her mother's chest instead of the abdomen. There is frequent reciprocally playful communication between mother and child.

Enjoyment of the child's communicative efforts by the parents is clearly shown in other ways: often the parents were observed to imitate a sign (usually nonstandard) or expression that seemed humorous to them: Ann putting her books to her mouth as if wanting to eat them (10 months), her "crabby" facial expressions (10 months), her tapping a spoon to her head (11 months), her surprise at dropping and "losing" a wooden ring between her legs (12 months), her gesture of index finger to side of nose (meaning unknown—12 months), her negative vocalization and cross facial expressions (16, 18½ months), her shrug and hunch of shoulders (17 months), her squeezing her doll (17 months), her version of the letter *"e"*—which looked like a "5" (18½ months), her swift, long-nosed *elephant* (18½ months), her answer of *old wrong* to the question of age (16 months), and her gesture of hand-over-heart as if saluting the flag (14½ months).

At other times the imitation carried the specific intent of approval or conversational reinforcement. We recorded parental imitations of Ann's pounding her highchair tray (8 months), clapping her hands when she finished a meal (11 months), signing *pretty* (12 months), waving *bye* (14½ months), signing *hat* and *eat* (14½ months), signing *one* and *old one* in answer to question of age (16 months), signing *apple, bird,* and *girl* in response to the alphabet cards (17 months), signing *funny* and pointing to the video camera (18½ months), and signing *elephant* in response to a picture (18½ months).

SIGN LANGUAGE ACQUISITION OF HEARING CHILDREN

We were fortunate to have the opportunity to review the parental diaries and language development records for two hearing siblings (Jason and Cathy) born to hearing parents who learned signs and fingerspelling in addition to speech because their deaf grandmother lived in the home during their childhood. Both parents were fluent in manual communication: the father had deaf parents, and the mother had learned sign language at age 12. Both parents value sign language and are interested in furthering research about it. They reported that their sign language alternated between English and sign language syntax, whereas the deaf grandmother used only sign language syntax. The diaries will be used to demonstrate an anecdote of the first sign, an abbreviated motor-language developmental table, variations from adult signs, and examples of "code-switching." Table 5 shows the motor-language development of Cathy and Jason.

TABLE 5
Motor-Language Development of Cathy, Jason, and Ann

Age	*Cathy*	*Jason*	*Ann*
5 months	sat	—	—
5½ months	—	1st sign? (*milk*)	—
6 months, 3 weeks	crept	—	—
6½ months	—	sat	—
7 months	—	crept	—
9½ months	—	walked	—
10½ months	1st sign; walked	—	—
11 months	1st spoken words	—	—
11½ months	—	1st spoken words	—
12 months	—	—	1st sign
14 months	—	—	—
15 months	—	—	1st spoken word
18 months	—	—	—
	Total spoken words: 245 Total signs: 113	Total spoken words: 81 Total signs: 51	Total signs: 106

First Sign Anecdote

The parents report that Jason was observed flexing his fingers, then his hands (at 5½ months), as if approximating the sign for milk. The incredulous, experimental parents first offered some juice, then some water—both of which were rejected in turn. He readily accepted milk which was offered next.

Deviations from Standard Signs

Both children often used variations of adult standard models.

cookie:

Index finger to palm of other hand with twisting motion of finger rather than whole hand in clawlike position twisting against palm.

apple:

Performed with "a" hand (closed fist with thumb up), or "g" hand (fist with thumb and index finger parallel outward), rather than standard "x" hand (in a fist except for crooked index finger to cheek).

water:

With two fingers instead of "w" (three fingers) against chin.

mother and *father:*

Both made with one finger instead of thumb to face with fingers spread.

Conjoining of Signs and Words

Cathy conjoined the following signs by 18 months. *Bathroom me, me eat, me sleep, mother milk, daddy work money, me sleep now* (18 months). Jason conjoined spoken words before signed words. (It will be remembered that Ann conjoined signs at 17 months.)

Code Switching

Both Cathy and Jason switched codes appropriately at age 2—signing only to grandmother and speaking to both parents. By age 3 years, Cathy also differentiated the syntax in code switching, using English syntax with her parents and sign language syntax with her deaf grandmother.

KAREN: THE BIRTH OF GRAMMAR [6]

Karen A., the second deaf child we shall describe, was observed at an older age period than Ann, and thus, interestingly

6. We are indebted to Peyton Todd, University of California, Berkeley, graduate student in Psychology, for helpful suggestions for this section. Anita Pitzer participated in the collection of some data reported in this section and incorporated some of our analysis in her M.A. thesis submitted to the University of California (Berkeley) in 1969.

illustrates the development of sign language syntax. In the first year of our three-year project, we collected data on the spontaneously signed complex constructions of this deaf child of deaf parents. She was then 2 years, 10 months old, and she had lived in a home where there was simultaneous sign/speech input since she was adopted at 17 months. To discuss the corpus of 200 combinations of two or more signs that we collected over a period of eight months (from age 2 years, 10 months to 3 years, 6 months), we draw on the framework of pivot grammars.

According to Braine (1963) the early grammars of children consist of the combination of two elements; one of these two elements is called the "pivot" word, the other the "open" word. Pivots are a small group of frequently occurring words, presumably found in fixed positions (i.e., either consistently first or last in the two-word combination), that are used in connection with a large, rapidly expanding class of "open" words. In the combination "there boy," "there" is the pivot word, which can, in this first position, combine with an unlimited number of open words, such as "boy," "girl," "mommy," "doggie," etc. Pivot words are like adult function words, while open words are like adult content words.

Our data on Karen correspond to those from previous studies of two-word utterances among hearing children, in that we can identify a number of pivotlike combinations of signs that fit into the functional classification by Slobin (McNeill, 1970*b*). Thus, table 6 compares Karen's sign language syntax with the typical pivot use of hearing children in standard English, German, and Russian.

Our data are consistent with the newest findings reported by Brown (in press) and others based on the utterances of hearing children. These data, like ours, call into question some of the earlier assumptions about pivot grammars.[7] For example:

> 1. Pivot words were said not to occur alone, yet Bowerman (1969) reported examples of pivots occurring alone in the data of Braine ("more") and of Miller and Ervin ("all gone"). We also have found pivot words occurring in isolation (*more*).

7. This discussion is drawn from a critique of pivot grammar by Brown (in press) in which he presents exceptions to pivot grammars, citing evidence from an unpublished study by Bowerman (1969) and Bloom's dissertation (1969).

2. Pivots were said not to occur in combination with another pivot, but again Bowerman (1969) found a few pivot combinations in Braine's data ("want get," "want more") and ten different examples in Miller and Ervin's data. Our data also show pivots in combination with each other (*please more*).

3. Pivots were said to occur only in fixed position —either initially or finally; however, in Braine's data, Bowerman (1969) found "all gone + ____ " and "____ + all gone." We noted a similar reversal with *come* + *eat* and *B-U-S* + *come*.

In addition the pivot grammar may be semantically more complex than was originally suggested. Thus, Bloom (1969) has proposed that children even at the two-word stage intend to express a variety of structural meanings, including locative, genitive, and attributive statements, and those indicating relations between an agent and an object.

Our data on signed constructions support this analysis of certain noun/noun combinations and are shown as follows:

1. Locative
   Daddy work
   The child is speaking of her daddy being at work —she also signed *Daddy come home* and *Daddy come later* soon after the above.
2. Genitive
   Barry train
   The child is telling the researcher that the train belongs to her brother.
3. Attributive
   Bed shoes
   The child is referring to a pair of slippers.
4. Agent-object
   Daddy shoe
   The child is trying to tell her daddy to take off his shoe and get in the sandbox with her.

If Bloom's analysis is correct, then again the pivot grammar model is inadequate due to its failure to differentiate all these structural meanings through its pivot + open class rule (Brown, in press). Perhaps children's early language really has more

TABLE 6
Comparison of Sign Language Pivots and Oral Pivots
(adapted from Slobin, in press)

Function	*Sign Language*	*English*	*German*	*Russian*
modify	my + (sweater)	my__	mein__	__bo-bo
qualify	(car)		(my)	(hurt)
	pretty + (lights)	pretty__	armer__	
	(tree)		(poor)	
locate	(open)	there__	__da	__tam
name	(wrong)		(there)	(there)
	(same) + that	that__		
	(pretty)			
	(leave)			
describe	(b-u-s*)	__come	__dort	__bay-bay
act	(mommy)		(away)	(sleep)
	(daddy) + come			
	(Nana)			
	(friend)			
	(Barry)			
	(Sally) + sleep			
	(there)			
	(Sh!)			
demand	want + (play)	want__	mehr__	
desire	(molasses)		(more)	
	(school)			
	(paper)	more__	bitte__	eschche__
	(crayons)		(please)	(more)
	(book)			
	(candles)			
	(church) + please			
	("put")			
	(that)			
	(milk)			
	(TV)			
	(straw)			
negate	no + (bed)	no__	nein__	net__
	(wet)		(no)	(no)
	(brush-teeth)			

* Fingerspelled.

structure than pivot grammars can suggest or, as Brown postulates in the early stages of sentence production "some children may adopt a pivot grammar as a strategy for beginning English while others do not."

The next two children, Ruth and Marie, will be discussed more briefly.

RUTH: DEVELOPMENT OF LANGUAGE

Ruth S. was 2½ years old when we first met her. She lives in a comfortable house on a military post with her father, her mother, and her three sisters, ages 6, 8, and 11. All other members of the family are hearing.

Her parents' history until the youngster was 1½ was hauntingly and tragically similar to many others. A clear-cut diagnosis of rubella was made in the first trimester of Mrs. S's pregnancy, followed by fears and uncertainties about the prognosis. However, at birth Ruth appeared to be a visibly intact infant.

The parents early suspected possible defects, but Ruth was an alert, intelligent baby. The physician wondered for months; finally nine months after her birth, several hearing tests confirmed the parents' early suspicion, and Ruth's odyssey as a deaf child began.

After the initial shock and depression, the family recouped and sought further help, including a hearing aid and early education. After several visits to a preschool program for deaf youngsters the mother said: "There was something extra special that existed between *that* parent (herself deaf) and *that* child that was not there in all other cases. So I seized upon that to find out what makes the difference. Essentially it wound up being the hand language." But, the parents added, "The oral approach has its merits also. So the simple addition of one-and-one-makes-two is why we started using simultaneous communication at 15 months."

Maternal Style of Communication

Ruth's mother worked arduously at providing verbal stimulation for her daughter. But the arduous quality did not preclude playful, enjoyable interchanges. The following dialogues have been chosen to show both the ludic quality of words and signs and to indicate how English syntax was introduced by this mother into the sign language. For the last year Ruth's mother has added an *"s"* to indicate plural, *"ing"* to indicate the present progressive tense, a gesture of the hand toward the back to indicate past tense, and special signs to differentiate between words such as "can't," or "couldn't," and "ly" to differentiate between adjectives and adverbs. Some of these endings resemble Seeing Essential English (see below), but others are frankly improvised by the mother. For example, although the "to" in an infinitive verb is usually omitted in the sign language syntax, Ruth's mother apparently feels more comfortable including it.

Ruth. Age 3 years, 3 months:

Mother: (reacting to Ruth "hamming") *"Why didn't you sing nicely? Now I want to say Mary had a little lamb . . ."*

Ruth: *"M-R-Y had a little lamb . . . OUT!"* (Ruth had been imitating her mother up until lamb.)

Mother: *"The teacher said out, but wait for that."*

Ruth: *"Teacher."*

Mother: *"She was so angry with Mary because she brought the lamb to school."*

Ruth: *"OUT!"*

Mother: *"it made the children laugh and play"* (Ruth is not participating, just watching mother who then says to her "come".)

Ruth: (imitating mother) *"laugh and play, it made the children laugh and play, laugh and play, laugh and play, to see a lamb at . . ."* (Ruth stops imitating mother and says: *"M-Y,* Mary. *Sew, deer, sew, follow"* in a sing-songy manner.)

Mother: "Oh, you want to sing 'Do, Re, Me'!"

Ruth: *"Nicely, nicely."* (See above where mother says why don't you sing nicely.)

Mother: "Joey? Oh, nicely. Are you going to be a good girl now?"

Ruth: *"Sew, sew, follow."*

Mother: *"Doe, a deer, a female deer, re, a drop of golden sun, mi, the name I call myself . . ."*

(This is sung and signed very quickly by mother.)

Ruth: *"Doe, a deer, re a . . . me a name, follow"* (Then she sees a motorcycle go by, imitates sound and spreads arms out as if holding handle bars.)

Mother: *"Did you see that? That boy! Daddy told that boy don't you ride that motorcycle in our y-a-r-d."*

"What about *H-M-Y? H-M-Y, D-M-Y sat on a,* what?"

Ruth: (imitating mother) *"H-Y, D-Y sat on a wall wall"* (Ruth does sign for wall on her own.) (H-M-Y or H-Y equals Humpty-Dumpty.)

Mother: *"H-M-Y, D-M-Y had a great fall"*

Ruth: *"H-D, D-Y had a great fall . . . fall"* (Ruth repeats fall for emphasis then she coughs and signs *napkin* [verbalization very faint]. Her mother brings her a napkin.)

Mother: "Oh, what a faker" (as Ruth pretends to spit in the napkin). *"All the king's horses and all the king's men . . ."*

Ruth: *"All the king's horses and all king's men, couldn't"*

Mother: "Couldn't . . . oh, that's right" (Ruth does sign for couldn't whereas mother had done the sign for can't—mother corrects hers) . . . *"put H-M-Y . . ."*

Ruth: *"put D-Y"*

Mother: *"together again."*

Ruth: *"together again."*

Mother: *"Poor H-M-Y, D-M-Y broken."*

Ruth: makes knitting motion with hands.

Mother: *"What happened to H-M-Y, D-M-Y . . ."* (Telephone rings, mother motions 'wait' to Ruth and starts to get up to answer the phone.)

Ruth: "Come back." (Mother has gone to answer the phone—mother sees this and sits down again with Ruth. Ruth's verbalization of "come back" is very clear.)

Mother and Ruth looking at Ruth's school book about Mark and Janet.

Mother: *"What is Mark doing?"*
Ruth: *"M-A-R-K, Mark in picture."*
Mother: *"Yes, he's in the picture—what is he doing?"*
Ruth: "The boy."
Mother: "*What, the boy what?* what? what?"
Ruth: "*Yours* (signs and says leaning toward picture of Mark in book) *bicycle broken,* fix it."

Age 3 years, 4 months: Ruth's classroom. Ruth and Carmen are sitting at a table together. Ruth's teacher, Carmen, has a "tiger" handpuppet which she playfully thrusts toward Ruth.

Ruth: "Stop it, *stop it.*"
Carmen: *"Tell him."*
Ruth: *"Stop it, tiger."*
Carmen: *"Say bite Carmen, tell him."*
Ruth: *"Go to bite Carmen."*

Ruth and two friends standing near rabbit cage with live rabbit inside.

Ruth: *"Come out rabbit."*

Ruth's friend touches the videocorder case top. Ruth goes over to her and says, "no," then signs (fingerspells *K*(atie), *A*(rline), *mad.*

Vocabulary Growth

The total number of signs Ruth used and responded to was checked at age 3 and 3 years 4 months and is reported in table 7. This table corroborates the impression (Moores, 1970) that language "explodes," growing very rapidly during short periods of time.

Receptive Grammatical Competence

Fraser, Bellugi, and Brown (1963) devised a test of grammatical competence in which children are presented with two pictures (each making a pair) involving the same agents and

TABLE 7
Vocabulary Growth—Ruth S.

	At 3 Years	*New at 3 Years, 4 Months*	*Total*
Nouns	227	132	359
Proper nouns	19	16	35
Adjectives	47	26	73
Verbs	34	70	104
Pronouns	5	4	9
Articles	—	2	2
Prepositions	2	—	2
Conjunctions	1	—	1
Adverbs	7	4	11
Interjections	6	2	8
Totals	348	256	604

actions but differing in the subject-object relation, in the apparent time of an action, or in the number of agents performing an action. Seven items were presented and four responded to correctly by Ruth at age 3. The items failed are marked by an "X."

X 1. Mass noun/count noun: Some pears/a pear.
X 2. Singular/plural, marked by inflections: The boy draws/The boys draw.
3. Subject/object in the active voice: The girl pushes the boy/The boy pushes the girl.
4. Present progressive tense/past tense: The paint is falling/The paint fell.
5. Singular/plural marked by *is* and *are:* The sheep is eating/The sheep are eating. Needed "two sheep are eating."
X 6. Present progressive tense/future tense: The girl is drinking/The girl will drink.
7. Affirmative/negative: The boy is sitting/The boy is not sitting.

At the same age Ruth was given a test in which she was expected to reproduce/imitate a sentence signed and spoken by her mother (adapted from Menyuk, 1963).

This test is difficult to interpret. Ruth's mother frequently engaged in "sentence and song" games where mother and daughter concurrently produce a signed/spoken sentence. Mrs. S. frequently signs slowly enough and keeps the sign in process long enough for Ruth to imitate while mother continues to sign it.

Transformation type	*Mother's evocative sentence*	*Ruth's response sentence (age 3)*
Adjective	I have a brown dog	"dog"
Conjunction deletion	I see a red book and a blue book	Concurrently: *"I see a red book and a blue book."*
Pronoun in conjunction	The boy saw the bicycle and was happy.	Mother: *"the"* Ruth: *"the"* Mother and Ruth concurrently: *"boy saw the bicycle and was happy"* Ruth omits "happy" Mother: *"happy"* Ruth: "happy"
Reflexive	I cut myself.	(Ruth first looks sympathetically at Mother's hand.) Ruth: *"I cut myself."*
Iterative	You have to drink milk to grow strong.	Mother and Ruth together: *"You have to drink milk to"* Mother: *"grow" "grow"* "say grow" Ruth: *grow* (signed with great difficulty) Mother: *"strong"* Ruth: *"strong"*
Imperative	Don't eat my food.	Mother: *"Don't"* Ruth: *"Don't"* Mother: *"eat"* Ruth: *"eat"* Mother: *"my"* Ruth: *"my"* Mother: *"food"* Ruth: *"food"*

The third task of grammatical competency performed at the same age involved Ruth's ability to understand prepositions when used in sentence form. (Test prepared by C. Geballe following Slobin's Manual, 1967.) Her mother signed and spoke the following sentences asking Ruth to perform these various tasks. (All recorded on videotape.) Incorrect responses are marked by an "X."

1. Put the book *on* the table.
2. Put the cup *on* the book.

X 3. Put the telephone *under* the table.[8]

4. Take the cup *off* the book.

X 5. Put the cup *on* the chair (put the doll on the chair and offered cup to doll).

X 6. Put the book *under* the telephone (picked up both objects and attempted placement).

7. Give the paper to ________ (research assistant).

Most linguists indicate that the age of emergence of grammatical structure has considerable variability whereas the *order of emergence* has an almost invarying regularity (as in the eruption of teeth). Menyuk (1963) demonstrated that the spontaneously *spoken* utterances of the children (around 3 years of age) do not indicate the level of grammatical complexity which is evidenced on the basis of *imitation.* Fraser, Bellugi, and Brown (1963) tap the same receptive versus productive grammatical competence. In these terms Ruth is acquiring the same sequences albeit somewhat more slowly than most of the hearing children reported. We intend to follow Ruth with continuing tests of grammatical competence during the next five years.

Expressive Communicative Modes

A pervasive fear exists among most parents of young deaf children that knowledge of sign language will inhibit the development of speech. Although evidence from learning theory, studies of disadvantaged children, etc., does not support this view, we were interested to see if we could statistically document the percentages of modalities used over a period of time. Figure 4 depicts the extent to which Ruth used the various expressive modes—sign language alone; combined signs and words; and spoken words alone—during three thirty-minute segments of

8. The first response was to put the telephone on the table, but when Ruth's mother repeated the sentence more emphatically, the correct response was elicited.

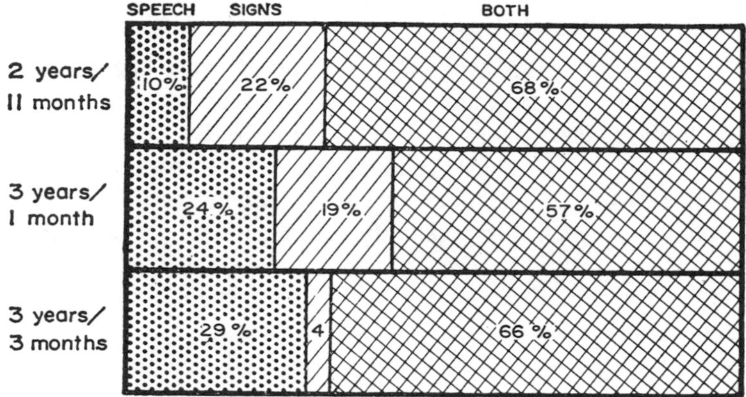

Figure 4 RUTH'S COMMUNICATIVE MODES Analysis based on Three 30-Minute Video Tape Segments Over a Period of Four Months

videotaped observation. Only expressions that were visibly and audibly clear to the researcher were counted. The first count was made at age 2 years 11 months. Arbitrary segments were chosen to represent the range of situations videotaped. The thirty minutes thus include a segment with Ruth outside in the backyard with her mother, sisters, and neighborhood children as well as a segment between Ruth and her mother alone. The second count was made when Ruth was 3 years 1 month. Ruth and her mother were alone drawing together, looking at a book, and playing store. The third count was made when Ruth was 3 years 3 months and refers to the first transcribed segment of interaction under "Maternal style of communication."

Figure 4 clearly indicates that over a period of time Ruth increased her use of speech alone, decreased her use of signs alone, whereas the combined mode of speech and signs remained relatively unchanged. Observations of mother-child interaction reveal that the mother's understanding increases when Ruth uses both modes of communication simultaneously; the mother is fully aware of this and frequently encourages the youngster "to speak" or "to sign" when questionable understanding occurs. This analysis, we hope, will allay the pervasive fear mentioned above, a fear which contributes to parental and child discomfort and may well interfere with optimal language development.

MARIE: FURTHER DEVELOPMENT OF LANGUAGE

The fourth child, Marie C., was adopted at age 6½ months. The adoptive parents knew of her "rubella deafness" at the time of adoption. The youngster lives with her hearing parents, two older sisters, and two older brothers. Marie's introduction to sign language came at age three when the parents attended some meetings at which this possibility was mentioned. The mother exclaimed shortly thereafter, "As much as I loved Marie before, I enjoy her more thoroughly now." Since then the parents have energetically joined parents' groups, met deaf adults and decided to use a system of sign language called SEE (Seeing Essential English) described by Anthony (1966). The essence of this approach is to visualize for the child the functional parts of English speech. Thus, plurals are indicated by an *s* at the end of the word, *ing* for present progressive by a sweep of the little finger, past tense by a backward flip of the hand, and the *en* suffix of certain past participles by an *n* configuration of the hand away from the center and to the side of the body. Although the parents state that they have committed themselves to SEE, the videotapes suggest that new users find it difficult to maintain at all times and that in talking to Marie the parents occasionally revert to English syntax without the endings, or to sign language syntax. Nevertheless, diaries and videotape recordings indicate that Marie used some Seeing Essential English signs appropriately in sentences at the following ages:

3 years 4 months:	*popped, broken*
3 years 5½ months:	*glasses, teachers, potatoes, shared, stabbed, working, cookie*
3 years 8 months:	*animals, finished, pulling*
3 years 9 months:	*friends, fishing*
3 years 11 months:	*wedding, clothes, riding*

Maternal Style of Communication

Besides the serious attempts to use SEE, Marie's mother placed great emphasis from an early age on fingerspelling of different words. The playful quality of the mother-child interaction which was portrayed in Ruth's case by songs is particularly striking with Marie in the anagramlike quality of vocabulary items. Two typical mother-daughter dialogues follow:

Age 3 years 8 months: Marie and Mother in playroom looking at picture cards of animals.

Marie: (Steps up to her mother) *pig!*
Mother: "It's a pig, O.K." Fingerspells P-I-G.
Marie: Fingerspells P-I-G.
Mother: Looking at the card of a monkey, *"like" like "you"* points to Marie, says "you know what this is."
Marie: Jumps back, raises both hands palms forward at shoulder level, looks down at floor, points to an animal on the rug.
Mother: "Yes, it's like you." "It's a *monkey,*" (fingerspells) M-O-N-K-E-Y *like you.*
Marie: Looks at mother, shakes her head no and fingerspells M-O-T-H-E-R and points to mother.
Mother: "No, wrong, it's *not Mother, it's Father."*
Marie: Points to father and fingerspells F-A-T-H-E-R.

Age 4 years 9 months.

Mother: Prints on the board H-O-M-T-E-R.
Marie: Points to her mother and touches her mother's chest.
Mother: "Me?"
Marie: "Mother."
Mother: "That's O.K., *I want* you *to tell me that"* (pointing to the letters L-E-S-I-G-N-S-C-H-R-E.[9] *"Think hard, that's a hard one."*
Marie: Looks at the letters (Mother points to the string of letters and shrugs her shoulders. Marie signs *psychiatrist* (*p* on wrist).
Mother: "Yes." Nodding her head. "Right!"

9. Anagram for (Dr. Hilde S.) Schlesinger, the medical director of the project. Marie's ability to decode this difficult name is probably partially dependent on numerous similar "games" played with her mother. However, mother states this is a first occurrence of this particular anagram.

Fingerspelling Games Carried into Reading Skills

At 4 years 5 months Marie demonstrated she was able to transfer her fingerspelling games to reading material (*Hear and Near*—The Sheldon Basic Reading Series, 1961).

Marie: *"Mother, Bill."*
"Help me."
"Come and help."
"Run, run, run."
"Linda, mother." (Puts her right index finger to her mouth as if thinking.)
"Linda and Rickey."
Mother: "Good."
Marie: *"Linda, Rickey come fast."*
"Daddy is helping." (Then she looks at mother.)
Mother: *"Wrong."*
Marie: *"Home, Home?"*
Mother: "Think." "Wrong."
Marie: *"Here."*
Mother: *Here,* "right."

Marie's mother did not use complete sentences as frequently or playfully as Ruth's mother did, and this difference may be reflected in Marie's lower grammatical competencies. But it is also possible that the more delayed onset of sign language input may account for this discrepancy. With this small number of children observed we can only report differences and speculate as to the reasons.

Receptive Grammatical Competence

The full text of the items for the Fraser et al. (1963) test are presented on p. 78. At age 4 years 9 months Marie correctly indicated three of the seven contrasts, as follows:

Mass noun/count noun: Some pears/a pear.
Present progressive/past tense: The paint is falling/ the paint fell.
Affirmative/negative: The boy is sitting/the boy is not sitting.

Marie's performance on the Menyuk test (1963):

Transformation type	*Sentence*	*Marie's sentence*
Adjective	I have a brown dog.	Correct
Conjunction deletion	I see a red book and a blue book.	*Book, blue, book*
Pronoun in conjunction	The boy saw the bicycle and was happy.	*Happy boy*
Reflexive	I cut myself.	Correct
Iterative	You have to drink milk to grow strong.	*I grow strong.* (After three maternal repetitions, Marie signed the sentence correctly)
Imperative	Don't eat my food.	Not attempted

NEGATION

There are two examples of stage I negation (Bellugi, 1964, and personal communications):

3 years, 5½ months: *pot, no.*
Adult equivalent: "I don't need to go."
3 years, 9 months: *spank no.*
Adult equivalent: "Don't spank me."

Some examples of stage II negation can be found at

3 years, 9 months: *Me don't cry.*
Adult equivalent obvious.
3 years, 11 months: *Teacher don't slap me.* Also obvious.

Some more complex examples were found at different ages:

3 years, 9 months: *Me jump, not John.*
4 years, 8 months: *Father is home, not work.*

Partially analyzed data from Marie's spontaneous language output also indicate she is acquiring grammatical competence in the usual sequence.

Marie's Lipreading Test Data

Marie's entire class was given a lipreading test (Butt and Chreist, 1968). The test was given without audible voice or auditory clues and consisted of seventy items with twelve different sections: i.e., identification of objects, picture identification, numbers, etc. Marie's score at age 3 years 10½ months was 60; the average score at age 4 is 27 and at age 5 is 34, indicating that Marie's precocious use of sign language and fingerspelling did not interfere with her lipreading facility and may well have helped it.

Communicative Modes

A communicative mode count based on three videotaped sessions was made for Marie, and the relative percentages of speech only, signs only, and signs and speech are shown in figure 5. The first count at age 3 years 4 months was based on a session in which Marie interacted in the project playroom with several alternating adults. In the second at 3 years 10 months, Marie was again in the project office with mother and father, while in the third at 4 years 8 months Marie was at the blackboard with her mother. Although neither the increase in spoken words alone nor the decrease in signs alone is as dra-

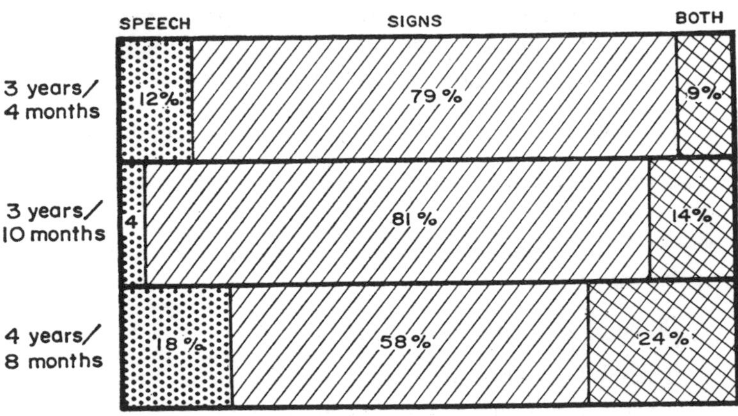

Figure 5 MARIE'S COMMUNICATIVE MODES Analysis Based on Three 30-Minute Video Tape Segments Over a Period of Sixteen Months

matic as in Ruth's case, the indications remain that as the child acquires sign language, the spoken output also increases.

SUMMARY

We have followed four children whose families make use of the language of signs and fingerspelling with concomitant use of speech. We have collected monthly observational and videotape evidence of language acquisition. The analysis thus far indicates that the milestones in sign language acquisition generally parallel the milestones of spoken language acquisition. We have also found that knowledge of sign language at these early ages has not interfered with speech acquisition; on the contrary, the number of spoken words and lipreading facility increased with sign language acquisition. Finally we were struck with the decreased level of communicative frustration in the four families observed.[10] We strongly recommend that continuing linguistic research be done on the sign language and speech acquisition of infants from the time their deafness is first diagnosed.

10. During the writing of this chapter we noted frequently and paradoxically that words may be accurate but insufficient vehicles to transmit some of the important aspects of language acquisition. In order to remedy this shortcoming a composite videotape demonstrating many of the above described linguistic events has been prepared. At this writing it can be viewed upon request at the Langley Porter Neuropsychiatric Institute.

5

The Developmental Process in Deaf Preschool Children: Communicative Competence and Socialization

All personality theories emphasize the importance of the events of early childhood in individual development. The major thrust of the research until fairly recently was directed toward an understanding of childhood socialization processes and was primarily concerned with the treatment and care given to the child. The contribution made by the child was, for the most part, neglected. While some of the important theorists from psychiatry and social psychology (Sullivan, 1953; Mead, 1934) have emphasized interaction and reciprocity, researchers more frequently utilized a cause and effect model that stated (implicitly or explicitly) that certain acts or attitudes on the part of parents created particular sets of responses or behaviors on the part of their children. "Descriptions by psychiatric clinicians suggest that failure to achieve mutual gratification in the nurturing relationship is likely to be associated with a long

Chapter 5 is by Kathryn P. Meadow, Hilde S. Schlesinger, and Constance B. Holstein. The assistance of Jeffrey Shapiro, Ph.D., Katherine A. Leland, Arline Cottrell, and Carole Geballe in the collection and organization of the data is gratefully acknowledged. The participation of Don Heath, Lois Karp, and Carole Ann Winfrey in the analysis of videotapes was a major contribution.

train of emotional difficulties for the child" (Clausen, 1968: 140).

Much important work related to psychopathology has emphasized the causal importance of distorted communication initiated by parents of disturbed children (Wynne et al., 1958; Lidz, 1963). Erikson offers an alternative, or an expansion, of this theoretical stance:

> I think one should consider that these (psychotic) children may very early and subtly fail to return the mother's glance, smile, and touch; an initial reserve which makes the mother, in turn, unwittingly withdraw. The truism that the original problem is to be found in the mother-child relationship holds only in so far as one considers this relationship an emotional pooling which may multiply well-being in both but which will endanger both partners when the communication becomes jammed or weakened. (Erikson, 1963:207)

As we have reiterated, the primary handicap imposed by early childhood deafness is that it jams and weakens communication between the child and others in his environment. The deaf child's inability to respond fully to parental communication may be compared to what Erikson has called the deficiency in "sending power" in the schizophrenic child. In considering the socialization process for the deaf child, it is important to emphasize that he is less likely to provide his hearing parents with the gratifications of parenthood they expect. The deaf child cannot respond as readily to the interaction initiated by the parent, nor, perhaps, does the child receive the gratification he needs from his efforts to communicate. While parental efforts to communicate are not responded to, the less frequent intrusion of the child's communicative efforts on his parents have an effect as well.

An analogous situation has been observed in the interaction of blind infants and their parents. These infants were found to be more passive, that is, to make fewer demands on their parents' attention. The parents responded by leaving their blind child alone in his crib more than is usual. Thus, the blind child, who probably needed more tactile stimuli, actually received less (Burlingham, 1967). Some of the mannerisms referred to as "blindisms" were traced to this pattern rather than being a direct consequence of blindness per se.

Bell (1964) reviewed five studies of families containing children with various kinds of handicaps. In each of the five studies, mothers scored higher for "intrusiveness" as measured by the PARI (Parental Attitude Research Inventory, Schaefer and Bell, 1958). Bell suggested that:

> an attitude described as "intrusiveness" can be induced in a mother as an effect of a limitation in coping ability in her child. . . . The possibility of children affecting parent behavior has been almost completely neglected in any explicit sense in current theories of socialization. (Bell, 1964:140)

In an experimental study of the effect of a child's behavior on the mother, mothers were found to reinforce independent behavior when the child acted in an independent manner and to reinforce dependent behavior when the child acted in a stubborn manner. "These findings lend strong support to the notion that changing child behaviors have a situational effect upon parental behavior" (Osofsky, 1970:403).

The true handicap of profound deafness is a consequence of barriers to the communicative process. Thus, by studying parent-child interaction in families where the child is deaf, we may hope to learn not only about some dimensions of the relation between deafness and mental health, but we may hope to learn more about childhood socialization in general.

METHODOLOGY

Selection of Research Subjects[1]

Forty preschool deaf children were recruited for partici-

1. A large number of directors and teachers of preschool programs for deaf children participated in the recruitment of subjects and in the collection of data. We would like to thank the following persons for their help: Dr. R. S. Kupfer, Marin County Public Schools; Mr. Gary Clarke, Mt. Diablo Therapy Center; Miss Patricia Jensen, Arcon Hearing Research Foundation; Dr. Richard F. Capano, Project "IDEA," San Jose; Miss Mary Ann Ceriotti, San Francisco Hearing and Speech Center; Mrs. Leahea Grammatico, Peninsula Oral School for the Deaf, Redwood City; Miss Michael Powell, California School for the Deaf Parent Orientation Program (Berkeley); Mrs. Adelaide McClatchie, East Bay Children's

pation in the study. They represent all children enrolled in the eight preschool programs for the deaf in the San Francisco Bay Area who met these criteria: (1) hearing level no better than an eighty decibel average in the speech range (500-1000-2000 cycles per second) in the better ear; (2) age between two-and-one-half and four years; (3) onset of deafness no later than twelve months of age; (4) family background not to include that of racial minority groups nor a language other than English spoken at home; (5) no additional known handicaps that might create additional problems for language development; (6) no twins; (7) no children with deaf parents.

A control group of twenty hearing children, matched with the deaf children for age and sex, was recruited from selected nursery schools in San Francisco.

Observation and Analysis of Mother-Child Interaction

Videotaped "scenarios" consisting of twenty-minute segments of semistructured mother-child interaction were collected for each of the sixty mother-child pairs participating in the study. The first ten minutes of the taped playroom interaction were spent in free play with blocks, dolls, and trucks. Additional activities included copying designs on a blackboard, looking at a set of picture cards, and sharing refreshments. Thus, an attempt was made to provide some structure, some variety, and some flexibility in activities.

After the sixty videotaped scenarios had been collected, segments were viewed intensively by staff members for guidelines to dimensions that appeared to differentiate the mothers and children behaviorally and that were important to our theo-

---

Hospital; Mr. Robert Shearer, Mt. Diablo Public Schools; Mrs. Maudis Foster, Richmond Unified School District; Dr. Ralph Richardson, San Juan Unified School District; Mrs. Ruth Jackson, Palo Alto Unified School District.

For help in recruiting and rating the children in the hearing control group we are grateful to Mrs. L. Baker, Presidio Pre-School Nursery, San Francisco; Mrs. Joyce Wilson, Laurel Hill Nursery School, San Francisco; Miss Mary Kay Jones, Telegraph Hill Nursery School; Miss Barbara Edwards, Edison Children's Center, San Francisco; Mrs. Nina Zimple, Noe Valley Nursery School, San Francisco; and Mrs. Frances S. Miller, Parent Education Programs, San Francisco Junior College District.

Financial support from the University of California, San Francisco, Research Evaluation and Allocation Committee enabled us to collect the data for the control group of hearing children.

retical framework. The set of rating scales eventually developed included ten dimensions descriptive of the mothers' behavior, ten dimensions descriptive of the children's behavior, four dimensions descriptive of the children's attributes exclusively related to deafness, and four dimensions descriptive of the reciprocal mother-child interaction.

A manual was written defining these dimensions in behavioral terms, including examples of behavior that would be rated at both ends of each scale. After this phase of the work was completed, a team of three outside observers was recruited to view the sixty tapes and rate each mother-child dyad on the entire range of dimensions.

These observers spent the first three days in orientation and training, including the rating of some practice tapes that were not among the sixty research cases. On two occasions during the orientation period a composite tape of excerpts from twelve research tapes was shown without comment, in order that the observers (who, by design, were unfamiliar with deaf children) might get an idea of the range of behavior to be expected among the deaf subjects. During the next fifteen days the observers watched four scenario tapes per day. After viewing a tape, each observer independently completed the rating scale, including written comments on the mother-child interaction. These ratings were then compared, and any dimension on which there was disagreement was discussed. ("Disagreement" was defined as a difference of more than two points on an eight-point scale.) In most cases, agreement was reached, although in some instances (1.3 percent of items rated) discussion did not eliminate differences in perception. In this event, ratings were averaged. Interjudge (Kuder-Richardson) adjusted estimates of reliability ranged from .90 to .65 for the twenty-four dimensions rated, with a mean of .83.

Parental Reports of Child-Rearing Practices

Interviews were conducted with each of the mothers of the deaf children in order to determine circumstances surrounding the onset and diagnosis of deafness, early educational experiences, and child-rearing practices. A questionnaire covering relevant items was substituted for the interview for mothers of the hearing children.

Assessment of Parental Personality Characteristics

The California Psychological Inventory (Gough, 1957) was utilized for an assessment of both father and mother. Three scales were used: "flexibility," "sociability," and "femininity-masculinity." A Self-Description Scale (Rosenberg, 1965) was also completed by both parents.

Assessment of Child's Communicative Competence

Several different measures of the deaf children's communicative competence were utilized in constructing an index reflecting communicative skills. These included the Mecham Language Development Scale (1958), scored on the basis of information supplied by the mothers; teachers' ratings for four dimensions of communicative skill (expressive communication, receptive communication, speech, lipreading); and ratings of deaf children from the videotapes. A combined score on these dimensions was utilized to place the forty deaf children in two groups (above and below the median index score): those who were more proficient and those who were less proficient in communication.

FINDINGS

Mother-Child Interaction: Comparisons of Mothers with Deaf and with Hearing Children

Comparisons of the judges' observations of mothers of the deaf and the hearing children are shown in figure 6. Ten dimensions were included in the rating scale, nine of which implied a positive or a negative evaluation of the mothers' behavior during the videotaped scenario. Mothers of hearing children received more positive ratings for all nine of these dimensions. Differences in six of the nine comparisons were great enough to achieve statistical significance. These included: permissiveness, nonintrusiveness, nondidactic behavior, creativity, flexibility, and approval of child. No significant differences between the two groups of mothers were observed for enjoyment of the child, effectiveness in achieving his cooperation, and the

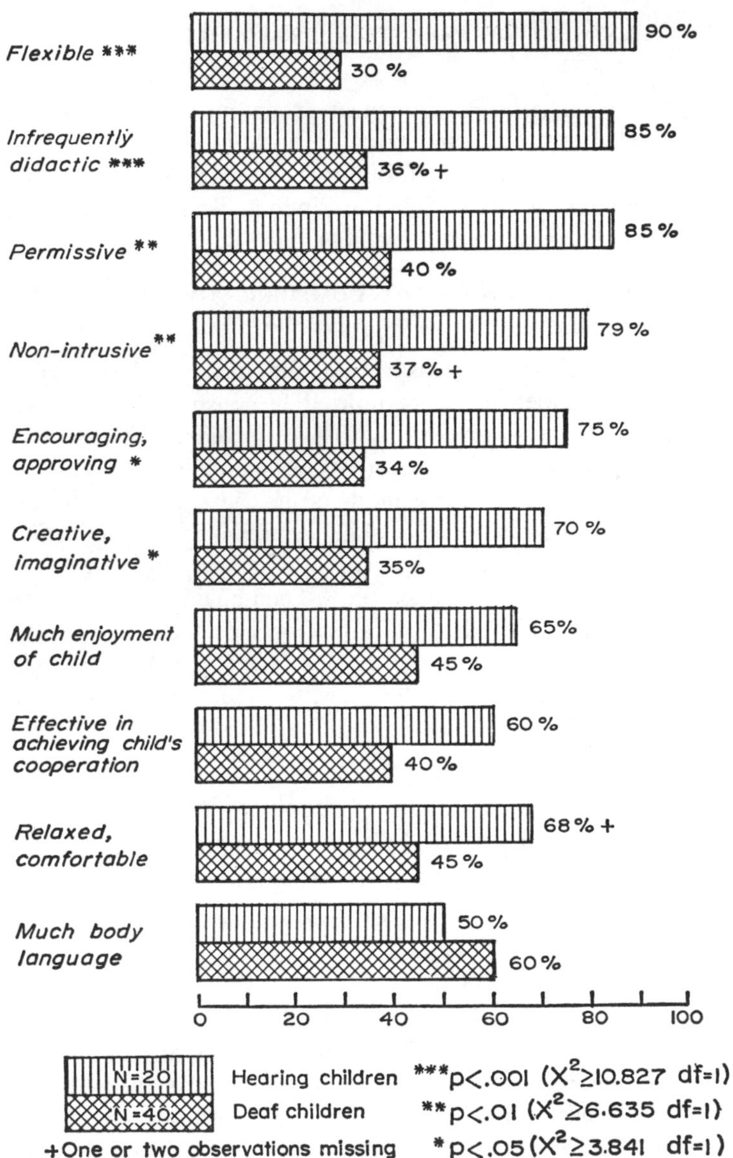

Figure 6 RATINGS OF MATERNAL-CHILD INTERACTION Comparisons of Mothers of Deaf and Mothers of Hearing Children: Proportion above the Median (N = 60)

degree to which the mothers appeared to be relaxed and comfortable in the studio situation.

Evaluation of the use of body movements showed very slight differences (10 percentage points in ratings above and below the median) with mothers of deaf children comprising the group using more body language.

When the two groups of mothers were compared within educational levels (that is, those with some college education and those without any college work), the observed differences in "creative" or "imaginative" behavior disappeared. Differences on the other dimensions were not affected by the application of the educational control.

A second kind of control factor applied to the comparisons shown in figure 6 was the personality variable reflected in scores on the paper and pencil personality inventories. When the two groups of mothers were subdivided on the basis of their scores for "self-image," "flexibility," "sociability," and "femininity" the original pattern of differences did not change. This finding is most interesting in that it strengthens the conclusion that the child's behavior and capabilities are extremely important in determining the quality of mother-child interaction, overriding at least some personality characteristics of the mother. However, since the personality measures were somewhat crude, the results are offered only as suggestive and as an indication of an area that would be a fruitful one for further research.

The assumption has been that it is the deaf child's communicative deficit that is the critical factor in differentiating mother-child interaction in the two groups. One test of this general hypothesis was provided in the data presented in figure 6. A second way of evaluating this factor is to look at interaction between mothers and deaf children with varying degrees of communicative competence. Although all forty of the deaf children included in the sample can be considered "severely to profoundly deaf" their receptive and expressive communicative skills vary greatly.

There are a number of known reasons for these differences, some suspected reasons for the variations, and probably additional reasons that are still shrouded in mystery. Thus, some children with identical audiograms may utilize their residual hearing to quite different degrees. This difference can be related to earlier or later diagnosis with consequent earlier or later use of hearing aids. It may be related to differences in "real" hearing thresholds that do not appear in responses to audiological testing. It may be related to differences in the ways children have been trained to utilize their residual hearing (or in the ways they have responded to attempts to train residual hearing). Lipreading skill seems to be unrelated to intelligence, in that many extremely bright deaf individuals do not master the art. Lipreading ability may vary with stress (Elliott, 1970), may be affected by "islands" of hearing in the very low or very high ranges of sound frequencies. Speech, for all but those with a great deal of useable residual hearing, is acquired by painful repetition and almost unbelievable hard work. The use of gestures or of formal sign language and fingerspelling is dependent on willingness of parents and teachers to provide this as an avenue of communication.

The forty deaf children were divided into two groups on the basis of their score on the "Index of Communicative Competence." Those with scores above the median were called the "High ICC" group or "High Communicators." Those with scores below the median were called the "Low ICC" group or "Low Communicators." Figure 7 shows the ratings for mothers of three groups of children (hearing children plus two groups of deaf children) on the five behavioral dimensions significantly differentiating the mothers of deaf and hearing children in figure 6. ("Creativity" was eliminated since it was confounded by mothers' educational level.) It will be seen that with the deaf children's communicative competence controlled, the mothers of hearing children continue to be rated significantly higher than mothers of either of the groups of deaf children. On four of the five dimensions (flexibility, nondidactic behavior, nonintrusiveness, and approval of the child) mothers of more competent deaf children rank second, while mothers of less competent deaf children rank lowest. Mothers of less competent deaf children were rated higher for "permissive" behavior than mothers of more competent deaf children.

Before discussing the implications of these observed differences in maternal behavior, let us examine the data resulting from comparisons of the behavior of the deaf and hearing children during the interaction sequences with their mothers. These are presented in figures 8 and 9. Figure 8 shows the ratings of

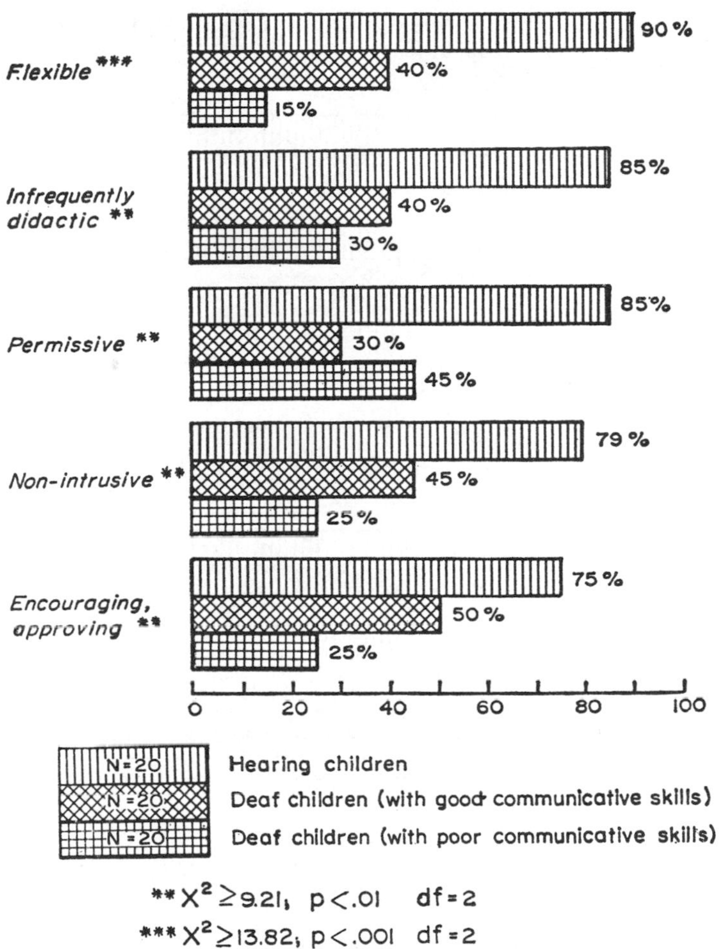

Figure 7 RATINGS OF MATERNAL-CHILD INTERACTION Comparisons of Mothers of Deaf and Mothers of Hearing Children (with Communicative Skill Level Controlled): Proportion above the Median (N = 60)

deaf and hearing children on the ten dimensions of child behavior included in the rating scales.

There are five dimensions on which the deaf and the hearing children differ significantly. All five comparisons favor the hearing children: compliance versus resistance; creativity versus lack of imagination; enjoyment of interaction with mother versus absence of apparent enjoyment; buoyancy, happiness versus

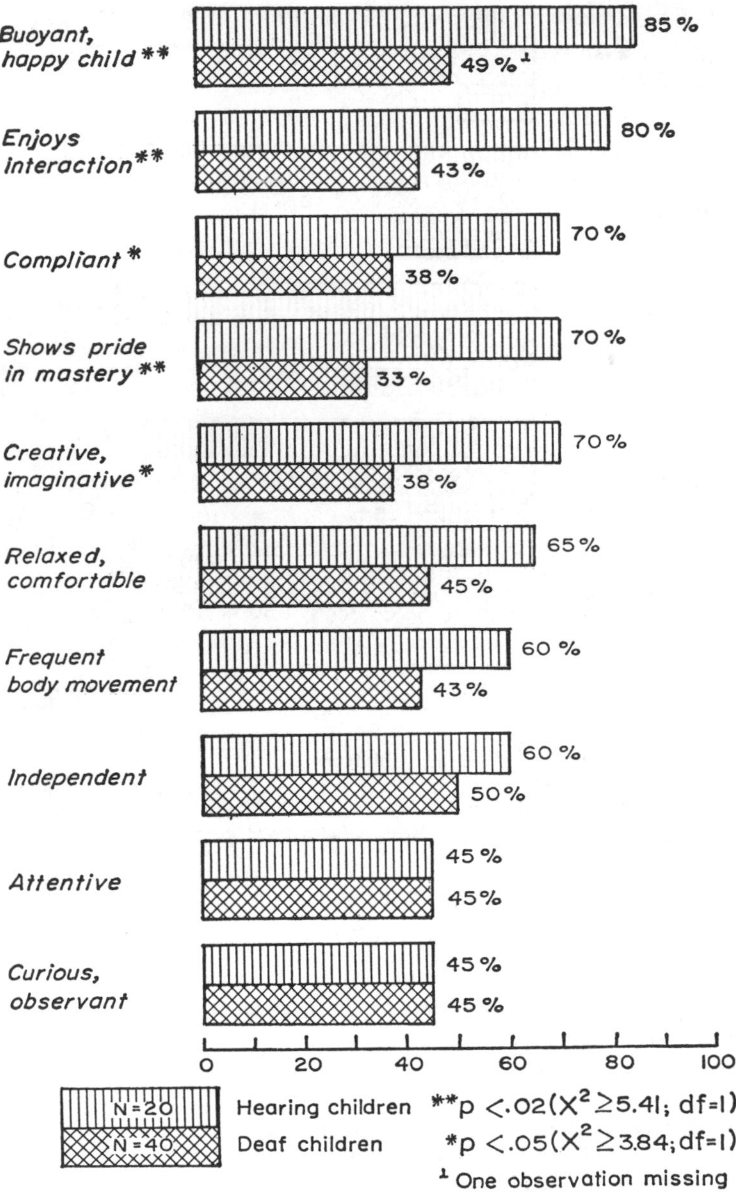

Figure 8 RATINGS OF MATERNAL-CHILD INTERACTION Comparisons of Deaf and Hearing Children: Proportion above the Median: (N = 60)

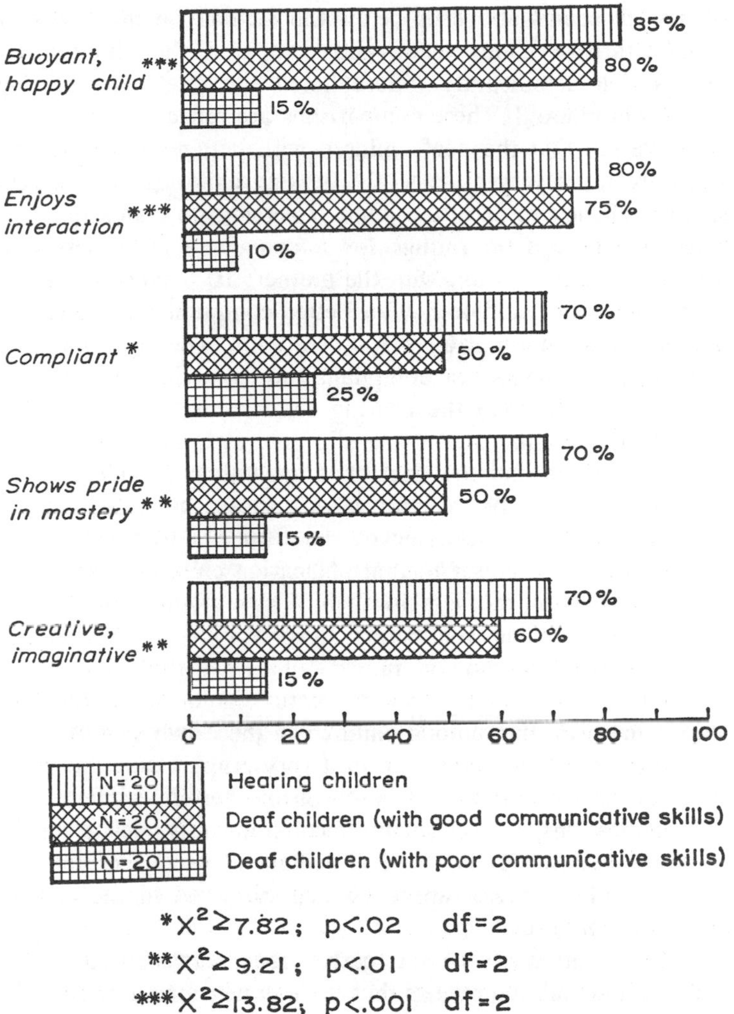

Figure 9 RATINGS OF MATERNAL-CHILD INTERACTION Comparisons of Deaf and Hearing Children (with Communicative Skill Level Controlled): Proportion above the Median (N = 60)

apparent sadness, unhappiness; pride in mastery versus absence of pride in accomplishments. The last three dimensions relate to the "joyful" quality of mother-child interaction.

We again divided the deaf children into two groups, according to scores above or below the median on the Index of Communicative Competence and compared the children on ratings that significantly differentiated the deaf and hearing subjects in figure 8. These comparisons are reflected in figure 9. Here we see that the deaf children with better communicative skills are rated very close to the hearing children with respect to three of the five variables. Only 5 percentage points separate these two groups on ratings for buoyancy or happiness and enjoyment of interaction with the mother; 10 percentage points separate the deaf children with better communication and the hearing children on ratings for creativity. The deaf children generally are seen as less compliant and as having less pride in mastery of skills than the hearing children. The deaf children with good communication are still intermediate between the hearing children and the deaf children with poor skills. Comparison of the graphs in figure 9 with those shown in figure 7 will show that the behavior of the deaf children with good communication is closer to that of hearing children than is the behavior of their mothers to that of the mothers of hearing children. Kogan and Wimberger (1966:1175–1176) analyzed mother-child interaction in pre-school "Headstart" and "non-Headstart" pairs. They found more significant differences among mothers than among children in these two groups.[2]

Figures 7 and 9 illustrate in a very graphic way the influence of absence of communication on mother-child interaction. The implications are that when the communicative deficit resulting from deafness is alleviated (in whatever way), both maternal and child behavior approach that observed in the control group of mother-child pairs.

Examination of the intercorrelations between ratings for mothers and children reveals that three dimensions of the child's behavior do not seem to be particularly related to his mother's behavior, as defined in the rating scales. These are curiosity, creativity, and independence. The child's enjoyment of the interaction with his mother is significantly related to every dimension of positively defined behavior on the part of the mother. (The ratings for buoyancy or happiness are similarly highly related, as would be expected.) The most highly corre-

2. We are continuing to follow the development of the deaf children described in this chapter, and are interested in whether these observed differences remain stable over time.

lated scales for mother and child are the ratings for enjoyment of the interaction for each member of the dyad ($r = .751$). (Correlation matrices are presented in Appendix A.) This is particularly interesting in view of the fact that "happiness" or "enjoyment" is a variable not included often in the literature of child development and child psychiatry.

Additional discussion of the implications of the ratings of mother-child interaction will be presented later in this chapter, following presentation of data regarding child-rearing practices, collected by interviews and questionnaires administered to the mothers of the deaf and hearing children.

The Impact of Communicative Deficit on Child-Rearing Practices

Parents of handicapped children are often advised by professionals to treat the child "as if" he were normal. Most parents in our sample conscientiously tried to follow the advice they were given and tended to believe that they had been successful in the normalization of the handicapped child. ("We treat him just like the other children. He's no different".) Comparisons of the child-rearing responses of the mothers of deaf children and those of the hearing control group reveal some striking differences—many of them somewhat subtly expressed.

Socialization for Safety

The balance between realistic assessment of the additional environmental dangers posed by deafness and overprotection of the deaf child is a delicate one. When means of warning or of explaining danger are lacking, parents are often "overprotective." This is illustrated by the data presented in table 8, reflecting responses made by mothers of the two groups of children to questions about methods of teaching children to avoid injuries from burns or accidents in the street.

Responses to questions in this area were categorized in four ways: (1) some verbal means of teaching or cautioning the child about danger. Examples are "I told them 'hot!' "; "I explained that the iron or the stove could hurt them"; "I just said 'No' when he started to go into the street"; "I explained what would happen if she got hit by a car." (2) A visual or tactile means for teaching avoidance of accidents: "Let him feel a

TABLE 8
Methods for Teaching Avoidance of Burn Injuries and Street Accidents

Methods of Teaching Avoidance	*Burn Injuries**		*Street Accidents*	
	Mothers w/Deaf Children (N = 40)	*Mothers w/Hearing Children (N = 20)*	*Mothers w/Deaf Children (N = 39)*	*Mothers w/Hearing Children (N = 20)*
Verbal method	70%	70%	20%	40%
Visual or tactile method	35%	15%	18%	15%
Control of child or environment	40%	30%	60%	25%
Child learned through mishap	35%	5%	3%	20%

* Based on more than one response per subject.

warm iron"; "Drew limits on the sidewalk to show him how close he could go to the curb"; use of pictures or pantomime. (3) Control of the child or of the environment in order to prevent an accident. This included "Constant supervision by parent or siblings"; "Child allowed to play only in a fenced yard"; "Ironed only at night"; "Always cooked on the back stove burners." (4) Learning through a mishap included a "close call" for the child in front of a car or an actual accident or burn. (None of the children had been seriously hurt, however.) One of the interesting facets of responses shown in table 8 is the greater volume of responses from the mothers of deaf children in regard to the question of teaching avoidance of burn injuries. Mothers of hearing children averaged 1.2 responses, compared to 1.8 responses for the mothers of deaf children (responses to two questions were combined: one related to the "hot iron," the other to the "hot stove"). The proportion of mothers with deaf and with hearing children who reported using verbal methods to teach avoidance of burn injuries was the same (70 percent in each group). However, almost all the mothers with deaf children utilized some other method in addition to the verbal one: about one-third of the group with deaf children reported using visual-tactile methods, and "accidental learning." These proportions are considerably higher than in the group with hearing children.

Responses to the question about teaching avoidance of street accidents suggest that this may be of greater concern to the mothers of deaf children than the possibility of burn injuries. Almost two-thirds of the mothers with deaf children reported using control of the environment to protect their child from this eventuality, compared to only one-quarter of the mothers with hearing children. Here again, a reality element is certainly operating since children with normal hearing can be expected to utilize their sound responses to car engines and horns to help them avoid traffic accidents. It is difficult to say where "reality" stops and where "overprotection" begins. Fully 20 percent of mothers with hearing children report some kind of "close call" with cars for their children, compared to only 3 percent of mothers with deaf children. Two possibilities occur here: one is that mothers with deaf children have been successful in controlling the environment and thus protecting the child from accidents, with attendant learning occurring. The second is that the close watch and control exerted by the mothers with deaf children at the preschool age only delays the child's ability to take responsibility for his own safety.

In view of the wide differences between mothers with deaf children and those with hearing children in behavior rated by the judges as either "controlling" or "permissive," these data become even more suggestive. The difficulties of separating *necessary* protectiveness from unnecessary overcontrol when a child suffers a profound hearing loss is difficult indeed. It points again to the problems faced by parents with deaf children, and to the importance of the child's capabilities and deficits in molding parental behavior.

PUNITIVE METHODS OF SOCIALIZATION

Mothers were asked two questions designed to learn about their beliefs and practices in regard to use of physical punishment for socialization. The first of these was simply, "How do you feel about spanking your children?" Almost three times as many mothers of deaf children indicated that they felt comfortable about physical punishment as did mothers of hearing children (71 percent compared to 25 percent. See Table 9).

TABLE 9
Feelings About Spanking as Form of Punishment

Mothers' Feelings About Spanking Children	*Mothers w/Deaf Children* (*N* = *38*)	*Mothers w/Hearing Children* (*N* = *20*)
Feels comfortable	71%	25%
Has some reservations	24%	50%
Does not spank	5%	25%

These responses included some mothers who stated that they spanked the child occasionally and felt that this was a legitimate control device. Other mothers, however, stated that spanking is "the only thing the deaf child understands." The latter statement, of course, reflects a situation that certainly is limiting to the parent, and unfortunate for both parent and child. About one-quarter of mothers with deaf children (compared to half of those with hearing children) have reservations about the use of physical punishment, using it only as a last resort. Some of these reported that they "only spank the child's hands." Five percent of mothers with deaf children and 25 percent of those with hearing children report that they "never" spank the child, preferring another method or feeling that spanking is not effective. Given the problems of collecting data about physical punishment from the mothers' self-reports, rather than from long-term observation, the differences in the responses of the two groups of mothers is extremely striking, and again may serve to confirm the importance of the child's handicap for child-rearing practices.

A second question in regard to physical punishment asked mothers to compare the use of spanking with the subject child and with his siblings. Table 10 shows that again there are striking differences between mothers with deaf and with hearing children. Differences between the two groups of mothers appear in two categories of responses: mothers with deaf children more frequently report they spank the subject child less than his sibs; they are less likely to report variations in spanking dependent upon age than are the mothers with hearing children. In view of data in table 9 indicating those mothers with deaf children generally feel more comfortable about spanking their children, a question must be asked about their state-

TABLE 10
Use of Spanking with Subject Child Relative to Siblings

Mothers' Use of Spanking with Subject Child	*Mothers w/Deaf Children (N = 31)*	*Mothers w/Hearing Children (N = 13)*
Subject child spanked more than sibs	16%	23%
Subject child gets same treatment	45%	54%
Subject child spanked less than sibs	35%	8%
Subject child spanked less than older sibs, more than younger sibs	3%	15%

ments that their deaf child is spanked less frequently than his hearing sibs. Again, several possibilities may be operative. First, it may be that mothers of families including a deaf child do indeed use physical punishment more frequently than mothers in other families, feel guilty about this, and attempt to rationalize the guilt by suggesting "this is the only method that children understand." A second possibility is that mothers with preschool deaf children are subjected to more strain than they can handle with equanimity. They do indeed spank generally more frequently than other mothers, but continue to protect the handicapped child.

METHODS OF TOILET TRAINING

The usual data collected from parents in regard to toilet training is related to the age at which they begin or complete this task. The *method* by which this chore is accomplished seems to be regarded as secondary, perhaps because verbal communication between mother and child is usually taken for granted. Table 11 shows some interesting differences in the methods used by mothers of the deaf and the hearing children for this "ordinary" task of child-rearing.

Table 11 suggests that older sibs are not models for toilet training to the same extent as they are when the younger sib can hear. Younger deaf sibs may be discouraged from following their brothers or sisters around simply because the interaction is generally negative, or they may have developed a

TABLE 11
Methods of Toilet Training

Method of Toilet Training	*Mothers w/Deaf Children (N = 38)*	*Mothers w/Hearing Children (N = 20)*
Siblings provide example	16%	40%
Frequent toileting	32%	15%
Other means	53%	45%

propensity to play alone due to their hearing deficits. The data show that mother takes over this task to a larger extent than for the hearing controls. Her personal supervision of this aspect of training may also reflect a greater preoccupation with the deaf child's total development.

FRUSTRATIONS AND IRRITATIONS OF PARENTING

The socialization of the young child calls for infinite patience on the part of the parents under the best of conditions. When the child is handicapped, and the handicap inhibits communication, the patience demanded of the parent is increased many times. The figures reported in table 12 are an eloquent reflection of the problems of parenting a deaf child.

Table 12 shows that 63 percent of the mothers of deaf children name some problem or frustration of parenting that

TABLE 12
Felt Difficulties of Child-Rearing

Felt Difficulties of Child-Rearing	*Mothers w/Deaf Children (N = 39)*	*Mothers w/Hearing Children (N = 20)*
Mother's inability to understand child	15%	0
Child's inability to understand mother	38%	0
Need for constant supervision of child (related to deafness)	10%	0
Large amount of time devoted to child (not related to deafness)	3%	30%
Problems of parental control	15%	50%
"Nothing" or "other"	18%	20%

is directly related to their child's deafness, and over half mention something related to the difficulty they find in communicating with the child. It is interesting that while 38 percent mention their child's inability to understand them as a felt difficulty, only 15 percent name their own inability to understand the child as a problem. (This would seem to reflect the nature of communication gap that is most annoying to parents, not a difference in direction of true communication flow.)

While half of the mothers with hearing children name problems of parental control as a felt difficulty, only 15 percent of the mothers with deaf children mentioned this area. It may be that their frustrations around communication are so great that other problem areas seem pale by comparison. Or, a less likely alternative may be that the greater amount of control exerted by the mothers results in more manageable preschool children.

DISCUSSION

To review very briefly the data presented in the preceding pages of this chapter, we can say that the behavior of mothers of deaf children differs radically from that of the mothers of hearing children, as observed in the videotaped scenarios of mother-child interaction. These differential behavior patterns are particularly pronounced when the deaf child lags behind his deaf peers in the development of a viable means of communication. In these instances, mothers are much more likely to appear inflexible, controlling, didactic, intrusive, and disapproving. Deaf children with fewer communicative skills appear to be less happy, to enjoy the interaction with their mothers less, to be less compliant, less creative, and to show less pride in mastery than either their deaf peers with additional communicative skills or the hearing children.

Data on child-rearing practices also reflected some wide-ranging differences in responses of the mothers with deaf children and those with hearing children. These included more constant supervision of the child to protect him from accidents, a more narrow range of disciplinary techniques, and feelings of frustration regarding mother-child communication.

In attempting to suggest some of the bases for and the significance of these differences in child and maternal behavior, some exceedingly complex questions arise. A recurring issue in interpreting interaction when deaf children are involved is that of balancing the reality of the necessity for shifts in style of interaction related to hearing deficit; shifts in style that arise because of the hearing person's discomfort or sense of frustration in reduced communication; and shifts in style that result from training or philosophy about "correct" ways of interacting with deaf children. (Some of these same issues arise in considering interaction between deaf and hearing adults, but they do not emerge with as much sharpness as when young children are involved.)

It would seem to be a "fact" in the lives of deaf children and those around them that it is more difficult to attract their attention than it is with the hearing children. Thus, the various tactile and visual and exaggerated auditory means of capturing the deaf child's attention are responses to very real problems faced by parents (and others). When a parent lifts the deaf child's chin to her face, takes hold of his shoulder or arm, physically restrains him, repeatedly calls his name loudly or stamps on the floor, we might say that these are methods of coping with the reality of the interactional world: that is, the deaf child does not hear—or at best, hears imperfectly—what is said to him. The mother's method of attracting the child's attention may well seem intrusive, authoritarian, or overly controlling to an observer. On the other hand, it is possible that the deaf child does not experience these behavioral mechanisms in the same way that the hearing observer does, or in the same way that a hearing child might experience them. Perhaps repetition is *necessary* if meaning is to be communicated to the deaf child. While the mother with a hearing child may be able to explain the meaning of a particular rule, and let the child know the kinds of occasions on which the rule may be broken, the limited nature of communication in the mother–deaf-child dyad may preclude the teaching of nuances that would allow flexible behavior on the part of the mother.

The second area of possible explanation for some of the observed behavioral differences may lie in the realm of the mother's reaction to the continuing frustration of impaired communication with her child. Thus, the constant repetition of the child's name, for example, in an attempt to get his attention may be experienced by the observer as an increasingly shrill, annoyed, critical, and irritated maternal mode. Mothers who have had little prior experience with deafness may well experience absence of communication as an annoying, irritating condition, even though they realize intellectually that their child does not hear them when he fails to respond to a vocal command. One of the frustrating, but realistic, situations often encountered is the variability of the deaf child's response to sound. On "good" days, he may respond to sounds that he fails to hear on "bad" days. ("Good" and "bad" days may relate to weather, mood, illness, hearing aid batteries, and so forth.) Thus, parents sometimes wonder whether the deaf child is being willful when he fails to respond. The ambiguity created by variations in the child's use of residual hearing adds to interactional frustration.

A third possible explanation for some of the differences in maternal behavior in relation to a deaf child relate to the "training" received by mothers from experts in the handling and socialization of their children. From the time that deafness is diagnosed, mothers are exposed to a multitude of dicta related to what they should or should not do with, for, and to the deaf child. Again, much of this advice is reality-oriented: the deaf child needs special training and treatment if he is to develop social and communication skills. However, if a mother is to retain her own style, and to incorporate the teacher's style rather than being engulfed by it, she needs self-confidence that often has been diluted by the difficult, guilt-producing process of adjusting to a handicapped infant. This area is probably reflected in the frequent ratings of mothers of deaf children as "didactic" and "intrusive." Many of the mothers whose behavior could be characterized in these terms seemed to be carbon copies of the child's teacher as they interacted with him in the playroom. Thus, every opportunity to "teach language" was seized upon with a vigor that often precluded pleasure and enjoyment. Rather than building a structure with the blocks, or encouraging the child to find his own activity with the blocks, many of the mothers of deaf children used the blocks as a way of eliciting the names of colors. Many of these mothers insisted that the child *say* the color of a cup, *say* "please" or "thank you," or *ask* for a cookie before they allowed him to have refreshments. This reflects the kind of instructions that teachers frequently give mothers, or show them by example. For some of the mothers observed, the investigators felt that they might have been able to predict the preschool program in which the deaf child was enrolled, so closely did the mothers pattern their behavior on that of the teacher. Some mothers appeared comfortable following the teacher's model. Others appeared to use the teacher's pattern as a facade—appearing unnatural and uncomfortable in a style they had not fully assimilated.

It will be recalled that the mothers of deaf children were rated as using gestures only slightly more than were the mothers of hearing children. This is strange and goes counter to what might be predicted, since deaf children rely on visual cues to a greater degree than do hearing children. This probably reflects the orientation that most of the mothers have received from educators. Only four of the forty mothers of deaf children have decided to utilize sign language. The remainder of the mothers, like their children's teachers, support the "pure oral" methods of education with greater or lesser degrees of fervor. While many of the mothers verbalize a belief in using gestures with the deaf child "when necessary," most have been trained to be aware of the use or nonuse of gestures, with a possibly inhibitory effect. This third area of explanation for shifts in maternal behavior related to the child's handicap is an indirect one. Nevertheless, it appears to be a powerful source of influence for mothers.

The data comparing behavior of mothers and children when deafness is present and not present would seem to provide powerful support for the notion that children's capabilities and behavior exert tremendous influence on the interactional style exhibited by the mother. This effect is both reciprocal and cumulative, with communicative deficit leaving its mark on every major area of child-rearing practices, and on the expressive and instrumental styles of both mothers and children.

6

Developmental Aspects of Deafness in the School Years

New problems and new possibilities await the deaf child as his world expands to include his school and his community. The tasks of developing industry, identity, and intimacy are the crucial ones for the years between six and eighteen. For deaf children, industry is required for the improvement of communication skills as well as for achievement in academic subjects; a sense of identity grows through development of self-image, in the acknowledgment or rejection of an auditory handicap and in positive identification with others; preparation for intimacy can come through the growth of maturity, and increasing personal-social adjustment. These are the areas we will evaluate in a search for insight into the developmental aspects of deafness during the school years.

In order to have a comparative basis for this evaluation, two major dimensions reflecting differential family and school conditions were selected. These dimensions, relating to the impact of the environment on the deaf child are: the hearing status of the deaf child's parents, and the nature of the school setting.

A consideration of the ways in which these major factors can be expected to influence the deaf child's development during his school years, and a review of previous research that takes into account either parental hearing status or differential school placement should be helpful in understanding the rationale for the research design.

Chapter 6 is by Kathryn P. Meadow.

PARENTAL HEARING STATUS

Parents' hearing status—that is, whether parents are themselves deaf or whether they have normal auditory contact with the environment[1]—can be expected to influence the deaf child's development in three major ways: (1) differences in attitudes about deafness that are reflected in their response to the initial diagnosis, and in their feelings about a deaf child later on; (2) differences in the knowledge of and attitudes toward manual communication during the deaf child's early years; (3) differences in social, economic, and psychological resources stemming from a prior history related to hearing status. Although there is much individual variation among families in all of these areas, we can expect that group differences will generally favor the deaf parents in the first two areas, but will favor hearing parents in the third.

Response to the Diagnosis of Deafness

Deaf parents' experiences with and reaction to the process leading to a diagnosis of deafness usually differ radically from those of hearing parents. Hearing parents are more likely to experience a long period of uncertainty about the precise nature of the child's difficulties. Since profound congenital deafness is relatively unique, it is usually a medically unexpected event. It is an "invisible" defect and thus objectively difficult to diagnose. Symptoms are ambiguous and often mistaken for developmental anomalies. During the process of diagnosis, when hearing parents are sent from one doctor to another, they often become increasingly more anxious and frustrated. Frequently, the medical experts whom they consult accuse them—overtly or covertly—of being over-anxious, inadequate, or incompetent. When the diagnosis is eventually made, it usually comes as a shock and is experienced as a tragic crisis with long-term implications for family life. Hearing parents often feel guilt, grief, and remorse. They are overwhelmed with prescriptions for

1. Two variations of this major dichotomy are theoretically and empirically possible: (1) the case where one parent has normal hearing and the other has impaired hearing; (2) the case where both parents are "hard of hearing" rather than profoundly deaf. Both of these variations involve small numbers of families. They were excluded for this reason, but also because the differences which are considered crucial for the developmental patterns of deaf children are not so likely to be present.

necessary auditory, speech, language, and lipreading training that they may feel incapable of meeting, particularly since they have come to feel themselves inadequate for many parental tasks during the period of diagnostic ambiguity.

Deaf parents, on the other hand, almost never experience the diagnostic delay when ambiguity about the child's condition becomes so debilitating to hearing parents. They half suspect their child will be born deaf. They usually make the diagnosis themselves—either accidentally or in a planned way. For example, one deaf mother reported:

> When M. was four or five months old, he was lying on the sofa sleeping. I was putting the oldest boy's toys away in his wagon. And I forgot that I was making such an awful racket. The baby slept through it. So I knew he was deaf. (Meadow, 1967)

Although most deaf parents express a desire that their children be hearing, they adjust quickly to the idea of deafness (Meadow and Meadow, 1971). More important, they feel adequate to communicate with their deaf child and to help him to cope with the disadvantages of deafness. They have a world in which they can imagine their deaf child will someday live. One difficult aspect of the adjustment made by hearing parents is the fear that their deaf child may someday choose (or be forced) to live in an exclusively "deaf world" while they, the parents, remain estranged in their exclusively "hearing world."

The Use of Manual Communication

The second way in which the hearing status of parents influences the deaf child's development is in the differential use of manual communication in the early years. Generally speaking, most deaf parents make use of manual communication as a matter of course, while most hearing parents learn sign language and fingerspelling only when their children reach adolescence, if at all. The New York group found that "in only 12 per cent of hearing families with a deaf child does anyone other than the child learn to use manual communication" (Rainer et al., 1963:112). Of the 493 deaf adults responding to the New York survey, two-thirds reported their means of communication as "mainly signs" or as an "equal use of speech and signs" (Rainer et al., 1963:119: computed from table 6). Of 71 deaf parents of deaf children responding to the Stuckless and Birch survey, only 5 stated they did *not* use "the language of signs" with their deaf child. Sixty-four percent stated they used the language of signs "when he or she was a baby" (Stuckless and Birch, 1966:458).

Of the 34 deaf families who had children enrolled in the California School for the Deaf (Berkeley) in 1966, 33 reported they had used manual communication with their children from infancy onward. None of the 34 hearing families interviewed had made early use of manual language. The hearing status of parents, then, has been a fairly reliable predictor of the communicative mode within the home.

Social, Economic, and Psychological Resources

By and large, hearing parents will be found to have more social, educational, and economic resources at their command than will deaf parents. This pattern is related to the unfortunate picture of low educational attainment in the deaf population as a whole, the job discrimination they often experience, even when their educational achievement and vocational attainment qualify them for jobs at higher levels, and the social isolation they suffer as a result of the linguistic handicap that is concomitant with their auditory one. A brief summary of some relevant statistics regarding the social, economic, and educational status of the deaf population will serve to illustrate the depth of the probable differences in any group of deaf and hearing parents.

Of 6,000 employed deaf men surveyed in 1955, 45 percent listed occupations in the "craftsmen and foremen" categories, compared to 19 percent of hearing men thus occupied in 1957 (Lunde and Bigman, 1959:21). Of 33 deaf families with children at Berkeley (residential) school in 1966, 3 percent were employed in white collar jobs, compared to 19 percent of the hearing families. It is estimated that the average deaf adult reads at about the fifth-grade level, or even below (Furth, 1966:205). An investigation of language comprehension of deaf students in 73 schools in Canada and the United States showed that only 12 percent of the sixteen-year-olds scored above the fifth-grade level on the Metropolitan Achievement Tests Battery (Wrightstone et al., 1962:13–14).

In terms of marital stability within deaf and hearing families, Rainer et al. (1963) reported that the rate of divorce among deaf women is higher than that for hearing women. Deaf adults are described as being "less mature" than hearing individuals, "more rigid," and "educationally retarded" (Brunschwig, 1936; Levine, 1956). The hearing population acquires much information regarding child-rearing methods from printed material (Wolfenstein, 1953). With the low reading level reported for deaf adults, it is not surprising that they do not enjoy reading, nor that their interest is confined primarily to daily newspapers (Rainer et al., 1963).

Deaf parents of deaf children appear to seek the help of experts in hearing and speech clinics less frequently than their hearing counterparts. This may be a function of their lack of communicative facility and general social isolation that leads to an absence of knowledge about community resources. It may stem from either a real or an imagined financial barrier to available services. It may also reflect a hostility toward the hearing world which they see as attempting to dictate rigid prescriptions and proscriptions regarding the use of hearing aids, speech training, and manual communication that can be interpreted as an effort to shut them away from their own children. Questions raised by experts about the capabilities of deaf families to provide a "proper" environment for their children (deaf or hearing) are not designed to build confidence in deaf parents. For whatever combination of these reasons, the deaf children of deaf parents are less frequently exposed to the hearing aids, speech training, and preschool education from which they could benefit. This may well be another consequence of the ubiquitous "oral-manual controversy" that reaches out to all areas.

Previous Research Involving Deaf and Hearing Parents

Six studies have been published that evaluate some aspect of the development of deaf children, and that include parental hearing status as a major independent variable.

Stuckless and Birch (1966) used a matched-pair design for comparing deaf children of deaf parents with deaf children of hearing parents. Of seventy-one deaf children with deaf parents in five different schools for the deaf, thirty-eight were selected who had been exposed to early manual communication as well as meeting other criteria. These were matched with deaf children of hearing parents on the basis of sex, age, age of admittance to present school, severity of hearing impairment and intelligence test scores. The authors found no significant differences between their two groups on scores for speech intelligibility, nor for "psychosocial adjustment" as measured by rating scales completed by teachers. Significant differences were found on reading scores, speechreading scores, and on written language scores. In all cases, higher scores were achieved by children with "early manual communication."

Stevenson (1964) compared the educational achievement of deaf children with deaf parents to the achievement of deaf children with hearing parents, using all children of deaf parents enrolled at the California School for the Deaf (Berkeley) between 1914 and 1961. "Of the 134 (children of deaf parents) only fourteen were found to be weaker educationally than the children of hearing parents with whom they were compared. . . . This would mean that 90 percent were better students and attained a higher educational level than the children of hearing parents." He found that only 9 percent of the children of hearing parents "succeeded in going to college," compared to 38 percent of deaf parents' children.

Brill (1960) compared the adjustment of forty-five deaf children of deaf parents to that of the same number in two other categories: (1) deaf children with deaf siblings and hearing parents; (2) deaf children with no deaf relatives. The two comparison groups were equated with the children of deaf parents on the basis of sex, age, and IQ score. No significant differences were found for the group as a whole. However, when boys were compared separately, differences were significant, with the children of deaf parents showing "better adjustment." "Children with deaf parents and with deaf sibs have more ratings at both extremes, while those children who are the single deaf person in a family do not have as many extreme ratings" (Brill, 1960:466). A subjective analysis of the twenty-eight deaf families revealed "at least fifteen (who had 26 of the 45 children) were families that had given very definite evidence of social and/or psychological maladjustment." Brill suggests that the maladjustment in the homes of such a large number of deaf children of deaf parents might more than offset the advantage of communication between parent and child.

Vernon and Koh (1971) report a study of deaf children attending the California School for the Deaf at Riverside. Three groups of children were matched on the basis of IQ, chronological age, and sex. One group had deaf parents, another group had hearing parents and had participated in the Tracy Clinic preschool program; the third group had hearing parents but had never had preschool training. Deaf children with no early manual communication and no oral preschool scored as high on educational achievement tests as the children trained in the Tracy Clinic preschool program. Both groups were far behind those with early manual communication.

Vernon and Koh (1970) also worked with another population of deaf children attending the California School for the Deaf at Riverside. They matched thirty-two pairs of genetically deaf children for sex, age, and intelligence. One group, consisting of recessively deaf children, had hearing parents and no early exposure to manual communication. On a standardized achievement test the early manual group's general achievement was higher on the average by 1.44 years. They were also superior in reading, vocabulary, and written language. No differences were found in speech, speechreading or psychosocial adjustment.

Quigley and Frisina (1961) compared day pupils to boarding pupils in residential schools. Although they did not set out to study children of deaf parents specifically, they did a separate analysis of this subgroup. Among the 120 day students studied, there were 16 who had deaf parents. The group with deaf parents performed at a higher level in fingerspelling and had a more extensive vocabulary. There were no differences in educational achievement or lipreading, but those students with hearing parents received higher ratings on their speech performance.

School Settings

Two of the major types of school settings available to deaf children are the state residential schools for the deaf (operated by most states) and local classes for deaf children, conducted by specially trained teachers within the public schools. To a greater or a lesser extent, these differing settings embody or reflect several differences in educational philosophy that have developed in the field over the years. These may be summarized under three headings: (1) dormitory versus home living arrangements; (2) the use of purely oral methods within the classroom versus the addition of some form of manual communication; (3) the integration of deaf and hearing children within a single school versus the segregation of deaf children in a homogeneous environment. A consideration of these three dimensions should provide insight into a number of additional social factors impinging on the deaf child's development, as well as providing insight into the reasons for the selection of research groups reported below.

Most educators would probably agree that the optimum arrangements for young deaf children are reflected in the situation of the child who lives at home with a loving, concerned family and attends a local school where his special educational needs are met. Unfortunately this is frequently not possible. When a family lives in a rural area where school districts are incapable of providing for the needs of every special child, it may be a case of educational necessity for a young child to attend a state residential school. Some of the disadvantages of the residential setting stem from the nature of dormitory life and the administrative hazards inherent in large institutions. The question of providing opportunities for independent activities, for encouraging children to take responsibility for themselves and their belongings, for providing for children's needs for privacy are all difficult ones. Parents are often partly responsible for the strictness of rules in residential schools because they are unwilling to grant the autonomy to school personnel necessary for encouraging students to take responsibility for their own actions. In spite of the difficulties of providing settings to encourage mature behavior in large institutions, it should be said that families with deaf children do not always provide these opportunities for the children when they live at home either. The frequent patterns of overindulgence of the child with a handicap point up some of the problems faced by parents as well as by school personnel.

The traditional differences found between public day and residential schools in the relative usage of oral and manual communication are grounded in the history of the differences in educational philosophy (Mindel and Vernon, 1971). The state residential schools have long been a focal point of the deaf subculture. In the absence of all formal instruction in sign language, the residential schools have become the setting for the communication of sign language from one generation of deaf individuals to another. It is a common belief among most deaf adults that the only "proper" place for deaf children to receive their education is in the state residential schools. Thus, the deaf children of deaf parents are much more likely to attend the residential than the day schools. These are the children who know sign language and who teach (their own version of) sign language to their peers. In this respect, it is interesting that of 256 records we reviewed of deaf children attending day schools in the San Francisco Bay Area, only three had a deaf father and a deaf mother. One of the three was hard-of-hearing, the other two were making plaintive pleas to school administrators to allow them to transfer the children to the state residential school. Thus, this difference in educational philosophy has not only resulted from the controversy but has created a greater chasm between educators who are likely to be divided not only on the basis of their commitment to a communicative mode but also on the basis of the type of school in which they teach.

In comparing the relative contact of deaf children with hearing peers in the residential and the day school settings, there is no doubt that a much greater opportunity for contacts exists for deaf children in day schools. The extent to which the opportunities are realized, and the feelings that these contacts evoke among both the deaf and the hearing members of the pairs, need to be discussed. Too frequently it would seem the deaf student is placed at a disadvantage in interaction with hearing students. His position vis-à-vis the hearing classmates is such as to almost guarantee inferiority. Frequently it is an accepted fact that the deaf students "cannot compete" with the hearing students in academic subjects, so are integrated only for physical education, home economics, shop, and the like, where academic ability is less important. The conflict between the possible advantages of learning to get along in a "hearing world" and the possible disadvantages of the "isolation of segregation" are issues that have been argued vehemently by deaf individuals and educators for some years.

An additional difference between the residential and the day schools is the presence of deaf adults as teachers and/or dormitory counselors in the residential schools. In contrast, it is relatively unusual for deaf children in day schools to have contact with deaf adults in these roles. In most public school systems it is impossible for administrators to hire deaf teachers, even if they are qualified. Many teacher-training programs in deaf education are reluctant to accept deaf students. In a few school systems, deaf adults have been hired as teachers' aides, but this is a recent development.

Although all of these differences between residential and day schools have a long history, it should be mentioned that many changes are taking place in both kinds of schools. In many parts of the country increased interest in "total communication" is becoming apparent in day programs, while more emphasis is being placed on speech and auditory training in many residential schools. These changes are apparent even in the span of time since this research was first begun in 1966.

PREVIOUS RESEARCH INVOLVING DEAF STUDENTS IN DAY AND RESIDENTIAL SETTINGS

Pintner and Reamer (1920) found that children who attended day schools scored higher on tests of academic achievement than those who attended residential schools. But differential selection is implied by the finding that those in day schools performed better on intelligence tests, had more residual hearing, and became deaf at a later age than the residential schools' students. Upshall (1929) reported essentially the same results but stated that differences in educational achievement of residential and day school pupils were reduced by 50 percent when the children compared were of equal age and intellectual ability, were deafened before the age of one year, and had never attended a school for hearing children. Myklebust (1960) reported that children in residential schools were more likely to have deaf relatives than were those in day schools. Barker's review of the literature regarding the social development of deaf children (1953) suggests that residential schools for the deaf "are not optimal environments for the development of social maturity" (p. 206). It should be noted, parenthetically, that all the studies cited in Barker's review were completed from twenty to forty years ago. More recently, Quigley and Frisina (1961) concluded that their data "provide no evidence that living in residential schools is detrimental to deaf children" in terms of educational achievement and psychosocial adjustment. It must be remembered that residential schools today are very different from those of several decades ago. Now there is a widespread emphasis on the importance of family life, and many schools require children to spend weekends and vacations at home.

RESEARCH DESIGN AND SAMPLE SELECTION

The preceding material was presented to illustrate the rationale for the selection of the major comparison groups of deaf children based on differences in parents' hearing status and school placement. When these two dimensions are combined, four groups of deaf children are theoretically possible:

1. Children attending residential schools whose parents are deaf.
2. Children attending residential schools whose parents are hearing.
3. Children attending day schools whose parents are deaf.
4. Children attending day schools whose parents are hearing.

For a number of practical reasons, the research has proceeded in two stages. During the first stage[2] data were collected from deaf children attending a state residential school for the deaf, with both deaf and hearing parents (Groups 1 and 2). During the second stage, children were recruited from day schools. The selection of research subjects during the two stages will be described separately.

Stage 1—The Residential Sample

The California School for the Deaf at Berkeley was the locus of the selection of the residential sample. Between January and September of 1966, when the sample selection was completed, 61 students were enrolled who had both a deaf father

2. The original study was submitted to the faculty of the Department of Sociology, University of California, Berkeley, as a doctoral dissertation. That work has been reported in Meadow, 1967, 1968*a*, 1968*b*, 1968*c*, 1969, and is available in toto from University Microfilms, Order No. 68-5785. It was supported by a fellowship (RF-265) from the Vocational Rehabilitation Administration, and indirectly by a Training Grant in Personality and Social Structure from the National Institute of Mental Health. Professors John A. Clausen, Herbert Blumer, and Susan Ervin-Tripp served as faculty advisors. Dr. Hugo Schunhoff and his staff at the California School for the Deaf, Berkeley, provided a great deal of assistance. Of special help were Myron Leenhouts, Jacob Arcanin, and Hartley Koch, then respectively Principal, Dean of Students, and Director of Pupil Personnel Services at the school. The late Harold Ramger, Mrs. Catherine Ramger, Mr. and Mrs. George Attletweed, and Rev. and Mrs. Roger Pickering played very special instrumental roles in the research process.

and a deaf mother. Two of these were members of racial minority groups and were excluded; one family did not give permission for their child's participation. Each of the remaining 58 deaf children with deaf parents was matched individually with a deaf child of hearing parents on the basis of sex, age, IQ test score, degree of residual hearing, and family size. Before the matching procedure was begun, children with hearing parents were eliminated if they had any of the following characteristics: (1) deaf siblings; (2) racial or ethnic minority group membership; (3) secondary handicap in addition to deafness; (4) deafened after the age of two years; (5) deafness resulting from maternal rubella, Rh incompatibility, or anoxia. The available pool of children with hearing parents included 225. Thus, the first phase of the research involved matched-pair comparisons of 58 pairs of deaf children: one member of each pair had two deaf parents; the other member of each pair had hearing parents.

Stage 2—The Day School Sample

After the completion of the original research involving deaf children attending the state residential school, it was decided to extend that study to include a group of similar deaf children attending day schools in the San Francisco Bay Area. Supervisors of special education programs for the deaf, representing six different school districts in the Bay Area, were contacted to obtain cooperation in the research.[3] Then records of deaf students in each of the school districts were evaluated in order to eliminate those who were ineligible for participation according to the criteria that had been set up in the original study.

Of the 256 records evaluated, 179 were eliminated because

3. The follow-up study was made possible by the cooperation of the directors of a number of special programs for deaf children in the Bay Area, to whom we are indeed grateful. These include: Mr. Valentine Becker, Supervisor, and Mrs. Shirley Hall, Resource Teacher for the Hearing Handicapped, both of the San Francisco Unified School District, Programs for Speech, Hearing, and Visually Handicapped; Miss Margaret Breakey, Director of Special Services for the Deaf, Burlingame School District; Dr. Barbara Nelson, Supervisor of Special Education, San Jose Unified School District; Dr. Al Tudyman, Director of Special Education, Oakland Public Schools; Mr. Ed LaPlace, Director of Special Services, Richmond School District; Mr. Robert Shearer, Supervisor of Speech and Hearing Services, Mt. Diablo Unified School District.

Most of the testing for the follow-up study was completed by Arline Cottrell and Katherine Leland, who have assisted in other phases of the research work as well.

of: the presence of deaf siblings (15), racial or ethnic minority group membership (63), secondary handicaps (10), postlingual onset of deafness (10), etiology (27), age (3), residual hearing (29), inadequate information, and so forth (22). Of the remaining 77 children, only three had deaf parents. Since this was too small a number for the collection of meaningful comparative data, these children were dropped also, and the decision was made to conduct an extension of the original research with three groups rather than four. A tabular description of the three groups for sex, age, IQ scores and residual hearing is included in Appendix B.

RESEARCH INSTRUMENTS

Self-Image Test

The development of a measure of self-image was one of the most difficult tasks of the entire research process. After much experimentation with existing tests and modifications, an instrument was devised that combined a graphic cartoonlike presentation with written words plus illustrations of the manual signs for the adjectives used. When the research was extended to the day schools, the manual signs were eliminated, since this form of communication was not used by the third group of students. Six adjectives were chosen as the basis for the child's self-evaluation: lazy, pretty or handsome, smart, nice, mean, silly. These six adjectives were familiar to even the youngest residential children. They were selected because they seem to describe a number of different dimensions of "self-hood." Three positive and three negative adjectives were chosen in an attempt to diminish the halo effect or response set in the children's answers. Students were asked first how they evaluated themselves on these adjectives, then how their mother, father, teacher, counselor (or principal), boys at school, girls at school, and hearing people felt about them. Administration was in small groups for older children, individual for younger ones.

Rating Scale

A rating scale was constructed especially for this study (see Appendix C) to be completed by teachers and counselors. Each child was rated independently by three "caretakers" (teachers or counselors) on dimensions of social/personal adjustment and achievement. Ratings were made on a scale ranging from one to ten, and summed. The analysis of these ratings is based on a rank ordering of the ratings in all cases.

Measures of Intellectual and Communicative Functioning

The rating scale described above contained items relating to communicative and intellectual functioning, but it was considered important to obtain more objective measures of each area. Thus, the Craig Lipreading Inventory (Craig, 1964) was selected as a measure of lipreading skill, while standard achievement tests administered by the schools were utilized as a measure of academic achievement or intellectual functioning. The lipreading test includes both single words and sentences, and it was constructed and filmed for a research project conducted by Professor Stephen Quigley at the University of Illinois.[4] The test includes thirty-three nouns, preceded by "Show me the ————." For example: "Show me the fire." "Show me the purse." The sentence portion of the test includes twenty-four simple sentences: "A coat is on a chair." "A top and a ball are on the floor." For each word or sentence, the child checks one of four choices pictured on his answer sheet.

Stanford Achievement Test scores were collected from schools for as many children as possible. Unfortunately these scores were unavailable for many of the students in the three groups. The tests are not routinely administered to children below the third grade in the residential school. Some of the day schools do not administer the SAT to their deaf students. This seems to reflect a nationwide pattern. The Babbidge report stated, for example, that "returns (of Stanford Achievement Test data) from public day schools and classes were fragmentary and inconclusive. Most reported that records were no longer available at the reporting schools, having followed the students to other schools" (Babbidge, 1965:22).

FINDINGS AND DISCUSSION

Industry Versus Inferiority: "I Am What I Can Learn"

During the early school years (ages six to eleven) the primary developmental task is that of industry, leading to com-

4. We are grateful to Dr. William Craig for the use of the filmed test for the original research, and to Dr. Stephen Quigley for the film used in the follow-up study.

petence. Translated into academic achievement, the deaf child is at a disadvantage, compared to his schoolmates with normal hearing. His difficulties in acquiring language usually are reflected in his lack of academic progress, in spite of normal intellectual potential (Furth, 1966). Translated into communicative achievement, his disadvantage is even more extreme: the painful process of learning to communicate through speech and lipreading is rarely a complete success for those with profound congenital deafness.

INTELLECTUAL FUNCTIONING

The measure of intellectual functioning most frequently used during the school years is that of academic achievement. Table 13 shows the average Stanford Achievement Test scores for the three research groups for reading, arithmetic, and overall grade level. Scores of the day students (Group 3) fall between those of the two groups (1 and 2) of residential students. While the residential students with deaf parents rank first and the residential students with hearing parents rank last, the differences between day and residential students are not statistically significant.

TABLE 13
Mean School Achievement Level for
Residential and Day Students
(Ages 11.5–17)*

	Group 1 *Residential* (*Deaf Parents*)	*Group 2* *Residential* (*Hearing Parents*)	*Group 3* *Day* (*Hearing Parents*)
	Mean (*N*)	Mean (*N*)	Mean (*N*)
Grade level	4.7 (26)	3.9 (26)	4.3 (21)
Reading	4.8 (26)	3.8 (26)	4.4 (26)
Arithmetic	5.6 (26)	4.7 (26)	5.4 (22)

* The original research, comparing Groups 1 and 2, included thirty-two matched pairs of students for whom achievement test scores were available: *t*-tests of the differences between members of the pairs favored Group 1 in each case ($p < .01$). In order to equate the three groups for age, the six oldest children in Group 1 and in Group 2 were eliminated. This reduced the differences in the score levels of the two groups (mean difference in grade level in the upper grades was 2.2 years). Separate *t*-test analyses, comparing Groups 1 and 3, then Groups 2 and 3, showed no statistically significant differences in either case. Tables reflecting these comparisons will be found in Appendix B.

Comparatively speaking, the differences among the three major groups of deaf children are not significant. More important than the differences between these groups of deaf children would appear to be the differences between the deaf children and their hearing peers. The average age of the deaf children whose scores are summarized in table 13 is 13.2 years. If their performance levels approached the norms for hearing children, they should achieve at least at a seventh-grade level. Thus, the lag in reading achievement level ranges from 2.2 to 3.2 years. This is not ununusual in relation to past findings of the achievement of deaf children. For example, Wrightstone, Aranow, and Moskowitz (1962) reported the average reading achievement of deaf sixteen-year-olds as 3.4, with 80 percent of sixteen-year-olds reading below grade level 4.9. The study conducted by the Advisory Committee on the Education of the Deaf reported on 920 deaf students who left public residential schools during or at the end of the 1963–1964 school year:

> At no age was the median grade average as high as the seventh grade despite the fact that the bulk of those included were at least of high school leaving age. (Babbidge, 1965:22)

Thus, the low achievement score levels of students participating in our research are not unexpected in terms of general academic achievement of deaf school children.

When the students were divided into two subgroups according to age (older or younger than age thirteen), analysis showed no significant differences among the three groups of older students, but the younger day students scored significantly higher than did the residential students with hearing parents. It was discovered that one school in the day student group had been exposed to total communication (i.e., the simultaneous use of oral and manual language in the classroom). Since this variable was a major reason for separating the two groups of residential students, a separate analysis was undertaken, comparing the school achievement of day students with and without exposure to manual language. Although only thirteen day students were involved in the comparison, statistically significant differences were found for reading level and overall grade level achievement favoring the day students in the total communication classroom. These analyses are summarized below in table 14.

TABLE 14
Mean School Achievement Grade Level for Residential Students and Day Students from Oral and Total Communication Classrooms (Ages 11.5–13)*

	Group 1 Residential (Deaf Parents)	*Group 2 Residential (Hearing Parents)*	*Group 3a Day (Oral Classes)*	*Group 3b Day ("Total" Class)*
	Mean (*N*)	Mean (*N*)	Mean (*N*)	Mean (*N*)
Grade level	3.6 (11)	2.8 (10)	3.8 (5)	4.5 (6)
Reading	3.3 (11)	2.7 (10)	3.6 (7)	4.4 (6)
Arithmetic	3.8 (11)	3.1 (10)	5.3 (7)	4.5 (6)

* Detailed statistical analyses appear in Appendix B.

Table 14 indicates that the differences between the younger residential and day pupils in reading and grade level were contributed primarily by the class of students with whom manual communication was utilized. These results provide some supportive data for the one extant experimental study comparing the academic achievement levels of deaf children using finger-spelling in their classrooms to those in oral control classrooms.

> The significantly superior ability in the reading of finger-spelling (after a four-year program) was accompanied by a general superiority on most of the other variables measured in the project. The experimental subjects were significantly superior in their speechreading ability on the sentence version of the Inventory although the difference did not reach statistical significance. The experimental group also was superior to the control group at a statistically significant level on five of the seven measures of reading ability, and had higher scores than the control group on the other two measures of reading ability although the differences did not reach statistical significance. (Quigley, 1968:89)

Returning again to a consideration of the intellectual functioning of the total groups of research subjects, table 15 shows teacher-

TABLE 15
Teacher-Counselor Ratings for Intellectual Functioning: Proportion above the Median for Residential and Day Students

	Group 1 Residential (Deaf Parents)	*Group 2 Residential (Hearing Parents)*	*Group 3 Day (Hearing Parents)*
	% (*N*)	% (*N*)	% (*N*)
Intellectual ability	71% (55)	29% (56)	48% (69)[a]
Use of intelligence	67% (54)	35% (55)	45% (69)[b]
Motivation for school work	68% (57)	40% (58)	51% (69)[c]
Written language	62% (50)	47% (51)	45% (64)[d]

[a] Kruskal-Wallis $H^* = 21.03$; $p < .001$.
[b] Kruskal-Wallis $H = 5.78$; $p < .001$.
[c] Kruskal-Wallis $H = 4.92$; $p < .09$.
[d] Kruskal-Wallis $H = 7.32$; $p < .03$.

counselor ratings of students' intelligence, and their use of intellectual abilities.

Table 15 shows that the teachers' and counselors' ratings for intellectual functioning yield the same rankings for the three research groups as did the academic achievement tests reflected in table 13. That is, the residential students with deaf parents rank first, the day students rank second, and the residential students with hearing parents rank last. However, the differences separating the three groups are much greater, yielding significant results for ratings on intellectual ability, use of intelligence, and written language. (Differences on ratings for academic motivation were not statistically significant.)

There are two important points to be made about the results of the teachers' ratings. First is the fact that they confirm the direction of the differences (that is, the rankings of the three research groups) that was reported in the tests of academic achievement. Second is a possible explanation for the greater degree of differences observed in the test scores and the teachers' ratings. This may well be related to the criteria of "success" or

* Kruskal-Wallis *H* is based on the rank ordering of the total distribution of scores, and thus takes more information into account than is reflected in the "percentages above the median" given here (see Siegel, 1956:184–193).

"acceptable performance" used by teachers in the two different school settings. The original analysis of the data from the residential students indicated that the academic achievement of both research groups (those with deaf parents and those with hearing parents) was greater than was the remainder of the residential school population (Meadow, 1967:161). The differences between the two residential research groups and the general population of the residential school stem partly from the fact that those children whose deafness has a genetic base are less likely to have additional handicaps. The deaf-parent group that formed the basic pool for matching had a mean IQ level higher than that of the school population generally. Thus, if teachers used the entire school population as their frame of reference in making ratings (as they were asked to do), the relative level of rating for both groups might seem somewhat inflated. The teacher-raters for the day students were requested to make their ratings using deaf students' performance as their reference point. However, with their increased opportunities for observing the performance of deaf students relative to that of hearing pupils of the same age in the same school, it seems likely that their assessment of deaf students might be depressed.

The implications of this point are broader than the rankings obtained by students on these particular scales. It may well reflect a relative degree of satisfaction with students' progress on the part of their teachers that has ramifications for (1) the teachers' own sense of accomplishment in contributing to the children's development, and (2) the sense of approval or disapproval that the teacher communicates to the students. The teachers' expectations for students' progress contribute to that progress, as some recent research has demonstrated in a dramatic way (Rosenthal and Jacobson, 1968). Data presented below reflect a depressed self-image on the part of the day students. This may be related, in part, to their teachers' low estimates of their intellectual functioning in the school situation.

COMMUNICATIVE FUNCTIONING

The second area to be considered under the general category of developing "industry" in the deaf child is that of communicative functioning. An auditory deficiency is a handicap primarily because it provides a barrier to communication, both receptive and expressive. Receptive communication refers to understanding others; expressive communication refers to making oneself understood. The success with which a deaf child masters various communicative modes is, in one sense, a measure of his success in dealing with his handicap—at least on a functional level. The hypotheses of the original study included a prediction that deaf children with deaf parents would exhibit more effective communication than would deaf children with hearing parents (provided they were matched for intelligence, hearing loss, and age at onset of deafness).

There were two reasons for this prediction. First was the fact that most deaf children with deaf parents have language from the time they are infants. It seemed logical to predict that this early system of communication would give those children a "head start" that might be transferred later to more formal modes of communication. The second notion behind the initial prediction related to the presence or absence of emotionally tinged conflicts regarding communication within the deaf child's family. Precisely because communicative skills are the crucial pivot for overcoming auditory loss, a great deal of understandable anxiety is generated regarding the acquisition of these skills, especially among hearing parents. In addition, the families of deaf children must come to terms with the oral-manual controversy that rages among educators. To some extent, this dilemma has been solved for deaf parents, in that they are less likely to have a choice about communicative mode. The "family climate" that encourages the development of the complete range of communicative skills is related to a complex of emotions, beliefs, abilities, resources, and values. Since lipreading and speech skills require formal training,[5] this training must be included. If the deaf child is to communicate effectively with the hearing world, he must acquire facility in speech, lipreading, and writing. If he is to communicate effectively within the deaf community, he must acquire both receptive and expressive facility in fingerspelling and the language of signs. In addition, he should feel comfortable about his own communicative skills, and be willing to attempt to communicate with strangers, both deaf and hearing. All of these items were included in the rating scale

5. Apparently, professionals in the field of speech therapy and deaf education agree that deaf children require special training if they are to acquire speech. However, some feel that lipreading develops naturally (Cawthorne, 1967; Hardy and Bordley, 1957).

completed by caretakers of the children participating in the study. In addition to teachers' ratings of communicative skills, an objective measure of lipreading skills was utilized, the Craig Lipreading Inventory.

Table 16 shows the results of two different comparisons of scores from lipreading tests: score levels on the word and sentence portions of the inventory for each of the three groups. Group 3 (day students) scored highest on the word portion of the test, while Group 1 (residential students with deaf parents) scored highest on the sentence portion of the test. None of these differences is significant. When the three groups are compared separately by age level, the older members of Groups 1 and 3 score significantly higher than their age mates in Group 2. Table 17 shows teacher-counselor ratings on three dimensions of communicative competence: lipreading, speech, and communicative confidence (i.e., willingness to communicate with strangers). Differences on ratings for lipreading do not discriminate significantly among the three groups. According to the teachers' observations, however, the residential students with deaf parents (Group 1) rank significantly higher than either the residential students with hearing parents or the day students (Groups 2 and 3) on communicative confidence. Day students, on the other hand, were rated significantly better than either of the residential groups for speech.

TABLE 16

Craig Lipreading Test Scores: Proportion above the Median for Residential and Day Students

	Group 1 Residential (Deaf Parents)	*Group 2 Residential (Hearing Parents)*	*Group 3 Day (Hearing Parents)*
	% (*N*)	% (*N*)	% (*N*)
1. Words	48% (46)	36% (47)	62% (72)[a]
Sentences	55% (42)	49% (39)	49% (71)[b]
2. Younger (−13 years)	39% (33)	47% (30)	46% (52)[c]
Older (13+ years)	82% (11)	51% (17)	89% (19)[d]

[a] Kruskal-Wallis $H =$ 4.81; n.s.
[b] Kruskal-Wallis $H =$ .44; n.s.
[c] Kruskal-Wallis $H =$ 1.59; n.s.
[d] Kruskal-Wallis $H =$ 10.43; $p < .01$.

TABLE 17
Teachers' Ratings for Three Dimensions of Communicative Competence: Proportion above the Median for Residential and Day Students

	Group 1 Residential (Deaf Parents)	*Group 2 Residential (Hearing Parents)*	*Group 3 Day Schools (Hearing Parents)*
	% (*N*)	% (*N*)	% (*N*)
1. Lipreading	49% (53)	45% (53)	54% (67)[a]
2. Speech	40% (53)	47% (53)	64% (67)[b]
3. Communicative confidence	65% (57)	40% (58)	36% (66)[c]

[a] Kruskal-Wallis $H =$ 4.56; n.s.
[b] Kruskal-Wallis $H =$ 7.64; $p < .02$.
[c] Kruskal-Wallis $H =$ 22.67; $p < .001$.

The juxtaposition of these two seemingly contradictory results is quite interesting. It would seem that deaf students with higher levels of spoken language would be more willing to communicate with unfamiliar persons. The fact that this is not the case may be a reflection of the depressed self-image of the day students (reported below). Their constant contacts with hearing peers may emphasize for them the poor quality of their communicative skills relative to those of their classmates with normal hearing. The deaf students in the residential school, on the other hand, probably are more likely to compare their skills with those of deaf rather than hearing people.

Thus, there seems to be ample evidence that for deaf children, even more than for hearing children, the development of industry during this period may contribute a great deal to the successful resolution of the question of identity during the next stage.

Identity versus Identity Diffusion: Where to Belong

There are a number of "identity options" open to the deaf adolescent as he approaches the ages eleven to eighteen. This is a time when all adolescents examine the avenues open to them for the future. They can choose their important reference groups, elect to identify with those groups that serve to ally them with their parents, with groups that can be seen as oppositional to their parents, or select some middle position. For the deaf adolescent, these choices are even more fraught with difficulty. The core of the choice focuses on electing to belong in a deaf world, a hearing world, or to prepare to rotate from one to the other, enjoying the rewards of both. The latter choice requires a firm acknowledgment of one's own self: of the possibilities and limitations of the condition of deafness. It requires that one know full well who and what one is in relation to those around him.

SELF-IMAGE AND DEAFNESS

The nature of the deaf child's self-image, and the relation of the development of the self concept and the acquisition of language, are of great importance to those interested in both theoretical and practical aspects of deafness. Language, as it relates to the development of the self, is central to the sociological perspective of symbolic interaction elaborated in the writings of Mead (1934) and Cooley (1922). At the core of this perspective is the notion that the individual is a human being, as opposed to an animal or a mere physical body, only insofar as he can see himself as others see him, and then act toward himself from the perspective of knowing, or imagining from prior cues, what their reactions to his acts may be. "The self" can become an object to itself by means of the manipulation of symbols, that is, through the use of language. Thus, the individual need not "see" the actual response of significant others to his behavior after the event in order to "know" how they might react. He can make symbolic indications to himself on the basis of previous experiences or imputed sentiments in a variety of situations, describing the interaction that is likely to follow a particular act.

Cooley was among the first to emphasize the importance of others' appraisals to the individual's self-appraisal. His concept of the "looking-glass self" (1922:183) implies that the individual's conception of himself develops as he sees a reflection of the kind of person he is, mirrored in the actions and responses of others to him. Thus, the self is a social self. It grows through contact and interaction with others. However, this process cannot be seen merely as a mechanical mirroring of the opinions of others. In order for the process to acquire meaning, the individual must interpret the actions and reactions of others.

Thus, the self-image test was designed to measure the ways in which the deaf child interpreted the ideas his mother, father, teacher, counselor (or principal), boys and girls at school, and hearing people generally had about him, as well as his own self-appraisal. Table 18 summarizes the scores for the self-image test for the three groups altogether, for boys and girls separately, and for younger and older children separately. Table 18 shows that students in Group 1 (residential pupils with deaf parents) score significantly higher than those either in Group 2 or in Group 3 on the self-image test. Boys in Group 1 score significantly higher than those in the two other groups, while there are no significant differences among the girls. Younger children in Group 1 score higher than those in the two other groups; older children in Group 2 (residential students with hearing parents) score higher than children in Group 1 or 3.

It is interesting that the pattern of differences among the

TABLE 18
Self-Image Test Scores: Proportion above the Median for Residential and Day Students

	Group 1 Residential (Deaf Parents)	*Group 2 Residential (Hearing Parents)*	*Group 3 Day (Hearing Parents)*
	% (*N*)	% (*N*)	% (*N*)
1. All students	62% (58)	46% (58)	46% (56)[a]
(Mean score)	(183.3)	(173.4)	(172.5)
2. By sex:			
Girls	66% (24)	52% (24)	59% (28)[b]
Boys	59% (34)	43% (34)	42% (28)[c]
3. By age level:			
Younger (−13)	63% (38)	35% (34)	50% (36)[d]
Older (13+)	50% (20)	63% (24)	30% (20)[e]

[a] Kruskal-Wallis $H = 4.82$; $p < .05$.
[b] Kruskal-Wallis $H = .89$; n.s.
[c] Kruskal-Wallis $H = 5.02$; $p < .05$.
[d] Kruskal-Wallis $H = 6.11$; $p < .05$.
[e] Kruskal-Wallis $H = 4.97$; $p < .08$.

older and younger children is similar for Groups 1 and 3 (residential: deaf parents and day school: hearing parents), and that residential children with hearing parents have a reversed pattern. It may be that these variables represent realities of particular importance for developing identity during the adolescent years. As discussed in Chapter 2, the primary task of adolescence, in the Eriksonian framework, is the resolution of the identity crisis: "the self-image cultivated during all the childhood stages . . . gradually prepares the sense of identity" that emerges in adolescence (Erikson, 1964:94). It may be that young deaf children with hearing parents come to the residential school from a hearing environment in which they were unique or "alone," where they were often unable to communicate with those around them. They may build increasingly positive ideas of themselves and their abilities with increasing tenure in the residential school where they are among deaf peers and some well functioning deaf adults (teachers and dormitory counselors). As they begin to learn in school, and as they make friends, they begin to have more positive feelings about themselves. Their parents, too, may be more able to relax and to enjoy their deaf child as their worries about the future are alleviated and they are relieved of their often constant care-taking responsibilities. This in turn is communicated to the deaf child, relieving him of another source of self-denigration.

The increasingly positive self-image of the residential deaf child with hearing parents can be contrasted to the postulated developmental picture for the residential deaf child with deaf parents. He comes to school from a world with very narrow boundaries. Where the young child with hearing parents is "unique" in a hearing world, the young child with deaf parents has very limited contact with that world. The contacts that he does have may be limited to sympathetic neighbors, relatives, or family friends. In his younger years at school, he may well feel superior to his peers from hearing families who are unable to communicate fluently in sign language (as he does), and who learn neither as quickly nor as well.

From this early feeling of superiority over peers, acceptance by deaf parents and their deaf adult friends, the deaf adolescent may react with a sense of shock to the realization that the hearing world sees him as peculiar: that most people are not deaf, and that the adult occupational and educational world is geared to hearing people. Since the pattern of self-image scores in the day school follows that of the residential school children with deaf parents, this lends additional support to the suggestion that the findings are related to a crisis in deaf adolescent identity, tied to peer group and school context. This is an area that needs additional research, important both theoretically and clinically.

SELF-IMAGE, DEAFNESS, AND FAMILY CLIMATE

Much previous discussion was aimed at providing insight into some of the factors that might provide differing environments for deaf children of deaf and of hearing parents. There is, of course, a good deal of variation within any three groups of parents in terms of the factors that may contribute to or detract from the development of positive self-image in children. For the families involved in the research being described here, an "Index of Family Climate" was devised, in an effort to summarize in short form some of these factors. A rating was assigned to each family on the basis of a combination of variables reflecting socio-economic status and parental emotional/marital stability. Those families that demonstrate a greater degree of stability, a higher degree of educational and economic resources, and higher participation in community activities were assigned to the group said to have "positive family climate." A middle group was designated "intermediate" for family climate and the lowest group was labeled as having a "negative family climate." In an effort to assess the influence of family climate on the development of self-image in the deaf child, self-image score levels were analyzed in terms of this index (see table 19).

Table 19 shows that "family climate" is an important determinant of self-image for Group 1 (residential students with deaf parents) and for Group 3 (day students with hearing parents). Residential students with hearing parents from different levels of family climate do not differ significantly in terms of their self-image scores.

The pattern of findings relating self-image to family climate raises some extremely interesting possibilities. If Groups 1 and 3 (residential with deaf parents versus day students) are considered, Group 1 scores higher on the self-image test than does Group 3 at each level of family climate. However, these differences are quite small (only 6 percentage points) among children whose families are rated most highly for stability and resources.

TABLE 19

Self-Image Score Level for Residential and Day Students from Positive, Intermediate, and Negative Family Climates: Proportion above the Median

	Positive Family Climate	*Intermediate Family Climate*	*Negative Family Climate*
	% (*N*)	% (*N*)	% (*N*)
Group 1			
Residential deaf parents	75% (16)	67% (21)	43% (21)[a]
Group 2			
Residential hearing parents	47% (15)	58% (24)	37% (19)[b]
Group 3			
Day hearing parents	69% (16)	40% (25)	27% (15)[c]

[a] Mann-Whitney $U = 282.00$; $p < .04$.
[b] Mann-Whitney $U = 378.00$; $p > .10$.
[c] Mann-Whitney $U = 254.50$; $p < .02$.

The hearing parents able to provide a better family environment are more likely to overcome the negative effects of stigma or other kinds of environmental stress that may lead to negative self-image in the deaf child.

It is interesting, in relation to this conclusion, to review Rosenberg's (1965) findings on the relation of adolescent self-esteem to parental attitudes. He found that parental indifference is more closely related to negative self-image than is parental punitiveness (p. 138). The deaf child of hearing parents may interpret being sent to a residential school as a rejection by his parents. This may be a contributing factor to the low level of self-esteem manifested by these children. Residential schools for the deaf have a very special place in the value system of the deaf subculture. These schools are seen by most deaf adults as the focal point for the promulgation of sign language, and the most appropriate educational setting for deaf children. Most adult members of the deaf subculture are themselves products of state residential schools, and many friendship groups have their basis in these schools. Thus, the meaning of residential school for deaf children may be similar to that of the public schools among upper class children in England: if your parents have attended the same or a similar school and all your friends continue in the same tradition, being sent away to a residential school will not be interpreted as parental rejection.

Rosenberg's data provide another insight suggestive for interpreting the findings. He concluded that membership in a religious minority group is related to negative self-image only when the child lives in a neighborhood where his religious group is a numerical minority: "It is only when the individual is in the distinct minority, when it is impossible for him to restrict his associations to members of his own group, that the deleterious psychological consequences of the dissonant religious context become evident" (Rosenberg, 1965:68). In terms of their definition of their situation, deaf students in day schools may be said to be located in a dissonant context, to use Rosenberg's term. Some data from a subanalysis of the self-image test support this idea. Of the eight subsections of the test, referring to the appraisals of self, mother, father, teacher, counselor (or principal), boys and girls at school, and "hearing people," the most pronounced differences between the day and the residential students are found in their ideas about the appraisals of hearing people. Of the Group 1 students (residential-deaf parents), 65 percent rank above the median for their ideas of the appraisals of hearing people, compared to 42 percent of Group 3 students (day-hearing parents). (This difference was significant at the 1 percent level of confidence.)

Table 19 indicated a strong positive relation between family climate and self-image for students in Groups 1 and 3. However, for Group 2, this relation is skewed: students from families with an intermediate rating for family climate rank highest on the self-image test. This discrepancy between the pattern of residential students with hearing parents and the two other groups might be explained by the gap between parental expectations for communicative and academic achievement, and the child's performance. That is, we can predict that hearing parents who themselves have achieved higher educational attainment (and are more likely to rate higher on the index of family climate) will place more emphasis on this kind of achievement for their children. Their disappointment in the child's inability to perform is greater, is reflected in their appraisal of the child, and contributes to a deflated self-image in the child. Data in the previous section indicated that the residential students with hearing parents perform at a lower level of intellectual and communicative functioning than either of the two other groups.

Intimacy versus Isolation: The Ability to Love and Work

In terms of Erikson's epigenetic model, the primary developmental task of young adulthood is that of the increasing ability to commit oneself to an intimate relation with another on a personal level, and to commit oneself to meaningful work on a more impersonal level. In either area, the ability to love and to work presupposes a certain degree of maturity: the capacity to put aside childish, selfish, self-seeking modes of behavior in preparation for living and working with other human beings on a give-and-take basis.

This global approach to the development of a capacity to love and work is conceptualized as a generally positive psychosocial adjustment. Table 20 summarizes teacher-counselor ratings of students on eight different dimensions reflecting adjustment: maturity, responsibility, independence, sociability, popularity with peers and adults, appropriate sex-role behavior, and positive adjustment to deafness.

On the eight teacher-counselor ratings reported in table 20, the residential students with deaf parents (Group 1) ranked first on six, tied for first on one, and ranked second on one. The day students (Group 3) ranked second on most dimensions, and the residential students with hearing parents ranked third on most. (All differences were significant at the 5 percent level or beyond.)

The three related variables of maturity, responsibility, and independence are of particular interest in the study of deaf students because this is an area in which deaf individuals, generally, are said to differ from the hearing population. It will be recalled that "immaturity" is a trait often used to describe deaf persons, both "normal" and "disturbed" (Rainer et al., 1963; Neyhus, 1964; Levine, 1956). Several researchers have evaluated the "social maturity" of deaf children, using the Vineland Social Maturity Scale, designed to measure degree of independence or self-sufficiency. Streng and Kirk (1938), Avery (1948), Myklebust and Burchard (1945), and Myklebust

TABLE 20
Teachers' Ratings for Eight Dimensions of Psychosocial Adjustment: Proportion above the Median for Residential and Day Students

	Group 1 Residential Students (Deaf Parents) (N = 58)	*Group 2 Residential Students (Hearing Parents) (N = 58)*	*Group 3 Day Students (Hearing Parents) (N = 69)*	*Kruskal-Wallis H*
1. Mature	60%	33%	51%	8.12[a]
2. Responsible	58%	41%	57%	7.38[a]
3. Independent	66%	41%	51%	12.52[b]
4. Sociable	67%	36%	49%	9.76[b]
5. Popular with peers	62%	35%	54%	10.51[b]
6. Popular with adults	59%	43%	46%	5.83[a]
7. Appropriate sex-role behavior	51%	40%	65%	10.14[b]
8. Positive adjustment to deafness	80%	50%	32%	39.75[c]

[a] $p < .05$.
[b] $p < .01$.
[c] $p < .001$.

(1960) all found that deaf children received lower scores on this scale than did hearing children. Myklebust (1960:215) reported that the discrepancy between deaf and hearing groups of children increased with age. Barker (et al., 1953) has hypothesized that the immaturity which seemingly characterizes deaf children and adults may result from the high proportion who attend residential schools, where the development of independence and responsibility may be stifled. Our results suggest a complex interplay of school and family environmental factors in the characteristically immature personality patterns of many deaf persons. In terms of the total deaf population, Group 2 is probably more comparable to the majority of those afflicted with profound congenital deafness. Group 1, with deaf parents, would be comparable to only about 10 percent of the total deaf population. Group 3 probably is smaller in comparable numbers. Both of these have an advantage in terms of family climate: Group 1 with deaf parents because they generally grant independence more readily to the deaf child; Group 3 has the advantage of living at home rather than at school. It may be that the tendency toward immature, dependent behavior is associated with institutional life. The ratings of the residential school children with deaf parents, however, suggests that residential living is but one of the factors contributing to patterns of immaturity among the deaf.

The most extreme differences to emerge among the three groups of deaf children on any of the ten differentiating social-personal variables are observed in the ratings of their "adjustment to deafness." Students rated highest on this dimension by their caretakers are the residential students with deaf parents (80 percent are rated above the median). Intermediate in ranking is Group 2, residential students with hearing parents (50 percent are rated above the median). In contrast, only 32 percent of the day school students were rated above the median. These findings confirm and extend the discrepancy between Groups 1 and 2 noted in the original study. This pattern is also congruent with the previously reported findings in regard to overall self-image scores in the three groups, and is particularly significant when related to the low assessment that the day students believe "hearing people" make of them. Resentment of and bitterness about the reality of their handicap is apparently stronger in the day school setting where they are constantly reminded, by both family and peer group, that they are different from and handicapped in comparison to others.

The final variable reflecting personal-social adjustment relates to the appropriateness of sex-role behavior (see table 20). The data presented in table 20 are also especially significant. They indicate that day school children are much more likely to rate high on the appropriateness of their sex-role behavior compared to residential children with deaf parents, and compared also to residential school children with hearing parents. Assuming that a strong model for sex-role behavior is important within the family if appropriate sex-role identification is to develop, this pattern would be congruent with expectations. That is, the day school children, living at home with (probably) both a male and a female role model available on a day-to-day basis, have the best opportunity for incorporating expected role behavior into their repertoire. Residential children with deaf parents rank second in this dimension: they might be expected to have had the next most frequent opportunity for observing so-called "correct" sex-role behavior, and to have been socialized through their early experiences (with more parent-child communication available to them than Group 2 children with hearing parents). Residential children with hearing parents might be expected to have had the least number of opportunities for both observation and interpretation of appropriate sex-role behavior within their families. The substantial differences among the three groups of deaf children are of great interest because there are some indications that problems of sexual adjustment may be more prevalent among the deaf generally, in comparison with the general population. In spite of difficulties of gathering reliable information in this sensitive area, Rainer et al. (1963) concluded sexual delinquency was a more frequent problem in the deaf population than in the hearing population. They suggest this may be related to general immaturity, to lack of education in the areas of sex and family life, and to residential school living:

> we were able to determine, with the aid of teachers and houseparents in our Eastern schools for the deaf, that sexual delinquency and immaturity, lack of preparation for a successful marriage and a stable family life, and the more extreme forms of deviant sex behavior are by no means less common among the deaf than in any other group of people. In our series of clinic patients, homosexual tendencies were found to be the main problem in more than ten percent of the cases. (Rainer et al., 1963:245)

Although the usefulness of arraignment data for comparative purposes is limited, "in the general criminal population, sex offenders, even including prostitutes, constitute the smallest number of arraignments. In our series (of deaf criminals), however, sex offenders formed the largest group (37 percent), although no cases of prostitution were involved" (Rainer et al., 1963:148). These figures are based on numbers that are quite small. However, in assessing the relative importance of any problem behavior in a group comprising less than 1 percent of the total population, we cannot expect to deal with large numbers.

Our data could be interpreted as suggesting that the combination of institutional living plus fewer possibilities for sex-role modeling within the family (illustrated by the residential school students with hearing parents) is detrimental to the development of appropriate sex-role identification. The significantly higher ratings of the residential school children of deaf parents (compared to their schoolmates with hearing parents) would indicate that weak sex-role identity is not a necessary consequence of residential living.

SUMMARY AND IMPLICATIONS

The results of comparisons among the three groups of deaf students, reported in the previous pages, are summarized in table 21, in the form of their comparative rank order for each of twenty-one descriptive variables. Fourteen of these comparisons resulted in statistically significant differences. It will be seen in this summary table that the children of deaf parents attending residential school (Group 1) performed or were rated at a higher level in most of the comparisons that were significantly different. Group 1 ranked first on eleven of the fourteen comparisons, and tied for first on one additional comparison. Group 1 showed particular strengths in areas that relate to positive self-image or identity and to social adjustment.

Generally speaking, the day school students (Group 3, all of whom had hearing parents) ranked second to the residential students with deaf parents. They are ranked first on two variables and tied for first on one additional (considering only those comparisons yielding significant results). They ranked second on six variables and tied for second on four others.

The residential students with hearing parents (Group 2) scored or were rated poorly on a majority of the dimensions: ranking third on eight of the fourteen with significant differences, tying for second on four additional.

Implications for Development of Industry

The original research with residential students showed that deaf children of deaf parents scored significantly higher than deaf children of hearing parents in reading, arithmetic, and overall school achievement tests. The present analysis, including

TABLE 21
Tabular Summary for Chapter 6: Rank Order

	Group 1 Residential Deaf Parents	*Group 2 Residential Hearing Parents*	*Group 3 Day Hearing Parents*
	Rank	Rank	Rank
1. Social Development			
Self-image	1	2.5	2.5[a]
Maturity	1	3	2[a]
Responsibility	1.5	3	1.5[a]
Independence	1	3	2[b]
Sociability	1	3	2[b]
Popularity with peers	1	3	2[b]
Popularity with peers	1	2.5	2.5[a]
Adjustment to deafness	1	2	3[c]
Appropriate sex-role behavior	2	3	1[b]
2. Communicative Development			
Craig Lipreading Inventory			
Words	2	3	1
Sentences	1	2.5	2.5
Written language	1	2.5	2.5[a]
Lipreading (teachers' ratings)	2	2	2
Speech	3	2	1[a]
Communicative confidence	1	2.5	2.5[c]
3. Intellectual Development			
Achievement Scores			
Grade Level	1	3	2
Reading	1	3	2
Arithmetic	1	3	2
"Highly intelligent"	1	3	2[c]
Good use of intelligence	1	3	2[c]
Motivated for school work	1	3	2

[a] $p < .05$.
[b] $p < .01$.
[c] $p < .001$.

the third group of day students, showed that they received scores intermediate compared to the two original research groups. When older and younger groups of children were compared, the younger day students were found to have significantly higher scores, apparently accounted for by a small number in one class receiving instruction by means of "total communication."

If, as these results suggest, academic achievement among deaf children may be greatest when they both live at home and receive instruction that combines speech and auditory training with manual communication, parents and teachers should be encouraged to experiment with this approach. Indications are that many changes are taking place in this direction, but a great deal of bitterness still surrounds the controversy.

The poor ratings of residential students for speech would indicate the need for an increased program of speech therapy in the residential schools. It may be that a generally more accepting atmosphere for the use of manual communication may promote more positive student attitudes regarding the use of all forms of communication. Large-scale investigations of carefully controlled experiments under optimum conditions, including wholehearted cooperation from parents and teachers of participating students, would seem to be in order.

Implications for Development of Identity

The evidence presented indicates unequivocally that deaf children of deaf parents attending a residential school develop a more positive self-image than the other deaf children participating in the research. This was indicated by significantly higher scores on the test of self-image and by significantly higher ratings on "adjustment to deafness," "communicative confidence," and assessment of attitudes of hearing people toward themselves. Changes in the pattern of differences at different age levels (i.e., before and after adolescence) suggest that additional research focused on the precise nature of the "adolescent identity crisis" among deaf children would be most useful.

It also suggests that the provision of mental health services is of great importance for deaf students and their families during the adolescent years. The special problems that are apparently faced by deaf students in a minority situation in day schools should be of special concern to their parents and teachers. Perhaps help should be offered to these students in participating successfully with their hearing peers. This could include specific orientation for the hearing students (related to the problems of deafness, effective means of communicating with deaf students) whether this be through speech, sign language, fingerspelling, writing, or a combination. Another possible approach would be the provision of opportunities for day students to meet deaf adults with a variety of communicative modes who are leading happy, productive lives. Too often parents of deaf children try to shield them from contact with the real world of the deaf.

Implications for Development of Intimacy

The original research concluded that deaf children of deaf parents were less likely to exhibit those personality traits that have been said to be "typical" of a large number of deaf adults: lack of maturity, inability to take responsibility and to engage in independent behavior. Deaf children with deaf parents in the residential school were rated higher on these dimensions than day school children. However, the degree of difference was not nearly so great (day school children ranked in an intermediate position between the two groups of residential children). In addition, the pattern of relations between this congeries of traits and ratings for "family climate" led to the suggestion that the influence of the family on the positive development of maturity is very great. These findings reinforce suggestions of previous investigators that the so-called "immaturity" of the deaf may be related to the prevalence of the residential schooling experience. Thus, the residential children with deaf parents have, perhaps, a firmer family foundation on which to base their residential school experiences. The day school children, who live with their families, may be more likely to be given responsibility and independence, thus developing greater maturity. Counseling with the parents of deaf children, and mental health consultation with teachers and administrators who work with deaf students, could focus on finding additional ways in which independence and responsibility could be fostered within the realistic limitations of the deaf child's potential and the requirements of institutional life.

Several areas might be suggested as examples. Many schools make sure that students take some responsibility in caring for their rooms and clothing. Some provide opportunities for kitchen and grounds helpers on a rotation basis. A few provide apartment living-quarters for high school students so they may practice planning, purchasing, and preparing their own meals. The question of the amount of freedom to offer deaf residential students in this increasingly permissive age is a difficult one, especially for adminstrators. They must have the support of parents if they are to provide opportunities for developing maturity. The area of boy-girl relationships is particularly difficult. Some residential schools do not allow their students to date. One quite progressive residential school (not the one where our research was conducted) published the following as its general policy (dated 1970):

> Dating, as such, is not permitted. The school provides as many opportunities as possible for boys and girls to mix socially. These activities are necessarily group activities since there are a limited number of staff members to provide supervision, and supervision, unfortunately (from the children's point of view), is necessary. No doubt there are many older students capable of behaving themselves at all times in unsupervised boy-girl relationships, and for such students, the presence of counselors might, or might not, be desirable. There is equally no doubt that there are students who would not be capable of behaving themselves at all times in unsupervised boy-girl relationships. Unfortunately there is no sure way of determining to which group any given student belongs. . . . Aside from the very practical consideration of avoiding pregnancies and sexual misbehavior, supervision of boy-girl activities provides counselors with the opportunity to promote attitudes of respect and mutual consideration among the students.

No doubt many practical considerations relating to administrative responsibility made this policy seem necessary. However, most residential schools permit students to remain until the age of 21 if they appear to be benefiting from the program. The idea that a 21-year-old leaves school never having had a "date" seems quite remarkable. The development of mature relations with members of the opposite sex, as preparation for intimacy leading to marriage and adulthood, is difficult under these conditions, to say the least.

Sex-role behavior is another personality dimension of special interest in relation to deafness. A good deal of literature suggests that deafness is associated with problems in the area of sexual adjustment. It has been suggested that these difficulties may be related to institutionalized living inherent in residential schooling. Results from analysis of data from teachers' ratings on this dimension tend to support this interpretation: day school students are rated highest among the three groups for "appropriateness" of sex-role behavior. Rated second are the residential students with deaf parents, followed by the residential students with hearing parents. Additional confirmation of the influence of residential living is the fact that day school students are rated high on this dimension even when they are ranked "low" for family climate. Family climate generally has very little influence on the ratings for this trait.

Research on the development of sex-role identity among deaf students should have a great deal of theoretical importance. Very little direct (or indirect) data exist on this facet of personality development and deafness. In the light of the importance of sexual adjustment for the total effectiveness of the individual, this is an unfortunate omission.

Findings suggest that programs of sex education should be considered essential in any residential school for deaf students. These schools serve in place of parents in conveying sexual information and indicating standards of sexual morality, as well as in many other areas. However, in the area of sexual practices, schools often do not have the freedom to fulfill their role as stand-in parents. The help of mental health consultants in this sensitive area of human behavior should be of unusual benefit. Clear-cut policies for dealing with sexual "misdemeanors" and positive programs for "prevention" should have high priority in all residential schools.

The pattern of differential behavior and adjustment among the three groups of children studied adds further evidence that the deficiencies noted for so long among deaf children—in terms of intellectual and social functioning—are not a necessary or innate result of auditory deprivation. They stem, rather, from the impact of the treatment received by the deaf child from various individuals and groups in his environment. Many changes are taking place at the present time that may serve to improve the developmental climate of deaf children generally. In fact, the aura of change in the world of the deaf child is one of the most striking things happening in educational circles today. Change is usually painful and often resisted. Through change, however, will come the opportunities that deaf children need to traverse successfully the developmental mileposts marked "industry," "identity," and "intimacy."

7

Deafness and Mental Health: A Residential School Survey

The relation between mental health and physical disability has rarely been explicitly examined, although there are numerous sociological and psychological expositions regarding personal consequences of disability (e.g., Goffman, 1963; Barker et al., 1953; Wright, 1960). The relation between mental health and deafness has special significance for etiological theories of mental illness, since it is generally accepted that the major handicap of early profound deafness is not one of auditory deficit per se, but rather one of communicative deficit in a global sense. A number of important theories explaining the genesis of mental disorder regard distortions in the communicative process as lying at the root of emotional disturbance (Ruesch, 1959; Bateson et al., 1956). Other theories directed to the more general nature of individual development rely heavily on interpersonal communication, particularly in the early years, to explain both "normal" development and deviations from the norm (Sullivan, 1953; Mead, 1934; Erikson, 1963). Well-known studies of the consequences of communicative deprivation in the early years of life (Spitz, 1945) and of social isolation generally (Kohn and Clausen, 1955) lend further support to the assertion

Chapter 7 is by Kathryn P. Meadow. The original data were collected by Hilde S. Schlesinger. The research assistance of Katherine A. Leland, Arline Cottrell, and Nancy Peterson is gratefully acknowledged. We are most appreciative of the cooperation of Dr. Hugo Schunhoff, Superintendent at the California School for the Deaf, Berkeley, and his staff, especially Mr. Jacob Arcanin, then Dean of Students.

that studies of deafness may contribute to the understanding of mental health.

The major study published to date that sheds some light on the relation between deafness and mental health emerged from work completed at the New York Psychiatric Institute (Rainer et al., 1963). These investigators concluded that the incidence of schizophrenia was not appreciably different in the deaf and in the hearing populations of New York State. However, they reported that the prevalence of "problems of living" appeared to be considerably higher in the deaf population of the state. These problems appeared as higher arrest rates, marital/sexual and vocational difficulties, and difficulties related to low educational attainment.

The study reported here was conducted at a California residential school for the deaf, as part of a general effort to determine the extent of the need for mental health services in the deaf population of the San Francisco Bay Area. The survey was undertaken with two purposes in mind: (1) to determine the incidence of behavioral problems in a population of deaf school children compared to that in a population of hearing school children; and (2) to determine the characteristics of those deaf children identified as exhibiting problems in the classroom and dormitory compared to the characteristics of deaf children in the same school who were not identified as exhibiting problem behavior.

METHODOLOGY

A questionnaire form was adopted that had been developed and utilized for a mental health survey of all school children in Los Angeles County. The definition of emotional disturbance proposed to teachers and counselors was as follows: "An emotionally disturbed child is one whose pattern of behavior over a period of time deviates markedly from the usual acceptable patterns of school behavior, and deviates in maintaining ordinary normal social relationships with his classmates at school, due to some cause other than physical." Clues to the behavioral identification of emotional disturbance included in the survey form were:

—few social contacts; reluctant to speak or play with other children

—classroom behavior unusually withdrawn; nonparticipating
—extremely compliant; submissive; over-dependent
—learning problems not due to lack of ability but to emotional difficulty
—nervous habits (tics, nailbiting, etc.)
—hyperactivity
—very aggressive; hostile, potential danger to others
—noncooperative; attention-gaining behavior
—disregardance of and persistent, open defiance of rules
—recurrent absences from school (apparently unwarranted); truancy
—accident-prone
—chronic headaches or stomachaches without identifiable physical cause

In November 1966, questionnaires were distributed to all teachers and counselors at a state residential school for deaf students, asking them to identify those students in their care whom they believed to be emotionally disturbed. Thirty-nine teachers and forty-six counselors participated in the survey. Teachers and counselors were asked to identify two groups of children, described as follows:

> *Type I:* Children who are severely emotionally disturbed and have been or should be referred for psychiatric help.
>
> *Type II:* Children who are not severely disturbed, but whose behavior necessitates a disproportionate share of the teacher's time or requires other special attention. (State of California, 1960:564)

Those responsible for the Los Angeles survey felt that the questionnaire should provide the Type II classification to enable teachers to record judgments concerning pupils who, though perhaps difficult in some respects, were not clearly cases of emotional disturbance. "Both the educators and the psychiatrists also recognized that this division might result in considerable numbers of disturbed pupils (Type I) being erroneously placed in the Type II group. This risk was believed to be warranted because of the increased confidence with which Type

I classification could then be accepted as a severely disturbed group undiluted by borderline cases" (State of California, 1960:308).

Two methodological issues might be raised: one in relation to the definition of emotional disturbance used, the other in relation to the identity of those responsible for "case-finding." Either definition or case-finding procedure can falsely inflate or depress the number of cases eventually included as emotionally disturbed. The definition adopted is based on observable behavioral traits. Thus, a child was not to be identified as "disturbed" on the basis of inferred covert "mental" disorder. This has the advantage of providing fewer ambiguous guidelines for teachers and counselors plus that of relating more directly to behavior that has immediate situational consequences for the students involved. That is, students who are identified as showing extremes of "acting-out" behavior often cannot be tolerated in a school setting.

> The behaviors defined as symptoms of "illness" may be as much characteristic of some particular situation or group setting as they are enduring attributes of persons. . . . Although seemingly obvious, it is important to state that what may be viewed as deviant in one social group may be tolerated in another, and rewarded in still other groups. (Mechanic, 1962:67)

In the case of the deaf students included in this study population, rejection by the school has profound and immediate effects. Thus, identifying "emotionally disturbed" students by means of specification by their teachers and counselors would seem to be a valid method of definition since these are the persons with the eventual power to retain or expel the student.

Using teachers and counselors to identify students exhibiting problem behavior has both advantages and disadvantages. For this survey, there was a decided advantage in providing data that would be comparable to the data collected in the Los Angeles survey. More generally, however, there is an advantage in using persons for case-finding who have had an opportunity to observe students over a prolonged time period. Outside observers might visit the school or interview a child on a day when his behavior did not follow his usual pattern. Both Berlin (1967) and Bower (1958) have commented on the fact that teachers' judgments about students' mental health are remarkably accurate. This is congruent with the experience of the project's psychiatric director: as a consultant at the residential school where the survey was conducted, she has been impressed with the high rate of agreement between her perception of students' behavior and that of school personnel.

FINDINGS AND DISCUSSION

Prevalence of Behavioral Problems

At the time of the survey, 516 deaf children were enrolled at the residential school for the deaf. Teachers and counselors identified 60 students as "severely emotionally disturbed" (Type I). An additional 100 students were considered to require a disproportionate share of teacher/counselor time because of behavioral problems. Table 22 shows percentages for the deaf students at the residential school and for students in the entire Los Angeles County school system. While 2.4 percent of the Los Angeles students were seen by their teachers as exhibiting severe emotional disturbances, 11.6 percent of the deaf students were so identified by their teachers and counselors. An additional 7.3 percent of the Los Angeles students were identified as exhibiting behavioral problems requiring a disproportionate share of their teacher's time; 19.6 percent of the deaf students were seen in this way. *Thus, using these criteria, almost five times as many deaf students are identified as severely disturbed, and over two-and-one-half times as many deaf as hearing students are identified as occupying a disproportionate share of*

TABLE 22
Proportion of Children with Severe Emotional Disturbance or with Milder Behavior Problems at a Residential School for the Deaf and in Los Angeles County Classes

	Deaf Students	*L.A. County Students**
Severely emotionally disturbed (Type I)	11.6%	2.4%
Milder behavioral problems (Type II)	19.6%	7.3%
Total	31.2%	9.7%
(*N*)	(516)	(532,567)

* Los Angeles County data taken from State of California, 1960:309.

teachers' time. Stated in another way, almost one in every eight deaf students was identified as being severely disturbed, compared to one in every forty-two hearing students.

These figures can be compared with the estimates of the Joint Commission on Mental Health of Children that approximately 2 percent of persons under the age of twenty-five "are severely disturbed and need immediate psychiatric care. Another eight to ten percent are in need of help from mental health workers" (Joint Commission, 1970:38).

We should consider a number of issues regarding the comparability of the data from the two populations shown in table 22. One possibility is that the residential schools for deaf students are used as placements for children whose parents and teachers find them unmanageable in their local settings, thus falsely inflating the proportion of severely disturbed compared to the hearing population. The absence of any special classroom arrangements for emotionally disturbed deaf children makes this contingency more probable. However, it is relevant in this respect to indicate that the Los Angeles survey includes special education classrooms: "These are special facilities for children with problems and handicaps and the enrollments of the schools are therefore heavily weighted with disturbed children." In these special classrooms, 29 percent of the children were classified as Type I or severely disturbed, and an additional 26 percent classified as Type II. In addition, experiences of the Project's clinical staff in consulting with teachers in day programs indicate that the prevalence of behavioral problems may be just as high as in the residential setting. One teacher in a day school program referred her entire class of young children to the project for therapy. Observations of these children indicated that the referrals were quite justified. It would be extremely useful to collect comparable data from teachers of deaf children in day programs to learn if the prevalence of problem behavior is indeed comparable to that discovered in the residential school.

Characteristics of Deaf Students Identified as Severely Disturbed

In order to learn something about the relation between emotional disturbance and a number of demographic characteristics, a list of the total population of the residential school was obtained. Names of all students identified either as Type I (severely disturbed) or Type II (mildly disturbed) were eliminated. A one-in-six random sample of the remaining students yielded a list of sixty-one names that was used as the basis for comparisons with the most severely disturbed group. Information on the sixty students in the severely disturbed group and on the sixty-one students in the comparison group was collected from school records. Results of the comparative analysis of twelve variables is shown in table 23. It will be seen that differences between the two groups on four dimensions could be explained by chance alone (race/ethnicity, residual hearing, father's occupation, parental hearing status). Differences for an additional four variables approach statistical significance ($p \leq .10$) but are not quite large enough to be considered significant (family stability, family size, age, religion). Four variables, however, significantly differentiate the emotionally disturbed students from the control group (at the 5 percent level of confidence or beyond). These are sex, IQ score, ordinal position, and etiology of deafness.

RACE/ETHNICITY AND OCCUPATION

Items 1 and 2 of table 23, reflecting race/ethnicity and father's occupation, show no significant differences between the emotionally disturbed and the comparison groups. Generally, research has shown the incidence of mental illness to be greater among members of racial minority groups and among members of lower socioeconomic groups (Malzberg, 1953; Hollingshead and Redlich, 1958). The absence of a relation between these two structural variables and emotional disturbance among the deaf students might suggest that deafness transcends other group memberships that more frequently summarize an individual's experiences in the wider society.

RESIDUAL HEARING AND PARENTAL HEARING STATUS

No significant differences appear in the relative proportions of disturbed and comparison groups with more or less residual hearing, nor with parental hearing status. Few children attending the residential schools have a significant degree of residual hearing (those children would be more likely to attend day programs). Therefore, this population does not afford a true test of the relative effects of "marginal" status in the deaf

TABLE 23
Distribution of Severely Disturbed and Comparison Groups of Deaf Students on Twelve Demographic Variables

Variable	*Severely Disturbed Deaf Students (N = 60)*	*Comparison Group Deaf Students (N = 61)*
1. Race/ethnicity:		
Caucasian	73%	69%
"Other"	27%	31%
2. Father's occupation:		
White collar	29%	20%
Blue collar	71%	80%
3. Residual hearing:		
80+ dB	81%	73%
−80 dB	19%	27%
4. Parental hearing status:		
Both parents deaf	5%	17%
One or both hearing	95%	83%
5. Family stability:		
Intact family	52%[a]	67%
"Other"	47%	33%
6. Family size:		
Smaller (1–2 children)	43%[a]	29%
Larger (3+ children)	57%	71%
7. Age:		
Younger (−13 years)	50%[a]	34%
Older (13+ years)	50%	66%
8. Religion:		
Catholic	48%[a]	30%
Other or none	52%	70%
9. Sex:		
Girls	52%[b]	33%
Boys	48%	67%
10. IQ score:		
−100	61%[b]	42%
100+	39%	58%
11. Ordinal position:		
Only or first-born	57%[c]	32%
Middle or last-born	43%	68%
12. Etiology of deafness:		
Unknown	55%[c]	16%
Known	45%	84%

[a] $x^2 \geq 2.71$; $p < .10$.
[b] $x^2 \geq 3.84$; $p < .05$.
[c] $x^2 \geq 6.64$; $p < .01$.

and the hearing world. The numbers of children with deaf parents in the two samples are too small to reach significant levels of difference. However, the direction of the differences (with fewer children of deaf parents found in the disturbed group) supports previous research on the relative adjustment of deaf children with deaf parents (Brill, 1960; Meadow, 1968*a*).

AGE

Fifty percent of the severely disturbed students are in the younger age group (less than thirteen years old), compared to 34 percent of the control group ($p < .10$; table 23, item 7). This difference may, however, be a spurious one, related to the ability of the school to absorb the more seriously disturbed older students. In spite of the efforts of school administrators to provide special classes for children with special problems, and their willingness to accept some students on a nonresidential part-time basis, there are inevitably some children for whom the school situation is too structured. Between 1954 and 1960, eighty-five children were dropped from the school in which the present survey was done. These children were distributed evenly between those who were twelve years of age or younger and those who were thirteen years of age or older. In the older group, however, 79 percent were dropped for behavioral or "emotional" problems, compared to 35 percent of the younger children who were dropped for this reason (M. Leenhouts, personal communication). These data suggest the apparent negative relation between age and emotional disturbance in the present study may indeed be spurious.

RELIGION

Table 23, item 8, indicates there is a larger proportion of Catholic students in the disturbed group than is found in the comparison group. Almost half of the disturbed students (48 percent) are from Catholic families compared to 30 percent of the students in the comparison group ($p < .10$). It is possible that religious orientation influences family response to handicap, although it is also possible that religion is related to other causal variables, so that the apparent relation may actually be a spurious one. Some speculative inferences regarding this interesting point will be offered below.

SEX

Table 23, item 9, shows a statistically significant relation between sex and mental health status: girls comprise 52 percent of the disturbed group, but only 33 percent of the comparison group. (This proportion of boys to girls in the comparison group is very close to the sex distribution at the school when the survey was taken, and reflects the fact that boys are at higher risk for deafness than girls.)

A study completed at a residential school for the deaf some years ago reported that "many more behavior problems exist among deaf males than among deaf females" (Burchard and Myklebust, 1942:352). The authors explicitly noted, however, that the instrument used in their study (The Haggerty-Olson-Wickman Behavior Rating Schedules) measures primarily aggressive kinds of behavior. The instrument used in the present survey gives equal weight to withdrawn, passive behavior that may be more prevalent among girls and thus help to explain their overrepresentation.

IQ SCORE

Differences in scores on intelligence tests are significant at the 5 percent level of confidence (table 23, item 10). Sixty-one percent of the disturbed children scored below 100 on an IQ test, compared to 42 percent of the children in the comparison group. In spite of the wide difference between the disturbed and the comparison groups on tested intelligence, this relation must nevertheless be viewed with caution. It is difficult at best to administer standard IQ tests to most deaf children and even more difficult to interpret the results. When there is some degree of disturbed behavior, the testing procedure becomes even more problematical. Thus it may be that tested intelligence in the disturbed group does not accurately reflect intellectual ability. Nevertheless, low academic performance is clearly expectable in a large proportion of emotionally disturbed deaf children, and remedial teaching may be even more important for this group than for the deaf school population as a whole. Williams (1970), in a report of children applying for admission to an English school for emotionally disturbed deaf children, states that 15 of 51 (29 percent) had IQ's lower than 75 (p. 9). He suggests that "there is as much need for a school for maladjusted/deaf, E.S.N. (Educationally Sub Normal) children as there is for maladjusted/deaf children in the ordinary range of intelligence" (p. 10).

FAMILY SIZE AND STABILITY

Differences in disturbed and comparison groups on the two family variables (items 5 and 6 of table 23) are not great enough to be statistically significant. The direction of the difference for family stability is as expected, with almost half of the disturbed group from nonintact families, compared to one-third of the other students. However, a larger proportion of the disturbed children come from small families (fewer than three children). There is some evidence to indicate that this is contrary to findings in the general population (e.g., Clausen, 1966:14). Perhaps deaf children from large families get additional support, attention, and sensory stimulation from the larger numbers of siblings. Since deaf children often are more limited than are hearing children to their immediate family circle for their early social interaction, the presence of many siblings increases the number of their social contacts.

ORDINAL POSITION

Table 23 indicates that ordinal position was one of the variables differentiating most clearly the two groups of deaf students, with the largest proportion of "only or first-born" children found in the disturbed group (57 percent, versus 32 percent of the control group).

Clausen, in his comprehensive review of the literature regarding the influence of birth order on socialization and personality, reports that "there is some consistency in the finding that first-born children are more often presented as problems at child guidance centers . . . but it is not clear whether this tendency reflects greater frequency of problems or the relative inexperience and anxiety of parents in dealing with the first-born through the childhood years" (Clausen, 1966:25). In a study of the relation among birth order, family size, and schizophrenia, Barry and Barry report that "there is a tendency toward over-representation of early birth position in small families, and of late positions in large families" (1967:436). They explain this finding by suggesting that "in small families the children are likely to receive more individualized parental attention, and to be subjected to more severe pressure of parental expectations and aspirations" (Barry and Barry, 1967:438). The same mechanism may well be at work among the deaf children.

ETIOLOGY OF DEAFNESS

Etiology of deafness was considered in terms of whether the cause was "known" or "unknown." Table 23, item 12, shows that etiology was unknown for a significantly larger proportion of the disturbed group (55 percent) than of the comparison group (16 percent). While this difference may be a function of a more general lack of information from parents of children in the disturbed group, it could also be related to parental attitudes toward deafness. We know from other sources (Meadow, 1968*b*) that lack of knowledge of a definite cause for deafness is often a source of great anxiety for the parents of a deaf child. Apparently the uncertainty about or absence of etiological information increases parental anxiety and guilt regarding responsibility for the child's condition (Davis, 1963). This in turn might contribute to emotional problems in the child.

Table 24 presents more specific etiological information, to the extent that it is available. The only etiological category that shows a significant difference between disturbed and comparison groups is the "known-unknown" dimension.

TABLE 24
Etiology of Deafness, Disturbed and Comparison Groups

	Severely Disturbed Deaf Students		*Deaf Comparison Group*	
Cause of Deafness	%	(*N*)	%	(*N*)
Heredity	30	(8)	37	(19)
Maternal rubella, Rh incompatibility, Anoxia	33	(9)	33	(17)
Meningitis	11	(3)	8	(4)
Other post-natal	26	(7)	22	(11)
Total	100	(27)	100	(51)
Data not available		(33)		(10)

Some Speculation about More Complex Relations

In an effort to specify further the conditions under which some of the relations reported above either increased or disappeared, the technique of multivariate analysis was applied to the data. Some interesting results emerged, but because of the small size of the two groups of children, numbers were reduced considerably. The material is suggestive and is reported here with the idea that it may provide some direction for future research hypotheses. (Tables showing these relations can be obtained from the authors by interested readers.)

When the relation between mental health status and sex was examined with ordinal position controlled, it was found girls were more likely to be in the disturbed group whether they were first-born or later-born. However, when this relation was viewed in terms of the religious orientation of the family, the difference in proportion of girls in disturbed and comparison groups decreased among non-Catholics but increased among Catholics. Thus, it appears that family orientation to Catholicism is related to emotional disturbance among girls and contributes to the over-representation of girls in the disturbed group. Partialing the cases even further, it appears that first-born Catholic girls are most likely to be over-represented in the severely disturbed group. There were nine first-born Catholic girls included: one was in the comparison group; eight were in the disturbed group.

In considering the relation between family definitions of children's abilities and disabilities in fulfilling their sex-linked roles, religious orientation may provide some valuable clues.

Among the strongly Catholic ethnic groups in the United States, there is a good deal of evidence to show that sons are more highly valued than daughters.[1] In addition to the low status accorded women in ethnic Catholic families, we can expect to find rigid sex-role differentation with lines firmly drawn between appropriate role behavior for members of the different

1. See Barrabee and Von Mering (1955) for research on this point in Italian and Irish families; Glazer and Moynihan (1963) for the pattern in Italian families; Opler (1959) for references to the role of women in Irish and Italian families; Langner (1965) and Diaz-Guerrero (1955) for the role of women in Mexican families.

sexes.[2] Studies of the incidence of mental illness in the Mexican-American population (Jaco, 1960), and of symptomatic behavior in hospitalized Mexican-American patients (Meadow and Stoker, 1965), indicate some of the ways these patterns of role expectation contribute to personal adjustment.

Material from studies by Zuk (1959), Farber (1968), and Davis (1963) gives interesting but conflicting suggestions about ways in which religion specifies family response to a handicapped child. It is possible that a defective girl who is also first-born is doubly stigmatized in families that prefer male children. A daughter cannot fulfill family expectations for a son, nor (perhaps) is she expected to perform her role as caretaker for younger children or eventually as a competent wife and mother. The kind of evidence necessary for confirming or denying these speculations is not available from our survey data. The research possibilities, however, are intriguing. Further study could contribute to expanded knowledge about the relation between family expectations and children's adjustment to a handicap.

SUMMARY

A survey was undertaken at a state residential school for deaf students in which teachers and counselors were asked to identify children in their classes and dormitory groups whom they considered to be "severely emotionally disturbed." They were asked to identify a second group with more moderate behavioral problems. Sixty of the students (from the total school population of 516) were identified as severely disturbed (11.6 percent). An additional 101 students (19.6 percent) were seen by teachers and counselors as having problems of a lesser degree. Compared to a survey of all children attending schools in Los Angeles County, utilizing the identical questionnaire forms, almost five times as many deaf students were identified as severely disturbed, and over two-and-one-half times as many deaf as hearing (Los Angeles County) students were identified as mildly disturbed.

A comparison group was selected from the residential school roster, eliminating all students who had been identified

2. See Glazer and Moynihan (1963) for examples from Puerto Rican families, and Lenski (1963:220–221) for material from a large-scale study of various religious groups in the Detroit area.

as exhibiting any degree of behavioral difficulty. Comparisons between these students and the severely disturbed students revealed no relation between mental health status and race or ethnicity, father's occupation, parents' hearing status, or degree of residual hearing. Differences between the two groups approached significance in comparisons of family intactness, family size, age, and religion, with a larger proportion in the disturbed group from nonintact families, those with fewer than three children, those who were younger than thirteen years of age, and those who were Catholic. Statistically significant differences were found between the two groups in terms of sex, IQ scores, ordinal position, and etiology of deafness. Etiology was a significant factor only in terms of whether it was known or unknown, with more disturbed children having an unknown etiology. As expected, those with lower IQ scores were more likely to be found in the disturbed group. Girls, and those who were only or first-born children were more often represented in the disturbed group. When the relation between mental health status and sex was examined in terms of both religion and ordinal position in the family, it was found that Catholic girls were especially high risk, increased if they were also first-born. Data from other studies were presented in an attempt at an explanatory formulation which emphasized the interaction of family values placed on sons compared to daughters, sex role differentiation within the family, definition of handicap and the role of guilt within Catholic families, as these influence developmental problems in a deaf population.

8

Mental Health Services for the Deaf: Patients, Therapeutic Procedures, and Evaluation

Our research, our clinical experience, our theoretical orientation, and the conclusions of others (Rainer and Altshuler, 1966) have made it clear that it is essential that mental health services for a deaf population have a preventive orientation. The program as it has been developed by our staff can be described as a working example of community psychiatry. Prevention is the fulcrum of such a program (see Hume, 1966; Caplan, 1964; Lamb et al., 1969).

Prevention can be thought of on three levels: primary prevention is community focused; "it involves lowering the rate of new cases of mental disorder in a population by counteracting harmful circumstances before they have had a chance to produce illness" (Caplan, 1964:26). Work in this area has primarily involved consulting with other agencies and individuals and providing inservice training. This aspect of our program is described in the following chapter.

Secondary prevention refers to work with patients with mild or incipient disorders; a major aspect of work with this group involves efforts at early identification of the disorder through prompt service or referral or both. A fair amount of the clinical work has been done in this area.

Chapter 8 is by Winifred DeVos, Holly Elliott, Kathryn P. Meadow and Hilde S. Schlesinger.

Tertiary prevention refers to the rehabilitation of individuals who have been diagnosed as having a definite psychiatric disorder of some duration. Work with these individuals is designed to reduce the rate of defective functioning at school, at work, in the family, and in general interpersonal relationships. Prevention in this sense refers to therapeutic intervention that forestalls continued or further malfunctioning.

A DESCRIPTION OF THE CLINICAL CASE LOAD

In the first four years of the project's existence, 215 index or "identified" patients received services. In addition, 201 collateral clients were also seen by the clinical staff. Most of these were parents, since a condition of therapy is that all patients aged eighteen or under are seen in therapy with their parents. Siblings and other relatives were also included if this was consistent with the therapeutic plan. (It should be noted that 91 of the collateral patients were given psychiatric diagnoses.)

Geographical Distribution and Referral Source

The majority of the project patients (65 percent) came from the San Francisco Bay Area. However, the fact that patients were seen from a total of twenty-six different California counties, located as far south as Los Angeles, and as far north as the Oregon border reflects an important aspect of the need for mental health services for deaf persons. Our facility is the only one in the west specifically designed for this purpose. Also, those patients whom we were able to accept with a limited staff were willing to travel the necessary distances to the project office. This is also an indication of one reason for the importance of consultation and collaboration with other agencies: when such distances are involved, it is often necessary to encourage other mental health agencies to work with deaf clients and their families.

Types of agencies referring patients to the staff included: social welfare and mental health agencies, hospitals and physicians, audiologists or speech and hearing centers, State Department of Vocational Rehabilitation, court officials or juvenile authorities, and churches. As the services being offered by the project became known more widely in the community, additional agencies and individuals referred new clients. After four years, almost every agency in the area concerned with deafness in any way has referred some individual for services. The schools remain the largest single source of referrals, with 37 percent of the total case load referred by school personnel. The average patient had been seen by at least two other agencies. The clinical staff, during therapy, averaged about 2.4 agency contacts per patient. This figure includes three patients on whose behalf six agency contacts each were made. In spite of this high rate of agency involvement at least ninety patients were felt to be suffering as a result of the paucity and lack of coordination of therapeutic services, particularly for the very young deaf child, the youthful delinquent, and the deaf youngster too disturbed for admittance into school.

Age Distribution of Case Load

During the early years of the project, the adult patients (age twenty-one or older) represented about 40 percent of the total. While the number of adult patients has remained fairly constant, patients twenty years of age and under have been coming to the project in increasing numbers. During the past year, 75 percent of the case load was under twenty-one years of age. This age distribution is illustrated in figure 10. Reasons for the changing age distribution are related to both the kinds of referrals that were made and decisions about who could be accepted. Numbers of referrals, especially those from schools, continued to increase each year, as the school personnel had more experience working with project staff through consultation, and saw positive behavioral changes in children referred for individual therapy. Staff members felt, in addition, that younger patients were more amenable to change through psychotherapy, and when treatment facilities were too limited to enable every applicant to be seen, preference was given to those of younger ages.

Sex and Marital Status of Patients

Sixty-one percent of the patients were male, compared to 39 percent who were female. This reflects both the higher incidence of deafness among males, and the greater likelihood that males will come to the attention of community agencies generally. Among the patients over twenty-one, 45 percent were single, 24 percent married, and 31 percent separated, divorced, or widowed. In 1960, the United States Census showed that 21

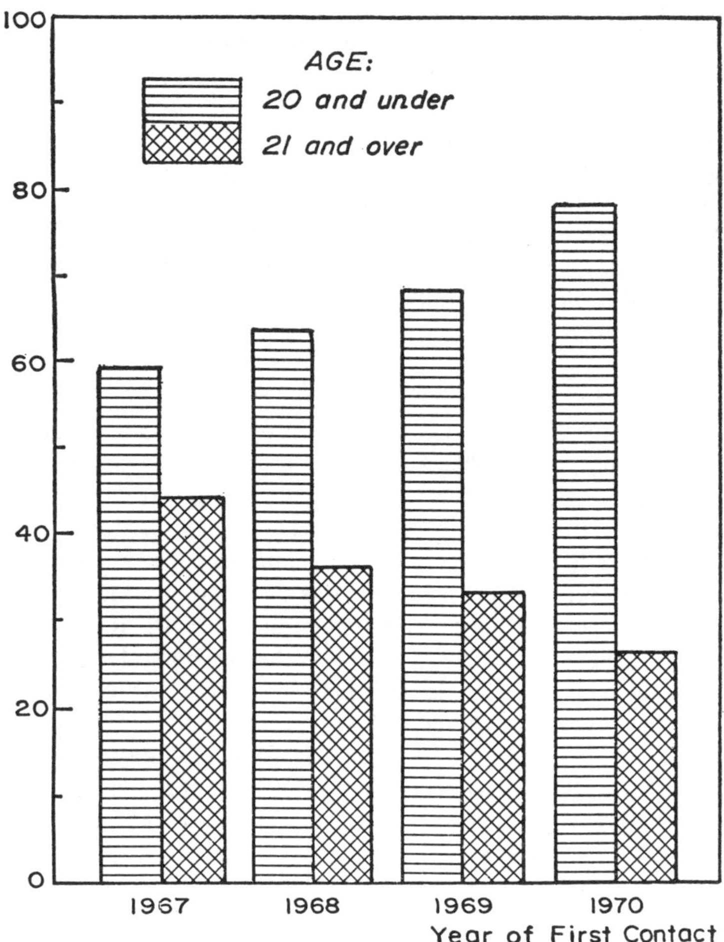

Figure 10 CASE LOAD BY AGE AND YEAR OF FIRST CONTACT

percent of all Californians over fourteen were single; 68 percent were married, and 12 percent were widowed or divorced.

Race, Ethnicity, and Religion

The proportions of various racial, ethnic, and religious groups in the caseload reflect the proportion of the same groups in the general population. The fact that 7 percent of our patients were black (only slightly below the proportion in the population as a whole) is interesting since deaf educators have sometimes remarked on the apparently low incidence of deafness among Negroes, as reflected by their numbers in school or general censuses. We are unable to draw any general conclusions about deaf persons who are also members of racial or ethnic minorities because of the small numbers involved in the caseload. However, this would be an important area for additional study, since these individuals may be subject to dual discrimination.

Occupational Distribution of Patients or Parents of Patients

The occupational level of our patients (or their parents) is somewhat lower than found in the general population. While 32 percent of the case load is employed in white collar jobs, almost half of the general population would be found in this category. Twenty-five percent of the patients are unemployed or on welfare, about twice the proportion found in large cities at the present time. This reflects the lower level of occupational skills among deaf adults, which is particularly handicapping in a period of high unemployment. The large proportion of patients on welfare also reflects their contact with community social agencies which may lead to a referral to our project.

Etiology and Age at Onset of Deafness

The etiology and age at onset for the patient population is about the same as for the deaf population generally. That is, 84 percent of the patients for whom this information was available experienced prelingual onset of deafness (before the age of two), while only 5 percent became deaf after the age of thirteen. The large proportion of patients with "unknown" etiology (53 percent) is also characteristic, with many of these cases probably related to genetic causes even though no other members of their families are deaf. The seven cases (4 percent) where hearing loss is not present represent hearing children of deaf parents.

THERAPEUTIC PROCEDURES

Types of Therapy Offered by Project Staff

Services offered during the report period were not limited to a particular type of patient with a specific pattern of symptoms. Thus, the clinical case load represents service at both the secondary and tertiary levels of prevention. Allocation of staff time to direct services is related to requests for consultation and education as well as to the volume of other kinds of requests. This broad range of function has been carried out through various procedures: referral, intake, diagnostic study, brief or long-term therapy, collaboration and case consultation with or without direct contact. In addition to the services provided by our own staff members, we may enlist the skills of outside diagnostic personnel who carry out clinical psychological testing, speech and language evaluations, educational and medical assessments. In turn, we constitute a resource for other agencies that may wish to make a referral or that may currently be working with one of our patients. Table 25 lists the various types of therapeutic intervention that have been used, with the proportion of patients for each.

The largest number in the case load, fifty-three (25 percent) were treated by consultation with other agencies. Long-term therapy (defined as therapy lasting longer than a six-month period) accounted for forty-one patients (19 percent). Fifteen patients (7 percent) were seen for crisis intervention therapy, intensive therapy over a period of from three to nine visits. Many patients who were originally referred for crisis intervention became long-term therapy patients. "Intake only" and "study" were often followed by referral to other agencies.

TABLE 25
Description of Therapeutic Intervention

Treatment Plan	%	(*N*)
Consultation	25	(53)
Intake only	11	(23)
Study	13	(27)
Crisis intervention	7	(15)
Short-term therapy	7	(15)
Long-term therapy	19	(41)
Hospitalization	—	(1)
Telephone or correspondence contact only	12	(25)
Awaiting intake	7	(15)
Total	101	(215)

In addition to the consultations included in table 25 the project psychiatrist has met with each of the fifty-six families of the fifty-nine children that have participated in the Parent Orientation Program at the California School for the Deaf in Berkeley. This included fifty-six mothers and twenty-two fathers, a total of seventy-eight parents.

Staff policy was to consider all referrals and to accept a case on the basis of individual need. No simple criterion was set for eligibility for services. In the important preliminary contact, discussion focuses on the relevance of our service to the problem being presented—i.e., how our staff can be helpful if the referring source continues to handle the case, or whether direct services should be offered. Many referrals do not require direct services if the referring agency can be assisted to carry out its own functions competently. When direct services are involved, the clinical staff felt that the relationship aspect of the therapy was of great importance. Therefore an attempt is made from the beginning to provide acceptance, understanding, and a sense of direction.

Communicative Mode

Communication is an aspect of deafness considered here not only for its importance in early language development and interpersonal rapport, but for the manner in which treatment is conducted. A major reason for the lack of services for deaf people is the difficulty most hearing people have in communicating with them. Our staff has acquired the orientation and the communicative skills necessary to surmount much of this difficulty.

The mode of communication used in therapy presented different problems in the adult and the child patient populations. Most of the adult patients required manual communication. Most were able to adjust the speed of communication to the proficiency of the therapist even at times of marked stress, when they were motivated for treatment and had good rapport with the therapist. "Transference crises" were subtly accompanied by an increase in speed and choice of signs unknown to the therapist. Other patients used the distortion of communicative mode as an artificial means to control the therapist or others, although not necessarily with conscious intent.

Case 1. Gregory was a 13-year-old, very intelligent boy who had succeeded in provoking his dismissal from school and had a close, albeit conflicted, symbiotic relation with his parents. He was very fearful that what we were about to do to him might topple his recently re-established "nest." Any questions bearing on school, parents, or his recent behavior were answered by a barrage of staccato-like signs accompanied by a knowing smirk. Uncontroversial questions were answered slowly and understandably.

Case 2. Jolyon, who had acquired deafness in young adulthood, had experienced marked difficulty in learning to lipread. Eventually he agreed to learn sign language with subsequent improvement of his lipreading facility. However, he wanted to force his parents to use sign language with him. When the father expressed willingness to do so, but did not progress at the speed his son desired, Jolyon went on a "silent strike" for five days.

Interestingly, with some patients, adult or child, it appeared that it was not the knowledge of signs but the attitude toward the sign language that facilitated successful therapy. Youngsters acquainted with the sign language were frequently ashamed or unwilling to use it, viewing the therapist as similar to the teacher or parent who might frown on signing. The therapist's acceptance and obvious enjoyment of the use of sign language tended to free the child to respond more spontaneously with signs and/or speech.

Case 3. In addition to her profound prelingual deafness, eight-year-old Joyce had a severe emotional block that interfered with learning and the establishment of meaningful relations, particularly with her peers. Joyce's teacher indicated that she was introducing signs and fingerspelling to her class, but that Joyce seemed reluctant to participate. In the uncritical atmosphere of the therapy playroom and before the TV camera it became obvious that Joyce had absorbed more signs and fingerspelling than anyone had suspected; in fact, she fairly exploded in appropriate manual communication. This occasion seemed to be a turning point, a key that helped to unlock Joyce's emotional block. With Joyce leading the way, her parents have shown their enthusiasm about this mode of communication. Joyce has reacted to their acceptance with greatly increased communication with them and others, in all modes available to her: speech, writing, fingerspelling, and signs.

Some patients indicated to the therapist that they were more willing to use speech in her presence than in the presence of others unacquainted with the sign language. In fact, under ideal situations the deaf patient was found to be able to use and accept all avenues of communication: speech, lipreading, fingerspelling, signs, or writing. All these modalities were used in the service of better understanding and welcomed in an atmosphere of good rapport. Difficulty with the effective use of any of these methods has generally been a symptom of a type of resistance encountered in therapy.

A further aspect of the problem is illustrated in case 4, in which the child was fluent in speech but not as well understood as he presumed. Discussion with the parents involved the introduction of combined modes of communication.

Case 4. Darrell at age 12 was a profoundly deaf child, using lipreading and speech as the prime means of communication in his hearing family and his special class at a regular junior high school. Presenting problems were school complaints about his agitated behavior, and denial of his share in mischievous behavior and competitive aggression with peers. Darrell's refusal to wear his hearing aid had become a point of struggle with his parents. His preference in the initial interview was oral communication. Despite the therapist's close attention, Darrell at times did not make himself entirely clear with articulation or pronunciation; at such times the therapist resorted spontaneously and inadvertently to fingerspelling in her own determination to try to understand. Darrell seemed to respond to this intent, replying with confirmation or correction also in fingerspelling.

After this interaction, the therapist talked with

the parents and got their approval for doing whatever seemed helpful in work with their son. Thereafter, on occasion in interviews Darrell himself spontaneously used not only fingerspelling, but sign language, showing that for him, too, manual communication could sometimes be more expressive and restore the flow of rapport.

Case 5. Jimmy came to us at age 4, profoundly deaf, with his 6-year-old hearing sister and 24-year-old hearing mother. All needed counseling over a prolonged period: Jimmy for hyperactive behavior at school and home; Barbara for diffusely anxious fantasies and learning problems; mother for distress at parental cares compounded by single parent welfare status. Jimmy had a hearing aid which he refused, broke, threw about. He did not speak, willfully sticking out his tongue in refusals or persisting energetically and often slyly to try to do exactly what he wanted. Sometimes, without his aid, he appeared to be hearing; with it, his actual reception was moderately good. A responsive child, Jimmy increasingly uttered sounds, their abundance especially notable when he was using the aid.

His mother, wanting to reach him in new ways, and to teach care-taking adults as well, started learning manual communication; at school the teacher worked at including speech training, special preschool teaching, and some acceptance of gestures. All these efforts carried on with good mutual cooperation were reflected gradually in Jimmy's interest in reproducing sounds made to him. Mother stressed "I love you"; school context and playroom brought out other useful language. In the waiting room, Jimmy was once noticed to be comprehending the conversation of two adult deaf persons using signs, and to be interacting with a surprising repertoire of signs himself. Although Jimmy had never been introduced to formal speech therapy his progress with the resources around him was considerable.

As Jimmy developed in communication, he also

> developed more acceptable behavior; the two were closely interrelated. His face, always very mobile and expressive, has become more often lighted up rather than frowning and angry. Therapy and collaborative efforts have improved not only Jimmy's communication, but his interpersonal setting, including a reduction in his mother's feeling of self-blame about his deafness, and of his sister's anxieties about why he is deaf.

While only 17 percent of the identified patients were using speech together with signs at intake, this figure increased to 38 percent. Writing was also occasionally used. One collateral patient (not included in the analysis of the clinical case load) communicated only through writing. Writing was especially useful for interim contacts, since deaf patients who cannot initiate or receive telephone contacts could experience a greater directness of communication through letters than through having someone else act as intermediary. This was recognized to have positive potential for treatment (Pearson, 1965), although a few patients used prolific writing to control and avoid rapport during therapy.

The child patients showed a high number of noncommunicators in any mode. Many of the children had never been exposed to the manual communication system and were in "pure" oral environments. In order not to produce or aggravate the ubiquitous conflict, an administrative decision was made to use only the language style preferred by the parents.

CONFIDENTIALITY

Always an issue in psychotherapy, confidentiality takes on added complexity in work with deaf patients and their families because of the closely knit communicating networks among deaf people. Thus, many members of the deaf community often knew of the alleged mental disorders, the behavioral misdeeds, and the infractions of the law of our patients before we did, and frequently asked us about such events. It invariably took great care not to violate confidentiality under such circumstances, while at the same time not rebuffing the frequently benevolent "informers." The deaf patients reacted in varying ways to this knowledge that others—even in different parts of the country

—might know of their difficulties; some anticipated the general knowledge and introduced the therapist even at social meetings quite openly as "my shrink"; others would carefully avoid meeting other patients in the office, and assume a paranoid air. A twenty-six-year-old patient would invariably at the beginning of each therapy session attempt to ask what other deaf person the therapist had seen that week and what, if anything, they had said about her. One year of utter silence in response to these requests was necessary before the patient believed and accepted the nature of confidentiality at our center.

MAJOR TYPES OF PROBLEMS TREATED

Problems treated by the clinical staff differed in terms of the presenting symptoms and the severity of disturbance as well as in terms of the demographic characteristics and type of treatment which have been presented in previous sections of this chapter.

Appendix D shows the precise diagnostic categories (from the nomenclature developed by the American Psychiatric Association) that were assigned to patients. Sixty-one patients were so classified. They constitute 28 percent of the total caseload of 215 identified patients. Of the remaining 72 percent, 66 patients (31 percent) were diagnosed as having behavioral disorders, social maladjustments, transient situational personality disorders or special symptoms.

Diagnostic labels attached to patients, however, do not tell a great deal about the kinds of practical therapeutic problems that are encountered and the ways in which the therapist attempts to deal with them. Using the developmental model presented in Chapter 2 as a framework for viewing the problems of deafness, we shall look at a number of case examples to illustrate the major types of problems treated.

Trust versus Mistrust—The Early Years

Children of all ages—even infants—are seen in our clinical services for problems involving deafness. Other physical problems besides deafness are particularly prevalent in "rubella children"; possibility of organic involvement must be considered in children showing delayed language development and unique learning difficulties. Assessment of these factors may be inconclusive in earlier years, and for some children "evaluative treatment" is undertaken. These are anxious and uncertain times for parents of the children involved. Their anxiety and lack of confidence in the way they handle their deaf child make it difficult for them to impart the trust which is the major task of the earliest years. The complexity of the diagnosis and remedial work with deaf youngsters is enormous. The amount of parental energy to be mobilized and sustained puts a tremendous demand on the ordinary family relations, often leading to personal or family disorganization. Parents need an opportunity to recover from distress before they can meet the successively occurring developmental crises of their children. One of our goals was to give parents as well as children an opportunity to express these concerns and to plan constructively about how to channel their efforts. Case 6 illustrates some of these points.

> *Case 6*. Warren, soon to be six, has been a complex challenge therapeutically and educationally. Physical problems based on rubella etiology were severe in early infancy, requiring surgical heart repair and several prolonged hospitalizations. Apparent profound deafness as well as possible visual deficits were presumed to account for the unique ways in which he responded to people. He avoided eye contact, did not attend to speech and did not use speech himself. Other behavior was bizarre as well: constant climbing, gazing at lights, short sleep periods, repetitive preoccupied play. Selectively attentive, he could be observant, curious, willful, test out, and even responded to limits.
>
> In placement for special education, teaching was so difficult that one teacher forecast a need for institutionalization, wondering about mental retardation or psychosis. The parents fluctuated between determination that there must be resources to meet his needs, resistance to despair, and occasional hope about his actual potential. All their strengths, previously marshalled toward speech therapy alone, have been applied in treatment in a multi-directed way: parent counseling as well as child play therapy; parent participation at preschool with half-day sessions at both public and private schools; periodic audiological and pediatric reevaluation. Collaboration among all the professionals has continued throughout therapy.

No labels have been applied, but milestones have been passed in relieving deep diagnostic concerns: no retardation was found on psychological testing; reliable consistent findings were eventually reached on audiograms. As some doubts were dispelled, the early premise of emotional disturbance took a chief focus as a likely explanation for the way Warren functions. This is understandable both in terms of early stress and subsequent unproductive lines of effort.

As Warren shows a continuous gain in social development, attention concurrently is going into facilitating his language development. Herein lies a still open question as to whether his lack of communicative skills results from a lag that is still reversible, or whether organic involvement is present at a level not evidenced on neurological testing. Despite the complexity of issues, a supportive therapeutic contact has resulted in improvement, which may be sustained and carried further assuming availability of long-continued optimal help.

Autonomy versus Shame and Doubt

It may be that the child must be in an environment where his significant others feel sure of their own autonomy if he is to develop into an autonomous individual. The clinical staff evaluated social problems of the parents as well as the children. The term "chaotic parenting" was applied in 60 cases, which represents 43 percent of the 140 cases in which it was felt there was basis for judgment. Seeking to define what we encountered, we find most relevant Goldfarb's (1970) concept of "maternal perplexity" developed in his work with schizophrenic children. Some of these components apply in the present context:

1. Outwardly, a striking lack of organized parental activity.
2. A lack of parental spontaneity and a lack of immediate natural awareness of the child's needs.
3. When pressed by the bizarreness of the destructive nature of the child's symptoms, the parent gives overt signs of bewilderment.
4. The child reacts as though there were no con-

> trols, either outer or inner. One sees perseverative, uncontrolled aimlessness, confusion and uncontained and enduring emotional responses of fear and rage. (Goldfarb et al., 1970:412)

Optimal adjustment to the diagnosis of deafness was rarely seen among the hearing parents. The handicap of deafness poses a tremendous extra challenge not only to the parent of a deaf child, but to the growth and change forces within the child himself. What affects the parent affects the child, and vice versa.

Numerous energetic steps are required (the search for a "cure," correspondence courses, hearing aids, medicine, day care, etc.), but do not appear sufficient or gratifying to most parents. Many parents, even those with grown children, continued to show vestiges of guilt, chronic sorrow, and over-involvement mingled with frank rejection. In many cases, the defect was magnified and all the difficulties in the family were attributed to it. On the other hand, some parents repeatedly denied the defect and saw the child "passing" as a hearing youngster. Chaotic parenting often alternated between over-indulgence and excessive demand, with inability to understand the dynamics of deafness, or the child's use of acting-out behavior as a mode of communication.

> *Case 7.* Nancy, age five, a child with moderate hearing loss, is the third girl in her family. She was brought by her parents because of whiny, clinging behavior, willful food-fads, restless sleeping patterns, unreasonable demands on time and attention. Most upsetting to the parents was their inability to reach her with explanations. The parents alternately acceded to Nancy's claims while also becoming furious at her impositions. Their problems with her were highlighted by the contrast noted in Nancy's relative compliance and cooperativeness with other adults. Eventually Nancy expressed direct verbal acknowledgment of her own awareness of the struggle with her parents.
>
> Many of her parents' concessions to her arose from their frustration and over-solicitude about her hearing loss—frank bewilderment about whether the hearing aid was really as uncomfortable as Nancy claimed; whether her range of vocabulary and con-

ceptual thought really did enable her to understand; whether her isolation from children her age reflected an acute sense of difference and troubled communication.

In counseling, realistic consideration of the direct effects of hearing problems was balanced by discussion of some of the parents' unworkable premises about child rearing in general. Practical planning for Nancy included speech training, extended attendance at play school (rather than starting formal school before she was ready) and, whenever possible, patient listening until her sometimes unclear meanings were satisfactorily understood. Initially Nancy had been so delayed in social development that there had been concern about possible retardation. Without help for the parents' anxiety about any degree of hearing loss, Nancy might permanently have been treated as profoundly handicapped. Instead, her eventually corrected hearing shows only moderate loss. She has now been placed in a regular school and is functioning in a way more appropriate to her real capacities.

The early childhood years were frequently described by parents as being clearly "child-centered" and replete with personal or financial sacrifice. Hearing siblings often felt or were described as "sacrificed." Most of the parents felt openly or vaguely uncomfortable about their tendency to hover excessively with advice, suggestions, and protection.

Among the children we have seen, the youngest tended to be aggressive and hyperactive. These youngsters had problems learning limits; they had few real guides for action, and their feelings of fear and rage often became overwhelming.

Case 8. Five-year-old Bradley has a family background of severe emotional trauma. His three siblings are all considerably older than he, and the father, who was an alcoholic, deserted the family shortly before Bradley was born. Meningitis at six weeks of age left Bradley with a profound deafness as well as occasional convulsive seizures. His first stepfather died of cancer when Bradley was three years old, and his mother remarried shortly before starting therapy. Bradley was suspended from school for aggressive and destructive behavior and psychiatric help was made a condition for readmittance.

The parents both work in order to pay their large medical bills. A succession of unsuccessful day care arrangements for Bradley has resulted in inconsistent handling, which has contributed further to his emotional distress. He has no speech and communicates primarily by an exuberant, nonhostile aggressiveness. Although he appears to be a bright, affectionate youngster, Bradley has problems in comprehending the damaging effects of his behavior on persons or objects and in interpreting the emotional reaction he evokes in others. When enraged he turns to physical assault on himself and others.

Attempts have been made to help the parents deal with their own deeply denied anger at Bradley. Therapy is construed by the parents as a means to get Bradley back to school, and in their attempt to resolve this issue, they tend to deny the extent of his problems. School admission is presently being considered and ongoing consultation with the teacher has been offered. It is our hope that the coordinate functions of parental effort, therapy, school, consultation, and consistent day care handling will help Bradley achieve the good potential that he undoubtedly has.

Industry versus Inferiority

During the years of elementary schooling and approaching adolescence, a child is involved in mastery of learning and relationships beyond the intimate confines of the family. His background of early security is carried forward in these new encounters. Complexity of problems that were encountered previously as well as those confronted currently enter into the capacity for adjustment at the next stage. Output of energies in latency years is aimed toward success in channeling capacities, both intellectual and emotional. Depending on how problems are resolved that occur at this stage, adjustment in terms of inferiority rather than competence may weigh in the balance.

Case 9. Doug, age 13, is oldest of 3 sibs and the only deaf member of his family. Diligent parental investment in early speech training, combined with Doug's high learning capacities and motivation, resulted in his achievement of good oral language skills. Identifying closely with his father in ambitious work incentives, and at the same time seeking to please his mother with his achievements, Doug has channeled much of his energy into self-initiated creative projects and into earning money. He wins awards with meticulous entries into model contests, and he buys expensive items with his own job proceeds. It is essential to his work to interact effectively with hearing customers and he has surmounted hampering factors of deafness in order to do this.

Contrasted with his positive achievements, Doug manifests behavioral difficulties which reflect the personal cost of his industrious output. He appears constantly tense, agitated, worried; and he feels that others are not sufficiently helpful to him when he needs them. This feeling is turned into a demanding petulance which alienates others and results in less dependency gratification than he legitimately needs. Although accepting his brother's participation in customer-contacts, he otherwise experiences keen rivalry with his younger hearing sibling. Doug's current adjustment in school reflects not only his high potential but his at times unmanageable behavior centering around competition with peers.

Future planning for Doug's school placement and occupational choice are already matters for consideration by the family and by the educators; they have not been discussed sufficiently with Doug as yet. His early adjustment difficulties, related both to deafness and to factors intrinsic to his particular family have been somewhat alleviated. They are not, however, resolved. Therapy with Doug and his parents has been aimed at elucidating some of their experiences with deafness so that a more realistic sense of needs and possibilities can be realized. Accomplishment of the therapeutic goal is complicated by the deep-seated frustrations in both him and his parents about his handicap—a wish to deny it.

Identity versus Role Diffusion

The adolescent years are difficult at best. Among the deaf patients seen, this was a particularly trying time as problems of identity and role diffusion became more central. Among our adolescent and adult cases, homosexual acting-out was a problem with sixteen patients. This is comparable to the incidence of homosexuality as reported in Rainer et al. (1963). Fifteen of these patients were fairly evenly distributed in two age groups: 16 to 20 and 21 to 30. One patient was in the 31 to 40 age group. Of the thirty-four patients aged 16 to 20, 21 percent had sexual problems. Sexual acting-out was sometimes diagnosed precipitiously as can be seen in the case of Michael:

> *Case 10.* Michael, a 17-year-old who lives with his mother and stepfather and spends weekends with his father and stepmother, was dismissed from school because of alleged homosexual activities. Psychiatric interviews with the boy indicated that some exploratory sex play had taken place, but that no irreversible feminine identification or homosexual orientation had been established. Consultation with the school successfully "detoxified" the label given to this youngster, and he was permitted to return. Both Michael and the school authorities expressed a preference for foster home placement rather than dormitory residence. Both "sets" of parents were seen for several interviews, and it became clear that in both families the mother predominated in the contact with the youngster. Both fathers, however, were willing to increase their contact with the boy and were encouraged to do so. Follow-up one year later indicated that Michael has made a good adjustment. He is dating and attending dances at school with no further behavioral problems.

The case of Jeremy illustrates some of the more generalized problems of identity formation faced by deaf individuals.

Case 11. Jeremy, 21, was expelled from residential school before graduation, tried leaving home and getting work in the city, but was restless and preoccupied by bizarre thoughts. It was highly problematical at first how therapy might be helpful to him. The approach that has evolved reflects a use of a combination of methods and resources: intensive individual outpatient work with Jeremy, similar work concurrently with his widowed mother with whom he returned to live; collaborative vocational rehabilitation counseling; brief interim inpatient mental hospital care; sheltered hotel living upon separation again from home; combined job training and supervised living. Environmental manipulation (including the therapists' interaction with cooperating resources) was an essential aspect of helping Jeremy establish some independence from an overanxious, protective mother, while gaining some mastery over feelings of abandonment by the earlier unexpected death of his father. Many alternatives were considered, including possible return to residential school, rather than moving directly into employment.

Accomplishment of goals for Jeremy required working toward compatible goals for his mother, since her ability to "let him go" and to feel gratified by his gains could only be achieved through her experiencing someone's interest in her needs as well as his. When temporary setbacks in plans resulted in disorganization in Jeremy's thoughts and behavior, hospitalization provided some protection and security. During this time his regular therapist maintained contact with him despite the 90-mile distance. Jeremy found our office a focal point of his reentry into city life, appearing very early for visits as though grateful for the hospitable welcome he received. As a mini-environment it had special meaning and in itself was an important part of the overall treatment. Interpretive work was of less relevance with Jeremy's situation than providing ways to meet his dependent and independent needs directly as well as symbolically.

Intimacy versus Isolation

In the adult caseload, the most prevalent psychiatric symptom was immaturity. While some patients showed psychotic ideation that was resistant to change, other patients evidenced experience gaps that were relatively amenable to intervention. Withdrawal tendencies were primary in about 13 percent of the cases, followed closely by a lack of social judgment in 10 percent of the cases. Depressive tendency, passive-dependence, and lack of moral judgment were common problems among the adults. True depression occurred only in patients with late onset of deafness.

Problems of immaturity, lack of experience and social judgment often prevent the intimacy that leads to meaningful adult relationships, and contribute to isolation in both social and occupational worlds. Some of these patterns are illustrated by the case of Ruth:

> *Case 12.* Ruth is a young deaf adult, a college dropout. Her concrete interpretations of the book of etiquette coupled with an intransigent "Old Testament" conscience immoblized her when she was faced with a personnel form or an employment interview. She could not be convinced that a youthful indiscretion did not give her a "criminal record." The fact that references from her previous employers were generally good had little effect on her inability to seek further employment. The therapist carefully shared with her the discussion of practical steps as well as possible reasons for her reluctance, and frequently accompanied her to agencies and job interviews to lend support and serve as sign language interpreter. Ruth finally accepted employment again and seemed thereby to have overcome some of her anxieties.

Generativity versus Stagnation

When the deaf individual marries and has children of his own, new problems arise. Sometimes those difficulties which have not been successfully resolved in earlier stages of the life cycle interfere with adequate parenting. Weakness in generational structure was noted in five of the six families we treated which included hearing children and deaf parents. One set of hearing grandparents had "adopted" the hearing grandchildren although the deaf parents staunchly maintained ignorance about such a court procedure.

The maternal role was unclear and passed from grandmother to mother in three of the families, and the youngsters clearly played one "mother" against the other. Unfortunately, social agencies, courts, schools, and welfare departments have contributed to this ambiguity by bypassing the natural mother in their work.

In the clinical interview and history and on psychological tests, the hearing children of deaf parents known to us were found to be impulsive, highly egocentric, immature, with intransigent conscience—findings hauntingly similar to those ascribed to the deaf by Levine (1956) and Altshuler (1964). Three of the families had two children. In these families, the younger child fit the description above while the older was more withdrawn and introspective. The older child in a family of two siblings tended to possess a pseudomaturity with certain regressive symptoms:

> *Case 13*. Peter H., now 12, is the younger of two hearing boys of a deaf divorced mother. Play sessions and interviews with Peter showed a likeable smiling boy, who seldom met direct gazes and who was rather inarticulate in speech. Observed with his mother, Peter could understand and communicate freely in the sign language of the deaf; he selectively adapted his mode of communication when turning from mother to clinician. When his feelings were elicited regarding proposed school away from home, he expressed his mother's need for him (answering the phone) rather than *his* anticipated loss of her.
>
> Raising her boys alone, Mrs. H. had involved her household closely with that of her elderly parents, relying on help with child care, meals, laundry, and so forth. Her mother alternately invited this dependence and scorned it. In the same way Mrs. H. requested and scorned the help. While grandmother indulged the boys, their mother was made to feel inadequate.

> Usurping Mrs. H's rightful role, the grandmother intervened at school, on the grounds that Mrs. H. could not hear and therefore was presumed (by the school as well) to be inaccessible. While the grandmother felt righteous, Mrs. H. felt increasingly resentful and the boys were caught in the struggle. Inconsistent discipline resulted in the boy's misbehavior outside the home. After the boys had been placed in temporary juvenile detention, Mrs. H. voluntarily chose residential school placement for the older boy one year, and for Peter the next year. A hearing Big Brother played a very significant (father) function for the boys throughout these years. Our project and the school also provided helpful support.
>
> A tendency in Peter "not to know" (to hear or look into) the rules in certain situations might possibly reflect an identification with his mother in some of the concretism attributed to deaf persons. Most hearing persons relating to the deaf mother and the hearing children usually took for granted that messages were clearly given and received, when in fact they were not. Peter had to make the best of very conflicting sources of information about plans affecting him from one day to the next.

Some hearing children of deaf parents are encouraged to assume household responsibility that may strengthen their sense of competence but may also pose burdens beyond their means. Whatever the needs of the deaf parent, care must be maintained to meet the legitimate dependent needs of the hearing child as well. Likewise care is required to sustain parental prerogatives, rather than playing into conflicts of allegiance for the child between deaf parent and hearing relatives or others. If, after effort, the deaf parent is found to have real problems in coping with the child's needs, realistic planning must be offered that is valid for the needs of all concerned and not simply compensatory for the deafness per se.

The deaf parents of hearing children were all desirous of being good parents, but most described themselves as feeling inadequate to the job. They tended to magnify the importance of the diagnosis of "hearing children" in much the same ways that hearing parents of deaf children magnify the diagnosis of deafness. Although the problems described by the deaf parents are found in all types of parents, the label of deafness was emphasized again and again. They all felt that fewer problems might have existed for them with deaf children. There is some indication from Rainer et al. (1963) that deaf parents do indeed "do better" with their deaf than with their hearing children.

The findings regarding hearing children with deaf parents are of sufficient interest to merit further investigation. Since guidance clinics sometimes appear to be at a loss when dealing with deaf parents, this group of hearing children suffers as much from the lack of appropriate mental health services as do the deaf children themselves.

EVALUATION OF THERAPY

Thus far we have presented a description of the individuals and families that have sought help from Mental Health Services for the Deaf during the four-year project, as well as considerations involved in their treatment. The most important questions are: To what extent was the therapeutic intervention successful, and what reasons can we suggest for the "successful" and "unsuccessful" outcomes?

Evaluation of the effect of therapy on the patient is extremely difficult (Rogers and Dymond, 1954; Eysenck, 1965; Meltzoff and Kornreich, 1970). On the one hand, the therapist is the one person other than the patient who has the most opportunity to observe behavioral and affective changes, to hear of differences in environmental responses or situational difficulties. On the other hand,

> In asking a therapist to evaluate how much a patient has changed during therapy one must expect distortions and inaccuracies that are both intentional and unintentional, consciously and unconsciously motivated. It is especially difficult for the principals in a therapeutic endeavor, each of whom may be intensely ego-involved in the process, to make accurate, unbiased observations and judgments. (Meltzoff and Kornreich, 1970:40–41)

The purpose of the assessment of improved-unimproved status of the patients seen during the four-year grant period was twofold: first was the interest in absolute rate of improvement, as defined by the therapist, and subject to the possibility of bias and personal involvement outlined above. These figures are presented tentatively and with realization of the possible inflation of proportion showing improvement. It can be pointed out, however, that our improvement rate is consistent with that reported by Rainer and Altshuler (1970) who worked with hospitalized deaf patients, while we worked with less severely disturbed deaf outpatients. The second purpose in assessing the improved-unimproved status of patients was the evaluation of subgroups of patients in the same case load to determine which categories of deaf patients may be most amenable to treatment as offered by our staff members. For this purpose, our method of definition can be considered more valid, since any bias in evaluation should operate in the same direction for all subgroups. This aspect of evaluation, therefore, will receive the most attention in the tables and discussion that follow.

Forward movement (Hunt and Kogan, 1950), in terms of behavioral change and/or situational changes that reduced the presenting problems, was considered to be the primary criterion in evaluating the effectiveness of therapy. Those patients rated as "improved" were by no means uniform in degree of improvement. The final decision (and classification) was reached in a conference that included the project director and one other therapist who had recourse to a wealth of recorded material: initial history; interview content; institutional logs; psychological, medical, and audiological reports; school records; staff conferences; and the extremely useful material obtained through videotapes of therapy sessions.

Improvement was often rated in terms of the receptivity of the environment to the patient, e.g., (1) school placement admission after prior dismissal, retention in school under prior threat of dismissal, eventual admission after delay or refusal; or (2) job placement following expulsion, ability to remain at work despite severe probation, obtaining a job for the first time. Some patients, particularly the most severely disturbed, were rated improved because they were kept out of the hospital. Other patients were rated improved on the basis of forward movement in interpersonal relations as reported by parents, teachers, siblings, and often the patient himself.

In the opinion of the therapists, 135 patients (63 percent

of the caseload of 215 patients) could be clearly classified as either improved or unimproved. This group consisted of 122 patients seen by the clinical staff, plus 13 patients that were followed closely in consultation. The ratio of improvement to unimprovement was approximately three to one, with 101 patients rated clearly "improved" and 34 rated as "unimproved." The criteria and results are consistent with those reported by Johnson and Reed (1947:271), who reported 74.1 percent considered "successfully" treated, and Rainer and Altshuler (1970:40) who reported 71 percent "improved."

Five different independent variables were selected as having a possible relationship to the treatment outcome. These included (1) age; (2) therapist's initial prognosis; (3) nature of the therapeutic intervention; (4) diagnostic category; and (5) patient's attempt to control the communication process.

Treatment Outcome and Age

The clinical staff has felt—and table 26 reinforces this belief—that early intervention represents the best use of time and energy. But it must be remembered that early intervention may require ongoing efforts if the results are to be maintained.

TABLE 26
Treatment Outcome by Age of Patients

Treatment Outcome	*Under Age 21*	*Age 21 and Over*
Improved	82% (80)	57% (21)
Unimproved	18% (18)	43% (16)
Total	100% (98)	100% (37)

$X^2 = 7.54$; $df = 1$; $p < .01$.

Treatment Outcome and Therapist's Initial Prognosis

The therapist rated each patient in terms of prediction of outcome after the initial intake. Table 27 shows that the therapist's initial prediction was a good indicator of the success of the therapeutic outcome. Ninety-seven percent of those patients with a good prognosis showed improvement and 41 percent of those patients with a poor prognosis showed improvement.

TABLE 27
Treatment Outcome by Therapist's Initial Prognosis

Treatment Outcome	*Good*	*Fair*	*Guarded*	*Poor*
Improved	97% (38)	80% (36)	67% (16)	41% (11)
Unimproved	3% (1)	20% (9)	33% (8)	59% (16)
Total	100% (39)	100% (45)	100% (24)	100% (27)

$X^2 = 28.71$; $df = 3$; $p < .001$.

TREATMENT OUTCOME AND DURATION OF THE THERAPEUTIC INTERVENTION

The nature of the therapeutic intervention varied because of need evidenced by the patient, but also because of limitations on the time of the therapists. Thus, some patients received crisis therapy only (from three to nine visits with the therapist for intensive treatment); other patients received crisis therapy plus referral to other agencies for further treatment; some who started in crisis therapy remained for long-term treatment. Many mental health clinicians feel strongly that long-term therapy may not be the best approach for every patient. Adjustive experiences at a time of crisis with prompt psychiatrically oriented intervention frequently enables patients to return to equilibrium. It was postulated that the length of treatment would not have a significant effect on the treatment outcome, provided that therapeutic intervention had been matched carefully to the patient's needs.

Thus, it can be seen that the percentage of improved cases in the short and long-term treatments are virtually identical: 86

TABLE 28
Treatment Outcome by Nature of Therapeutic Intervention

Treatment Outcome	*Crisis Intervention and Short-Term Therapy*	*Long-Term Therapy*
Improved	86% (25)	85% (35)
Unimproved	14% (4)	15% (6)
Total	100% (29)	100% (41)

$X^2 = .009$; $df = 1$; n.s.

and 85 percent. Also, it will be noted that the "rate of improvement" shown in table 28 is higher than for the total caseload as it does not include patients seen for study, intake, referral, or by consultation only. This may be seen as an indication that therapists with specific training and experience in working with deaf patients have an advantage over those without this additional expertise. Possibly this advantage lies in the increased confidence of the therapist which is reflected in increased confidence and trust on the part of the patient. The fact that one of the staff therapists is deaf may also have led to increased rapport with patients and their families.

Treatment Outcome and Diagnostic Category

Much better success was anticipated with the personality, behavior, and transient situational disorders than would be shown by those patients with diagnoses of psychosis, neurosis, or mental retardation. Table 29 confirms this assumption.

TABLE 29
Treatment Outcome by Diagnostic Category*

Treatment Outcome	*Psychoses Neuroses Mental Retardation*	*Personality, Transient Situational and Behavior Disorders*
Improved	56% (23)	83% (69)
Unimproved	44% (18)	17% (14)
Total	100% (41)	100% (83)

$X^2 = 9.11$; $df = 1$; $p < .01$.
* The number of cases (124) in this table represents those patients who were given APA diagnosis classifications.

Treatment Outcome and the Patient's Attempt to Control the Communication

During the pilot project we observed that many of our deaf patients attempted to control, directly or indirectly, the therapeutic situation by means of their communicative mode. Some might choose to sign too rapidly for the therapist to follow. Others who preferred to avoid communicating with the therapist at a particular time or on a particular topic might close their eyes, turn their back, or look away from the therapist. This is particularly likely to occur among children, and while with a resistant hearing child, auditory communication can continue, with deaf children who communicate visually, communication can be shut off entirely.

As an index of communicative resistance, a patient was classed as flexible if he was willing to "adapt" his communicative modes to the therapist's abilities, and did not often attempt to "cut off" visual communication. If a patient did cut off visual communication and/or attempt to "control" the therapist by his communication mode he was classed as rigid. It was predicted that flexibility in communication would be related to the successful outcome of therapy. Table 30 shows that this prediction was supported by the data.

A much higher proportion of the patients classified as "flexible" improved during the course of therapy, as compared to those judged as "rigid." Interestingly enough, thirty-six of the forty-seven patients (75 percent) who attempted to control the therapist with their communicative mode were judged to have a severe disability at intake.

TABLE 30
Treatment Outcome by Patient's Use of Communication to Control Therapist

Treatment Outcome	*Flexible*	*Rigid*
Improved	92% (55)	62% (29)
Unimproved	8% (5)	38% (18)
Total	100% (60)	100% (47)

$X^2 = 12.28$; $df = 1$; $p < .001$.

SUMMARY AND CONCLUSION

Mental health service has been provided by the project to deaf persons and members of their families representing all age ranges, social backgrounds, modes of communication, and emotional-behavioral-situational problems. The 215 requests for service during the four-year grant period have been reviewed in terms of problems presented, service offered, and the manner in which the specific handicap of deafness shapes both the problems and the treatment. Referring sources comprise a wide spectrum of community agencies that recognize the value of our program in gaining either direct or indirect services for their clients or themselves. In addition to meeting requests with appropriate professional attention, the clinical program has demonstrated the extent of need for service that is specifically oriented to deafness. Our focus on understanding deafness and on helping those for whom it is a problem has enabled others—parents and professionals alike—to cope better with its complexity. Thus, those persons provided service include not only the identified patients, but collateral family members and other members of the community relevant to the treatment plan. As we become known to the larger community as well as the deaf community, more deaf patients can avail themselves of our specialized services.

All of our cases have in common the deafness, or suspected deafness, of one family member. Problems requiring help tend to cluster in certain configurations at various age levels, according to the developmental stress involved. Among young children there are often multiple handicaps related to behavior and learning; older children present problems of self-identity and emancipation; among adults there are difficulties of social adjustment in job and marriage. Family context is relevant at all ages, as parents and other family members experience stress in regard to deafness. For their needs as well as the needs of the patient, they enter into the treatment program. We feel that our policy in this regard contributes significantly to accomplishing effective service.

In response to the need for professional help for deaf children and adults, which is insufficiently available elsewhere, our staff has employed a broad repertoire of mental health skills. Our approach encompasses aspects of many helping fields: psychiatry, social work, psychology, and education. With prevention of disability our goal, and at whatever level of intervention we feel may best suit the needs of a given case, we have chosen an eclectic rather than traditional psychotherapeutic role.

Assessment by our staff regarding improvement of the patients referred to us has shown favorable movement in 75 percent of the cases. Our criteria for successful treatment have been positive behavioral and situational change. Our experience shows that early intervention, important in the preventive context, represents the best investment of time and energy. As expected, improvement varies inversely with the severity of the disorder. Our studies also indicate that therapists with specific training and experience in working with deafness may have an advantage over those without this additional expertise. The therapists' understanding of the dynamics of deafness as well as their proficiency in the communicative mode of the deaf contributes to a relationship of confidence and trust, which in turn allows forward movement.

We have accepted for direct service as many cases referred to us as assessment of needs and time would permit. We have also offered consultation as a way of extending knowledge about deafness and of promoting provision of services elsewhere. Although consultation is effective in facilitating the work of others, our experience suggests that consultation must continue over a long period of time before comfort and skill are acquired by other nonspecialized professionals in this work to the degree necessary for them to do meaningful work. This points up two things: the desirability of our having sufficient staff and time to undertake more direct service, and the importance of providing specialized training in consultation to more mental health professionals in the problems of deafness and in work with the deaf.

The primary level of prevention can be implemented not only through the continuation of our own program, but also through identifying areas of unmet need for deaf children and adults and promoting the services and the skills that will best meet those needs. Resources such as placement homes, halfway houses, and extended day care services are critically needed. Within existing facilities more must be known about deafness; a good deal more of our time could therefore be spent profitably providing inservice training to large existing agencies such as welfare, probation, and schools.

In conclusion, the activity of the clinical program has been significant in three respects: (1) as a direct provider of services; (2) as a resource center for supplying intensive data about problems of the deaf as well as problems in working with the deaf; and (3) as a facilitator of community service.

9

The Preventive Aspects of Community Psychiatry: Mental Health Consultation and Education

> Primary prevention is the concern of all of the mental health professions, but the responsibility of no one group. Much preventive gold can be mined from clinicians and therapists by encouraging them to translate their clinical experience into programs with preventive possibilities.
> BOWER, 1963:836

Primary prevention refers to a process designed to reduce the rate of onset of emotional disorders in a given population,

> by counteracting the stressful or potentially harmful social conditions which produce mental illness. . . . A primary prevention program will necessarily involve significant members of the community and engage those institutions of our society which by virtue of their role have a crucial impact on the bulk of our citizenry . . . The principles of primary prevention are implemented by social agencies, schools and

Chapter 9 is by Hilde S. Schlesinger.

> churches, physicians and health professionals, local government leaders, and most important, the individual's family and other significant people in his life. (Visotsky, 1967:1537)

Mental health means many things to many people. It can mean the successful resolution of the life crises outlined in Chapter 2. Or it can be said to include the following criteria:

> Positive feeling toward the self, realistic perception of self and others, relatedness to people, relatedness to environment, independence, curiosity and creativity, recovery and coping strength. (Biber, 1961:326)

In general, mental health professionals are not the prime promoters of mental health. They can only provide corrective experiences to the individual who has lacked them. Or, in an indirect way, they can promote mental health by helping the individuals and agencies, parents and schools, that originally provide sensory and cognitive stimulation and foster healthy interpersonal relations. Perhaps the most useful contribution a mental health professional can make to an agency that desires help is to offer consultation. Consultation can be defined as a process by which an expert attempts to help a less knowledgeable consultee to solve a problem. Both parties must recognize that the expertise of the consultant is limited. In mental health consultation the expertise exists only in the area of the mental health of the "client," or on the mental health implications of the work situation in the agency. The expertise of the consultee in his own area of specialization must be accepted, and the consultee must always be free to accept or reject the suggestions of the consultant (Caplan, 1970). In general, in a task-oriented consultation, the consultee knows how to perform his task—how to be a teacher, or be a counselor, or a priest, or an audiologist better than the mental health expert does. The mental health expert, however, is able to give mental health education in his particular field of expertise—namely interpersonal relations, and individual psychosexual development. He can thus apply the expertise he may have both to the cases of specific clients and to personal relations within the agency, helping to reduce those tensions that exist in any work milieu without "judging" the individuals involved.

Mental health consultation is particularly important for agencies dealing with the deaf because the deaf child, invariably, and the deaf adult, frequently, come in contact with myriad individuals and agencies having different aims. The agencies range from physicians to speech and hearing centers, to hearing aid dealers, schools, departments of vocational rehabilitation, churches and others. The aims encompass such varied goals as acquisition of speech, promoting or preserving residual hearing, acquisition of academic and vocational skills, and spiritual guidance. Ultimately, of course, the aims are all congruent with mental health goals and indeed these agencies are (along with physicians) the prime providers and promoters of mental health, second only to the parents. The problem is to help coordinate their activities and to assist the deaf individual in threading his way through the maze.

Our staff has been asked to provide consultation to several agencies in the Bay Area. Here we will describe our experience in consultation with (1) a residential school for the deaf, (2) a city school system's program for deaf preschoolers, (3) a pilot project for deaf-blind children, and (4) professionals working with children in crisis, pediatricians, and psychiatric residents.

CONSULTATION AT A RESIDENTIAL SCHOOL

Before discussing our experience in consultation with a state residential school for deaf students, we should like to outline its history, structure, and problems. The school was established in Berkeley in 1860 and was initially supported by public and state funds. In 1866 the school was relocated on its present campus site and was incorporated into the California system of education. In 1970 the student body was comprised of about 500 pupils, with a waiting list of many more. The staff of 225 included 88 teachers, 50 counselors, and 86 supportive staff. It is a handsome Spanish-style campus, farflung over 130 acres, and strangely quiet for a school of 500 pupils ranging from 5 to 22 years old.

The administration includes a superintendent, an assistant superintendent, and a psychologist. The teaching staff is divided into six subgroups—according to the age of students—with a supervising teacher in each. A similar age-group division is found in the residential staff under the dean of students, consisting of supervisors and counselors. The ratio of children to each teacher is about eight or ten to one, a small ratio compared to public schools, but deplored by the staff as too high.

Our consultation at the school was requested in 1966. Consultation consisted of weekly two-hour meetings with either individuals or groups composed of teachers or counselors or both. The dean of students and/or the psychologist attended the group meetings as representatives of the teaching and/or residential staff. Some of the meetings consisted of lectures on such topics as psychological development of children, the usage or nonusage of drugs, the inherent difficulties of teaching or counseling, and mental health principles of importance in school settings.

Most of the meetings, however, consisted of actual consultation. This usually featured a description of "difficult" children by the staff, either individually or in a group and collaborative effort to find solutions to problems. As indicated previously, the proportion of difficult children at the school exceeds that in usual school settings. Valiant and frequently successful attempts were made to integrate these youngsters into the regular program of the school. On the whole, personnel had a good working knowledge of mental health factors in school settings. In general the school was effectively providing those educational, psychological and social services that are calculated to promote "mental health" in the growing child. Psychiatric referral was usually thoughtful and appropriate. Some of the youngsters presented to the consultant eventually found their way to direct clinical services. The description of their treatment can be found in the preceding chapter.

But the large number of disturbed youngsters and the paucity of trained staff suggested we should provide consultee-centered consultation to teachers and counselors at the school. While consultee-centered case consultation relates to the management of a particular client-student, it focuses primarily on the reasons for the consultee's difficulty in the management of the student. Four major difficulties can interfere with a consultee's ability to deal adequately with the mental health problems of his pupils:

> Lack of understanding of the psychological factors in the case, lack of skill or resources to deal with the problem, lack of confidence and self-esteem, and lack of professional objectivity. (Caplan, 1964)

The first three reasons for requesting mental health consultation did not differ either in number or content from the requests of teachers from other schools. Consultation involving these three types of problems is of sufficient interest to warrant further discussion through case examples later in this chapter. But the most typical of the requests from the school for the deaf involved the fourth problem—lack of objectivity. This difficulty can result from individual idiosyncrasies or from idiosyncratic perceptions inherent in the entire work milieu. We shall focus on the latter, in the belief that it has the greatest potential importance for primary prevention.

In analyzing the idiosyncratic perceptions of the work milieu we found that in the school for the deaf, as in any system, the staff is: (1) subjected to certain environmental stresses; (2) prey to certain intrastaff conflicts; and (3) possessed of certain stereotypes about each other, the students and the students' parents.

Stresses Inherent in a Milieu

The work milieu of a residential school for the deaf was characterized by a school superintendent as early as 1902 as breeding "provincialism and despair." This might be said to be true at present as well.

Provincialism, as observed by the consultant, took the form of a firmly held belief that only teachers of the deaf could really help the deaf. This attitude was held tenaciously by many teachers and was modified only slowly through the course of many successful consultations. The administration did not share this attitude, as evidenced by their sanction of our entry into the school. However, this widely held belief has probably delayed the participation of behavioral scientists in change designed to ameliorate the environment of the deaf.

Provincialism could also be seen in the relatively infrequent participation of teachers of the deaf in other collaborative educational events and delayed the free interchange between teachers of the deaf and those of other "exceptional children," thus depriving both groups of potentially fruitful resources.

Despair was manifested in the disappointment over the levels of achievement attained by the pupils. There were frequent discrepancies between anticipated and actual levels of achievement. The anticipated levels were frequently governed by teachers' expectations formed at training institutions. Many of the young teachers had attended training institutions geared to particularly high levels of student achievement and found it hard to adjust to average or below average performance. Many of these teachers reacted to poor pupil performance with guilt and anger.

Despair was also, paradoxically, produced by levels of expectations that were too low. Some teachers were so convinced that they were dealing with noneducable children that they despaired of positive achievements. This despair could arise from unrealistic expectation. It could also arise in reaction to those students whose ability was felt to be normal, even superior, but whose achievement was lowered by emotional disturbance. Consultation enabled the teachers to reach more realistic levels of expectation and a greater clarification of their teaching goals. With a reduction in the guilt and anger released by nonproductive students, the teachers were more relaxed and freer to teach more productively.

Competition was another stress frequently felt in the work setting. Competition among different schools for the deaf appears to be keen and tends to be measured, among other things, by the number of successful candidates to Gallaudet College and to the National Technical Institute for the Deaf. This competition produced a marked conflict in the staff. On the one hand they wanted to have a large number of successful graduates, but on the other hand they were interested in helping a wide variety of multiply handicapped youngsters whose academic future was dim. Consultation in this case only clarified the underlying problem since admission to the school was considered to be a purely administrative function. The school indicated, however, that they were more willing and able to admit and keep certain previously "unacceptable" youngsters with the help of the consultant.

Conflicts in the Work Milieu

Conflicts among adult caretakers can have a direct influence on those who depend on them. Psychiatric literature abounds with examples of conflicts between parents, particularly covert conflicts, placing the child in the untenable position of having to perform two diametrically opposed behaviors to fulfill two contradictory sets of expectations. It seems clear that the child, dependent as he is on the love and care of adults, will initially work hard to please them. But when pleasing one adult invariably displeases another, the child's behavior reflects the adult conflict. He may then become erratic in his attempts to please, or he may withdraw, never really expecting that his behavior can be pleasing to anyone in his environment.

Psychiatric literature also has many examples showing that children, and others who continue to depend on significant adults, will attempt to mirror the behavior that they have encountered in adult models with which they are familiar (Haley, 1962). Having reproduced the conflicted behavior, the children do not know what to do about it. Thus when adults in a work setting have conflicts, they can reactivate in the child the old pattern of conflict between the parents; when these conflicts are resolved between the adults, the child can resume his freedom to grow. Stanton and Schwartz (1954) have found such results in psychiatric hospitals, and we have noted them in the school.

Two of the conflicts present in the school were seen by the consultant as most important to the welfare of the pupils and also most amenable to change. One was a frequently expressed conflict between teachers and counselors. Both groups felt that their ministrations were "really" the most important and saw little or no value in the work of the other group. This tension was aggravated by existing or perceived status differences between the two disciplines. This conflict was partially resolved over the years of consultation by several processes. Teachers and counselors were invited to joint consultation sessions in which they gradually recognized, without the explicit intervention of the consultant, that indeed both groups were important to the child in question. Their conflicts, which were primarily covert, were brought out into the open, to the immense relief of the combatants, who increasingly became collaborators in the task of caring for the child. Incidentally, the status of the counselors was raised by some administrative moves which raised their salary and their accompanying titles.

The other ubiquitous conflict was between the adherents of the oral and manual methods of instructing the deaf child. Most professionals in the school clearly aligned themselves on one side of the conflict or the other. Most saw the controversy as an either/or question. Belief in a methodology was invariably more than an intellectually held tenet; it became a strongly emotionally invested crusade. As in other crusades it was accompanied by a dislike growing into hatred and devaluation of the opponent. Again psychiatric literature suggests that a specific technique may not be the only crucial variable and that parents (or other adults) can disagree about behavior provided they have a modicum of respect for each other. Talking about a child patient, one psychiatrist states that:

> When the parents were emotionally close, they could do no wrong in their management of the patient. The patient responded well to firmness, permissiveness, punishment, "talking it out," or any other management approach. When the parents were "emotionally divorced," all "management approaches" were unsuccessful. (Bowen, 1959:370)

We are postulating that the deaf child is frequently surrounded by adults who are "emotionally divorced," and that the use or nonuse of sign language becomes one of the prime reasons for the divorce. One youngster referred by the school and seen at our center for therapy illustrated this quite clearly.

> The play therapy room contained a large blackboard and the six-year-old youngster undoubtedly saw the therapist as the teacher. He remained fearful, immobile, with his hands at his sides, and gave no indication of understanding directions given to him in sign language. A few minutes later, the therapist encountered the youngster in front of the food machines at the clinic, and the same youngster now signed freely. Consultation about this youngster indicated that his teacher had strong inhibitions against signing, while his counselors encouraged it. Each professional clearly indicated his disapproval of the other. The child had apparently incorporated the conflict to the extent that blackboards meant "teacher and no signing," while food machines indicated "counselors and permissible signing." However, this switching was accompanied by marked fearfulness, inhibition of learning, and impulsiveness. Consultation reduced the conflict between teacher and counselor. Although neither changed methodological allegiance they

> reached a truce in which each respected the other's behavior. This change was followed by marked relaxation on the part of the youngster.

In summary, we found that covert conflict with lack of respect for the opponent is more noxious than clearly expressed differences of opinion held with a modicum of respect.

Stereotypes in the Work Milieu

Caplan (1970) refers to stereotypes as distortions of reality in which consultees act by placing certain of their charges into some "initial category" which must inexorably lead to an "inevitable outcome." Thus some teachers and counselors felt deeply that deafness affects all aspects of life and the inevitable outcome of deafness was a poorly functioning, immature human being. Others felt that deafness does not in any way affect normal functioning, and that deaf people could be like others in all respects. One stereotype about deafness—the belief that all deaf people end up being dependent—can be seen in the following consultation vignette:

> An impulsive group of young boys was seen as destructive and lazy. The counselors felt that these boys would be helped by being forced to perform clean-up duties without adult help, but with a surplus of adult supervision "in order to make them more independent." However, the maneuver was not effective and the youngsters worked less and less as the counselors demanded more and more. The consultant asked what would happen if the boys were helped rather than supervised and this question enabled the counselors to act collaboratively with the pupils which in turn permitted the youngsters to act more independently.

Stereotypes about teachers' roles also abounded. Teachers and counselors expected themselves to be everything to the deaf child—educator, surrogate parent, psychiatrist, friend, nurse, etc. They also expected that an understanding of psychodynamic principles would produce immediate and dramatic results. Good teaching was defined to include helping all children at all times, socializing the children, and helping the parents with personal problems. Some shared impossible ideals of the sort found in teachers by Parker (1962):

> Anger is always unprofessional; understanding of a problem is always followed by an immediate solution; permissiveness is good, authoritarianism is bad (or the other way around); teachers and counselors should always be able to help any child at any time.

A stereotype held by many teachers, and by teachers and counselors for the deaf, is that of the always loving, patient adult who either does not experience feelings of anger, or at least disguises them. But when a person tries to hide an attitude or feeling, the impact of the hidden attitude upon others is apt to be even greater than it would be if the attitude had been openly expressed (Parker, 1962). Consultation thus focused on a clearer understanding of the feeling of anger occurring in the teaching or counseling process.

The most common kinds of anger directed at a child fall into two categories: the first—realistic anger—stems from provocative behavior on the part of the child who places himself or others in immediate danger, who painfully attacks another, or who disrupts necessary activities. These anger-provoking behaviors are generally felt to be purposeful and controllable on the part of the child. The second kind of anger is displaced anger: that is, anger originally directed toward other counselors or teachers or parents and displaced onto the child. Frustrations and feelings of helplessness about the child's problems produce anger and make the child seem unlovable. Feeling unloved by the child also arouses the ire of the adults who must work with him.

Consultation focuses on the acceptance of feelings and on tracing their realistic etiology. Displaced anger can be refocused against the real source, with subsequent resolution of the conflict. If adults feel that they cannot love a child they can be helped to overcome their guilt. In both cases—realistic and displaced anger—a clear, nonhurtful expression of anger can be seen as helpful to the child and to the staff. Incidentally, this clarification of the anger experienced by the teachers provided new avenues of helping the students to express their anger more acceptably. This proved to be an important by-product of consultation, since deaf pupils deprived of adequate words to express anger frequently resort to unacceptable explosive behavior which in turn provokes revengeful behavior on the part of the adults.

We worked on dispelling the stereotype of the always helpful teacher or counselor by clarifying role definitions. The teacher's greatest contribution to mental health was clearly defined as her role of teaching, increasing the child's skills rather than solving his emotional problems psychotherapeutically. The counselor's main role was to enable the child to acquire those skills necessary in home (or surrogate home) settings: self-help skills and skills involved in recreational activities. All consultations were task-oriented, focusing on the specific task at hand rather than on the child's global intrapsychic difficulties. For example:

> An activity particularly distressing to school personnel was the misbehavior of several youngsters in the dining room. This misbehavior involved a creative, but unappetizing competition to see who could most accurately throw spinach onto the cathedral-like ceiling. This consultation involved two related themata. The counselors were clearly very angry at both the youngsters and the dean of students for this occurrence—at the youngsters because of their provocative behavior, and at the dean because he had come by, noted the event, and told the counselors that he expected this behavior to stop forthwith. The counselors, who had not been given alternatives, but had been scolded for their lack of intervention, felt increasingly helpless and threatened. The consultant acted as a model by stating her own feeling of helplessness in regard to such behavior, but added that maybe the entire consultee group—which included the dean—could indeed come up with alternatives. Alternatives sprung forth. The necessity of cleaning the ceiling and in some way involving the youngsters in the restitutive process were enumerated. Watching out for initial clues prior to spinach throwing and early intervention possibilities were clarified. The most important issue was that when the feelings had been expressed clearly, *approaches to the task* became paramount. At no instance was the focus on the guilt of the children (or the adults), but always on how the task could be better performed.

Teachers and counselors also generally felt that they could solve not only the child's intrapsychic difficulties, but also those of the parents who had contributed to these problems. Both groups of professionals harbored intense anger at the parents of difficult children, along with intense desires to reform them. Again, acceptance of their feelings toward the parents was encouraged, but at the same time their role with the parents was clearly redefined: the staff's main function was to listen uncritically to the parents' difficulties. The teacher's suggestions, if needed, were to focus on ways of improving the school work; the counselor's suggestions, if needed, were to focus on ways of improving behavior. This limited field of activity proved much more helpful to the staff than well-meaning but dangerous probings of the neurotic quality of child-parent relationships. Again, task orientation proved more helpful than pathology orientation.

This role clarification also helped to dispel the stereotypes held about parents, namely, that they were responsible for all the problems of their children and could easily and successfully change their attitudes when advised to do so. When parents did not take their advice kindly and immediately, the staff felt strong anger and expressed a denigration of the parents. The parents then withdrew, producing evergrowing anger on the part of the staff. Consultation focused on the difficulty of producing change in human beings solely on the basis of advice. Stress was placed on the existence of conflict in the parents, and the staff was helped to see that at least they must not increase the conflict in order not to hurt the child further. The consultant frequently drew on her clinical experience to demonstrate the slowness of human change. She also attempted to help the staff to see parents as people with problems rather than as "bad adults" who willfully interfered with the smooth functioning of the school. Very clearly, teachers often act toward their difficult students (or parents of students) as consultants have acted toward them (Berlin, 1967). In general, such reduction of the stresses and conflicts and dispelling of the stereotypes frequently resulted in spurts of development on the part of the children.

CONSULTATION TO A CITY SCHOOL SYSTEM FOR DEAF PRESCHOOLERS

Four to five teachers involved with preschoolers in the San Francisco School District had referred a large number of extremely disturbed youngsters to the project. Some of the youngsters were admitted to our clinical services, but because these children shared certain problems, we felt that consultation on a group basis might be useful to sustain other deaf children within the school system.

The chief complaints about the youngsters were nonachievement and aggressive, uncontrollable behavior. A considerable part of the consultative process was spent discussing techniques of controlling aggressive behavior: nonpunitive restraints, nipping potentially destructive behavior in the bud, and the differentiation between acceptable aggressive feelings and nonacceptable aggressive behavior. The problems of aggression are not unique to deaf children, of course. But there were three main themes that did pertain with special force to deaf children and were so frequently repeated as to be considered significant.

The "Ignorant Parents"

Most of the teachers were obviously middle class, while most of the children came from so-called working class families. Most of the teachers had great difficulties seeing the working class parents as potentially helpful allies in the cause of education. They felt they could not engage the parents in meaningful interchange. They frequently responded to the parents as ignorant people who needed to be taught, and the teaching had a supercilious flavor. The parents predictably reacted by withdrawing from contact with the teachers until they could be accepted as adequate, or at least potentially adequate, human beings.

The Depreciation of Deaf People by Others

Some of the classes for deaf children were held in a dilapidated building generally considered inferior by both parents and teachers. Serious attempts were made by the school board to integrate the youngsters into more pleasant and effective surroundings. However, the number of changes and the uncertainty about the changes were frequently seen by the teachers as a symbolic depreciation of deaf people by society at large, with an accompanying devaluation of their efforts.

Endorsement of Oral Communication Without Adequate Facilities for the Implementation

All the teachers sincerely believed in the effectiveness of oralism for teaching all deaf youngsters. Since none of the parents involved were deaf, the usage or nonusuage of sign language never came up for discussion. But although the teachers held such beliefs, both their training and the equipment available were clearly inadequate for optimal implementation. Concomitant arrangements were made for further training in audiology for the teachers and more adequate testing of the children. Serious attempts were also made to bring the auditory equipment in the classes up to par.

Again, the focus of the consultation was task oriented: namely to demonstrate that effective teaching can proceed even if parents at first are seen as uninvolved; that an effective teacher can proceed even if others feel that deafness is "bad"; and finally that in order for effective teaching to proceed, the teachers must know the full range of techniques and must have adequate facilities for their implementation. At all times it was recognized, however, that the feelings of helplessness engendered by uncooperative parents, discrimination against deafness, and students with learning problems, were indeed understandable and acceptable.

CONSULTATION AT A PRESCHOOL PROGRAM FOR DEAF-BLIND CHILDREN [1]

Supported by a two-year federal grant and codirected by members of the Special Education faculty of San Francisco State College, the Deaf-Blind Preschool in Hayward had nine children enrolled, ages three to six, with widely varying degrees of multiple handicaps in vision and hearing. Most of the referrals to the school came from the Variety Club Blind Babies Foundation, a private organization serving fifty-five countries in northern and central California.

The main objectives of the program were to serve as a teacher training center and as a service center for deaf-blind children; to observe the educational needs of this group of multiply handicapped children; and to develop suitable teaching methods and curricula to meet these needs. The staff consisted of two codirectors, one trained in deaf education, one in education for the visually handicapped; a head teacher; an assistant

1. This section was written by Winifred DeVos, A.C.S.W., who served as consultant to the preschool program described.

teacher; and student teachers from San Francisco State College. Parents of the children also participated.

In the second year of the two-year program, our staff was requested to provide consultation about behavior problems of some of the children. One child was hitting himself, and his parents had felt obliged to fit him with a restraint jacket; another was aimlessly pacing around the room or compulsively drumming on objects. Consultation was addressed to such specific case-oriented problems, but was also focused on the staff's attitudes toward such problems, as well as toward problems of overall program planning. The consultant spent one half-day a week at the facility, combining observation of the children and staff-parent interaction with attendance at staff meetings and occasional discussions with parents.

One purpose of this consultation was to help these dedicated and sensitive teachers find further ways of individualizing care for each of their young pupils, for they require more attention than most singly handicapped children. Another aim was to help the staff become more comfortable in what is almost by definition an often hopeless and anxiety-producing situation.

Consultation has centered chiefly on three major areas:

Referral and Collaboration

With multiply handicapped youngsters such as these, it is often important to use the consultant's knowledge of the handicap and of community resources to refer parents and children for special help, most often psychiatric. Such recommendations were made. In addition, the whole problem of referral and, indeed, what help-seeking means to parents was explored with the staff—including the issue of parental autonomy and of parents' need to feel that a decision to seek additional help is their own decision—not something foisted on them by someone else. Although staff should not take on clinical tasks, neither should referral be used as an escape from school-focused parent contact.

Sometimes referral also requires that the program staff collaborate with outside agencies. So, for example, Carl, one of a set of twins, had been seen with Carl's twin brother, Bill, at a child study unit. The parents' distress over a possible diagnosis of autism soon was reflected in completely atypical hyperactive behavior by Carl; the consultant helped both the clinic workers and the school staff to exchange information and insights. It is hoped this collaborative success will serve as a model when other such issues of relations to outside agencies arise.

Clinical Diagnosis and Its Implications

While a mental health consultant is not to function as a diagnostician, she can help by insisting on the importance of keeping careful observations, of reviewing diagnostic records, of revising them in light of new experience with the child, and of finding the diagnostic gaps that exist and calling in substantive experts in this area to help fill the gaps. The mental health consultant can also respond to the staff's feelings of uncertainty and despair that grow out of diagnostic problems. She can raise with the staff questions like: How many imponderables exist in problems of multiple handicap? How many answers can workers in this field legitimately expect of themselves or of others? How long a period of professional help is needed to accomplish significant improvement? What are ultimately valid expectations?

Parent Involvement

The program's policy of parental participation in actual teaching was based on the notion that parents and staff—and ultimately, the child—have much to gain from a meaningful interchange. One goal of consultation was to emphasize the importance of enriching parental involvement by giving parents more explicit assignments, thus helping them to become more task oriented and less anxious. In their turn, as the staff have focused on helping to structure the program so parents' roles could be more clearly defined, they were able to introduce innovations in play activities and sequences.

In addition to helping parents become more usefully involved in the teaching program, the consultant was, of course, available for consultation with individual parents about the problems and expectations of their own children.

Because the program was slated to end at the close of the academic year, several problems were connected with its termination. Parents and teachers wondered about the progress and prognosis of children exposed to new teaching methods in a relatively new area of special education. In light of the termination and the mixed feelings it aroused, the staff with the help of the consultant, when requested, had an obligation to plan for the children; to summarize for the sponsoring agency; to define their accomplishments and raise unanswered questions; to share plans with the parents and to plan also for themselves.

CONSULTATIONS WITH PROFESSIONALS

Brief consultations were requested by a variety of professionals working with deaf children and adults in crisis situations. They illustrate a number of difficulties characteristic of working with the deaf.

Non-Achievement of Deaf Children

The teacher of an eight-year-old girl seen at our project requested consultation because this youngster was not participating at school. This teacher illustrated all the difficulties that Caplan (1964) described as interfering with a consultee's work and these difficulties bear discussion here.

LACK OF UNDERSTANDING OF THE PSYCHOLOGICAL FACTORS IN THE CASE

The youngster was a seriously emotionally disturbed child with massive negativism towards adults and peers and a withdrawn quality in her interactions. She was, nevertheless, particularly sensitive to events around her, but the teacher had stereotyped Josette as a child living in a shell, oblivious to events and persons around her. The consultant shared with the teacher similar examples of apparently withdrawn youngsters with exceeding sensitivity to others and the teacher was asked to observe Josette carefully for such evidence. Two days after this consultation the teacher wrote an exultant letter stating that Josette had asked about the absence of two classmates, revealing for the first time her awareness and her interest in others.

LACK OF SKILL AND RESOURCES

The teacher was relatively inexperienced in her field. She expressed fearfulness about "pushing" Josette because of the youngster's frequent outbursts. This fearfulness resulted in non-expectation of achievement on the part of the child. Taking these cues, Josette rarely did achieve. Consultation was directed at clarifying expectations and recognizing the danger of self-fulfilling prophecies about low achievement. The gratifying bursts of achievement on Josette's part, over a period of several months, led to a highly positive evaluation of the results of this consultation.

LACK OF CONFIDENCE AND SELF-ESTEEM

The school district had recently given positive sanction to the use of sign language, and although the teacher felt well-disposed toward it and had made arduous attempts at learning sign language, she considered herself vastly unsuccessful in using it. Upon being asked to demonstrate a teaching event with sign language, the teacher demonstrated to herself that she knew far more sign language than she realized. Upon this realization she was able to be more relaxed in her use of signs. When she was helped to recognize additionally that teachers were human and could be effective without having complete mastery of every technique, the teacher's stance became more self-confident.

LACK OF PROFESSIONAL OBJECTIVITY

This difficulty was most clearly demonstrated in the teacher's initial dislike of the child, which interfered with her use of her actual technical competencies. These negative feelings were expressed, clarified, and relieved. The consultant gave sanction to their existence.

Shock-Withdrawal-Paralysis

We had frequently remarked upon the fact that professionals competent in dealing with other problems and handicaps seem to lose their competencies when they deal with deaf clients. Two cases will be used to demonstrate this phenomenon:

> 1. Johnny's probation officer, Mr. O., competent and especially sensitive to the problems of adolescents, called the project office one day in near-panic. "I was assigned this deaf-and-dumb kid of seventeen who's in trouble for stealing cars. Will you take him off my hands?"

Since the project psychiatrist had worked with Mr. O. previously in cases involving hearing youngsters, she found this request surprising. In dealing with hearing youngsters, Mr. O. had always been able to collaborate with the psychiatrist without attempting to turn a case away. The psychiatrist suggested a conference to discuss the youngster's problems. Mr. O. came into the office in an angry mood, feeling strongly that it was impossible to work with this "deaf-and-dumb offender." The psychiatrist listened quietly, occasionally asking questions. "What is the youngster's name?" Mr. O. sheepishly admitted that he didn't know, that he had assumed the label "deaf-and-dumb" would be sufficient to identify him. "What happened the first time you saw him?" "I haven't seen him yet. I was told he wouldn't understand me."

The psychiatrist acknowledged it must, indeed, be difficult to do probationary work in the absence of usual avenues of communication. Substitute means of communication were discussed, such as using paper and pencil (which often does not occur to professionals unaccustomed to working with deaf clients), obtaining the services of an interpreter, and even the simple expedient of speaking more carefully than usual.

Mr. O. departed after telephoning the youngster's parents to set up an appointment. He felt somewhat more confident of his ability to deal with the case. At a second appointment for the consultation, Mr. O. entered exuberantly. "That Johnny is really smart," he said. "The label deaf-and-dumb doesn't fit him at all. But what plans can be made for a deaf delinquent?"

The psychiatrist asked what kind of plan might be formulated for a hearing boy in the same situation. Mr. O. outlined an excellent probation plan, then stopped with amazement. "There I go again, forgetting that Johnny is a youngster in trouble, not just a 'deaf-and-dumb' kid."

To Mr. O.'s surprise, the plan he had suggested

for a hearing boy was fully applicable to Johnny, despite his deafness.

2. Two welfare workers came for consultation about a particularly impulsive, manipulative, intelligent young deaf woman by whom they felt absolutely defeated. Consultation revealed that their usual techniques had not been used or did not stand them in good stead. For example, their deaf client invariably asked them for money, and the workers indicated that they had given her some on several occasions—something they indicated they would never do with their hearing clients. The deaf client frequently was late for her appointments or did not keep them at all. They described their prolonged but tense willingness to accept this behavior by repeatedly rescheduling appointments, and staying late after working hours. Again this kidglove treatment was not usually followed with their hearing clients. Interestingly enough, the following stereotype emerged: "Workers cannot be angry with poor handicapped clients." But as both sophisticated workers said this, they burst into gales of laughter, for they suddenly realized that they had been angry, but had attempted to hide or cover up the anger with extra gifts of time and money. With this recognition, their work with the young woman in question became easier and less conflict-riddled.

The Use of Hearing Aids

An audiologist requested consultation because a patient in his clinic was refusing the recommendation of a certain type of hearing aid. The youngster wanted a more esthetic but less effective hearing aid, while the audiologist was opting for the more functional aid. The audiologist was fearful that his usual recommendation might prove harmful to a youngster who was "psychiatrically disturbed." Consultation focused on the fact that youngsters—particularly disturbed youngsters—perform better when adults can feel confident about their opinions, firm in their expectations and able to transmit this confidence and firmness in a clear-cut, albeit kind way. The youngster was subsequently able to follow the audiologist's recommendations and is wearing the aid successfully.

The Use of Sign Language

Consultation about using or not using sign language took many forms. The author's general views about the mental health implications of sign language were developed in Chapters 3 and 4. They can be summarized, however, by stating that sign language is generally considered helpful in the development of deaf children when it is used with positive affect, without conflict, is accompanied by speech and auditory training and is used early before a feeling of communicative impotence occurs between mother and child.

> A teacher who had initially felt comfortable and effective with most of her deaf students and with the oral method suddenly encountered a deaf youngster of deaf parents. The youngster who had at first appeared alert and well adjusted changed drastically in behavior and intellectual achievement after several months in school. His speech achievement had never been up to the standard of his development in other areas and when speech became his only acceptable mode of communication he developed a failure syndrome in all subjects. The teacher felt very uncomfortable and requested help from the consultant. She had entertained and rejected the notion of using sign language sub rosa. She had considered taking the youngster aside and signing to him out of view of the other children. Neither of these alternatives was acceptable to her, and she did not know how to proceed. The teacher indicated that she would like to use sign language with this pupil, but felt hampered because of school regulations. The consultant agreed that this youngster appeared to need resumption of a suddenly forbidden means of communication to regain his former equilibrium. Consultation focused on the theme that such a "mental health prescription" could not be effective unless sanctioned by school officials. The teacher shared her concerns and the consultant's opinion with her supervisor who agreed to the open use of sign

language in this case. The youngster subsequently was able to regain his former state of adjustment and learning ability.

The administrator of a school district located about fifty miles from the project office requested consultation about the introduction of sign language in district classes for deaf children. This policy change had been requested by a parents' group, but was opposed by some of the teachers. The consultant made it clear that she would be happy to share project research results and clinical experiences, but that she felt strongly the actual decision must be an administrative one. Her role as a consultant was to share experiences, to suggest some of the difficulties that might accompany either a decision to change or a decision not to change. Again, some of the same principles of mental health discussed previously were utilized: that conflict among teachers, parents and administrators creates difficulties for the children in their care; that if a change was to be forthcoming, both teachers and parents would need help during the transition period; that mutual respect and understanding was extremely important in any potential conflict situation. The school administrator decided to begin one experimental class using the combined method (sign language and fingerspelling used simultaneously with speech). A teacher with previous experience and enthusiastic commitment was employed for the special class. The class was not designed for children believed incapable of achieving speech and lipreading skills, so discouragement and failure did not permeate the atmosphere. To date, the experiment has met with enthusiasm, and all those involved are extremely pleased with the children's progress. A second similar class has been inaugurated.

Consultation with Pediatricians

An arrangement was reached with the University of California San Francisco Medical Center whereby all pediatric residents would experience working with deaf children in order to increase medical interest in and knowledge about deafness. The consultation took two forms; one general meeting was held with each rotating group of residents (about 10 each, for a total of 30) and a videotape of our work with deaf patients was shown and discussed. Such a discussion usually focused on the following themata: early diagnosis and the need to listen to parental concern, the impact of deafness on cognitive and psychological development, the need for parental support at the time of diagnosis and, subsequently, the need to collaborate with other professionals throughout the life span of the deaf patient. Attempts were made to provide one "deaf family" to each pediatrician rotating through the service to acquaint the young physician with the range of diagnostic, therapeutic and prognostic problems encountered in the life of a deaf child.

Consultation with Trainees at the Langley Porter Neuropsychiatric Institute

A similar arrangement was also made with the Langley Porter Neuropsychiatric Institute, Children's Service, whereby some social work trainees, some general psychiatric residents and all child psychiatry fellows were provided the experience of working with one deaf child and his family. It was interesting to note that every trainee so involved expressed initial reluctance or fearfulness about the deafness of his prospective patient. All had prior experience with mute schizophrenic children, but deafness was "different." The fright expressed was identical whether the youngsters used sign language or not. One resident was consumed with anxious ruminations about encountering a deaf child. Another anxiously discussed what he considered the nonexistent chances of helping a deaf child. It is of some interest to note that the generalized fearfulness was usually associated with frustration at not being understood by the child, rather than at not understanding him.

Exposure to the child and his parents and knowledge gained about deafness enabled the residents to use their competencies more fully and to envision deaf youngsters as potential future patients.

SUMMARY

We have attempted to demonstrate the range and usefulness of consultations possible in the area of psychiatry for the deaf. We feel that many of the problems that have been identified in this work are amenable to early intervention. Professionals working with the deaf can benefit from contact with mental health consultants, and mental health professionals need to be exposed to the field of deafness to increase their knowledge and decrease their fear. Optimal early intervention can have a vast impact in preventing the disorders of living so frequently found among deaf individuals.

10

A Model Program of Community Psychiatry for a Deaf Population

The previous chapters have dealt with various aspects of our research on the incidence of mental health problems among deaf students, selected approaches to therapy with deaf patients, developmental studies of language and behavior in deaf children. We have noted that despite the problems of definition and measurement, the incidence of mental health problems is considerably greater in the deaf community than in the total population. Emotional problems at the residential school we studied were five times the expected rate. Our developmental studies indicate some ways in which these problems may evolve. The research on therapy suggests some approaches to dealing with these and related problems.

In this last chapter we should like to propose a model that will incorporate our findings in the form of policy recommendations for community psychiatry for the deaf. We have already discussed the scope and goals of community psychiatry at some length. We emphasized the three levels of prevention—primary, secondary, and tertiary—and pointed out the need for all three types in dealing with deaf individuals and their families in the larger community. While primary prevention is the unique aspect of a program of community psychiatry, an essential part is still the traditional direct services to individuals at the levels of secondary and tertiary prevention.

Chapter 10 is by Hilde S. Schlesinger and Kathryn P. Meadow.

Within this general framework, we shall offer both a conceptual and working model of a program of community psychiatry for the deaf. We will describe the eight ingredients of any comprehensive community psychiatry program as delineated by Hume (1966). In discussing each of these components, we shall give illustrative examples based on our experiences with special emphasis on the preventive aspect of each component as related to a deaf population. The eight components of what we believe to be a model program are:

1. clinical services
2. collaboration with other agencies
3. mental health consultation
4. research
5. community organization
6. public education
7. administration
8. staff development and in-service training

CLINICAL SERVICES FOR DEAF INDIVIDUALS AND THEIR FAMILIES

Clinical services for deaf persons were nonexistent in California until late 1967 when the program at Langley Porter was initiated. The deaf had not formerly been recognized as a group needing specialized mental health services. New York, Illinois, and the District of Columbia also provide specialized services. Each program has reported a deluge of demands for services as the backlog of need responded to an opening floodgate. Our experience has been similar. The clinical staff consists of the project director, who is a child psychiatrist, and two psychiatric social workers. All devote only a portion of their time to the project and have been unable to keep pace with requests for treatment, which have come from twenty-one counties in California and from several additional western states. Requests for service include a wide range of demands resulting from the previous vacuum. Some patients came with a history of many prior agency contacts experienced as fruitless, frustrating, or ambiguous. Some were seeking a panacea for their problems that was nonexistent within the framework of medical, educational, or mental health knowledge.

Our clinical and developmental research has convinced us the ability to provide clinical services to a deaf population depends upon a broad understanding of the environmental and developmental stresses to which deaf individuals and their families are subjected. A willingness to make therapeutic contacts in a wide range of communicative modes is required. In working with many clients, a command of sign language is helpful. With some, indeed, sign language is imperative—either used directly or through interpreters. More important than the ability to communicate manually is the therapist's acceptance of unusual methods of communication, and a willingness to work with persons whose communicative abilities—in any medium—may be extremely limited. For professionals whose chief stock-in-trade is the spoken language, this requirement can impose a real strain. This may help to account for the paucity of clinical services for deaf clients. However, even psychiatrists who are accustomed to working with children with communication disorders have been reluctant to work with deaf children.

During the four years of the project's existence 215 identified patients were referred to the clinical staff. Rehabilitation, which is conceptualized as "tertiary prevention" by community psychiatrists, was the goal for 28 percent of these persons. Illustrations of three cases of such tertiary prevention follow:

> Ralph, age 18, is a profoundly deaf teenager with severe behavioral disturbances including stealing, lying and sexual acting-out. His dismissal from school could not be avoided. However, intensive weekly therapy and collaboration with innumerable agencies (ten conferences) enabled this youngster to go through job training successfully.
>
> Maurice, age 21, has been followed by various psychiatric facilities since he was 4 years old, in an attempt to obtain a differential diagnosis between deafness and schizophrenia. Although the differential diagnosis is still not clear, psychiatric support has enabled Maurice to finish school and work training.
>
> Jonathan, age 19, discharged from school because of florid psychotic manifestations, illustrates a less successful case of therapeutic intervention. Hospitalization was considered to be necessary, but unfortunately Jonathan was sent to a hospital in which the staff was unfamiliar with the problems of deafness. Jonathan's total inability to use spoken communication, and the staff's total inability to use sign language prolonged his hospital stay unnecessarily. It was even-

tually possible to have him discharged, however, and his therapy (conducted in sign language) is continuing at our center. He has been able to obtain gainful employment.

Jonathan's case illustrates the acute need for a facility for inpatient treatment of deaf persons on the west coast. Several pioneer efforts to provide inpatient settings for deaf populations have proved successful in New York, Washington, D.C., and Chicago. All these projects have emphasized the need for grouping deaf patients together so they may be served by a staff trained both in knowledge about deafness and in manual communication.

Secondary prevention, characterized by early identification of disorder and prompt referral for treatment, was the goal for about 50 percent of identified patients seen during the four years of the project. Families with young children have accounted for an increasing proportion of the referrals. Our work with children under eighteen typically also includes seeing both parents individually. The parents in this group are characterized by massive anxiety regarding the deafness itself, the developmental effects of deafness, the incipient emotional disorder, and/or their own feelings of guilt and sorrow. The high incidence of these feelings among parents of young deaf children, compared with the frequent apathy of the parents of deaf adolescents, permitted early intervention and positive shifts of parental feeling toward the child with a subsequent improvement in the parent-child relationship. These parents of younger children were also characterized by overwhelming feelings of helplessness, frequently provoked by overanxious attempts to provide optimal assistance for their child. Parents may well be bewildered and immobilized, or simply expected to do too much, in tracking down a multiplicity of avenues for help.

Examples of some successful cases of secondary prevention would include these two:

Nancy is a 5-year-old youngster with only a moderate hearing loss. However, her emotional problems were severe enough to interfere actively with her utilization of any audiological aids or speech therapy. She therefore functioned as a profoundly deaf child. A year of psychotherapy brought the following prediction from her speech teacher: "Nancy will be able to participate in regular classes due to her increased utilization of hearing and her advances in speech."

Lee, age 3, was a severely neglected child who had been misdiagnosed as mentally retarded in early infancy. Project staff members were instrumental in clarifying the diagnosis of deafness and in helping the deaf foster parents to work with the youngster. Lee is showing indications of at least average, if not superior, intellectual potential after one year of monthly visits.

Our clinical work and our field research with younger children, their parents, and the professionals involved with them have been most helpful in providing insight into some of the shared hazardous circumstances which occur early in the life span of a deaf individual. These insights, in turn, have provided a basis for a framework for a possible program of primary prevention of mental disorders in the deaf, and have suggested important areas for research.

These commonly hazardous circumstances include a *general lack of information about deafness* among physicians, which prolongs the family crisis at the time of diagnosis of deafness. During this critical period, many parents report a lack of support from the medical profession because of misdiagnosis, false reassurance, or distorted and delayed treatment plans. *A bias against deafness* resulting in a subtle, persistent, and destructive idolizing of normality frequently interferes with adequate crisis resolution for both parents and professionals. *Conflicting advice from experts* due to a century-old battle regarding the optimal education for the deaf robs the parents of support and can precipitate a prolonged conflict. *Frequent absence of gratifying, reciprocal parent-child communication* in the early years may rob both parent and child of interpersonal relationships necessary for emotional growth and development. The investigation, alleviation, and elimination of these commonly hazardous life circumstances could help to reduce the life problems of deaf individuals and their families, and should be included in planning a program of primary prevention.

COLLABORATIVE SERVICES TO OTHER AGENCIES

As we have already noted, deafness is more than a medical diagnosis. Social, emotional, linguistic, and intellectual patterns combine to create multiple difficulties. Thus, the deaf individual requires services from a variety of disciplines. These include medicine, audiology, speech therapy, special education, vocational counseling, as well as services from agencies which do not specialize in deafness, such as welfare departments, courts, and probation departments. It has not been unusual to find that our patients have simultaneous contact with eight or more agencies or professionals. Unfortunately, the multiplicity of necessary agencies specializing in deafness has sometimes produced unintentional side effects.

> Mrs. S. had felt so submerged by the multiple requests of her son's eye doctor, ear doctor, audiologist, surgeon, orthodontist, hearing aid dealer, and teachers that she remained paralyzed for a period of several months after the diagnosis of deafness had been made. A frank and open discussion with the therapist of how overwhelming the numerous tasks were helped her to mobilize both time and financial resources for effective problem-solving.

In the case of the S. family, the parents had been bombarded with advice and instructions, but the suggestions were parallel and not conflicting. Often, however, different agencies will give opposing advice to parents, thus precipitating additional conflict within the family. Also, personnel in agencies that do not specialize in deafness sometimes have a subtle and pervasive fear of deafness that may prevent them from extending the same degree of help to the deaf client as to his hearing counterpart. Thus, an effective program of community psychiatry requires collaboration with other significant agencies in order to provide coordination of services, reduce possible fragmentation and redundancy, as well as reducing conflict between community agencies.

MENTAL HEALTH CONSULTATION AND EDUCATION

The third ingredient of a comprehensive program of community psychiatry is the provision of consultation and mental health education for nonpsychiatric agencies and professionals. Unlike a comprehensive program of psychiatric services for the broader community, that concerned with the deaf community will provide consultations to psychiatric as well as to nonpsychiatric agencies and professionals. For example, our staff members have helped psychiatric agencies to see that some modes of adaptation to deafness can represent realistic means of coping with hearing loss or with some crisis produced by the hearing defect, rather than as a neurotic solution on the part of the individual or the family. Some requests for help must be seen as realistic needs rather than neurotic needs, e.g., the use of a telephone is impossible without sophisticated electronic gadgets or the help of a hearing intermediary.

The process of consultation may vary from one practitioner to another, but it usually consists of (1) the diagnostic evaluation of a patient or client; (2) advice and direction to a consultee; or (3) the joint undertaking by consultee and consultant of a solution to a mental health problem encountered in the consultee's professional work setting or in his work with clients (Hume, 1966). Although the community psychiatrist may perform any of these three functions, he would probably choose the third alternative most frequently.

A considerable number of consultations conducted by the project's specialist in community psychiatry have been directed toward eradicating what we have called the "shock-withdrawal-paralysis" syndrome that occurs frequently when professionals or nonprofessionals are called upon to deal with deaf clients. A part of our work has been to try to understand the reasons for this reaction when professionals are faced with the need to communicate with a deaf person. We are concerned that an encounter between a deaf client and a hearing professional is often colored by feelings and attitudes that further impede an already difficult pattern of communication for both. When this happens, the human interaction that results tends to be uncomfortable and either to proceed at a level below potential, or not to proceed at all. The further investigation of this phenomenon would have both theoretical and practical value.

Other aspects of consultative work around deafness are more familiar. For example, the project director has been engaged in ongoing consultations with a residential school for the deaf since the inception of the program. This work consists of weekly consultative sessions with teachers and administrative staff.

We feel that the community psychiatrist can act as an agent

for social change in the area of education of the deaf, where conflict and distrust have existed for years. Many observers are dismayed by the slow rate of change in this field (in spite of research that has repeatedly demonstrated the lack of success among students taught by present methods). It may be that this is precisely the kind of situation where interpretation of research findings must be attempted on an individual face-to-face basis, rather than through the impersonal medium of professional journals. When the consultee regards the mental health consultant as a basically sympathetic noncombatant, research findings may become more acceptable and more closely related to immediate problems of mutual concern.

THE ROLE OF RESEARCH IN A PROGRAM OF COMMUNITY PSYCHIATRY FOR THE DEAF

Research is an important part of any comprehensive program of community psychiatry. When a program is directed at a specific population of deaf individuals, however, the research requirements are broader: basic research must be carried on in a model program for the deaf as well as the more customary applied or evaluative research. The need for basic research arises because there is still relatively little available knowledge on a number of aspects of the social, psychological, and cognitive consequences of deafness (Schlesinger, 1970).

Very little is known about the acquisition of sign language, which is used by a majority of deaf adults. Problems of child-rearing in families with deaf parents and hearing children have not been explored systematically. Additional information is needed on the effects of differing educational techniques, since the oral-manual controversy still rages in the field of education for the deaf after four hundred years (Levine, 1963) and is a major concern of parents of deaf children. No longitudinal study of the physical, cognitive, social-emotional development of deaf children has yet been conducted, apart from the one in which our group is currently engaged. (The study reported by Fiedler, 1969, focuses primarily on academic development of deaf children over a seven-year period.) Analogies between the cognitive and emotional functioning of deaf children and of "culturally disadvantaged" children is an area for future exploration. Also valuable would be a research-demonstration program to evaluate the possibilities of using "Headstart" curriculum materials and frequent teacher-psychiatrist consultations with preschool deaf children who are emotionally disturbed. The relative efficacy of individual psychotherapy, group psychotherapy, and mental health consultation for deaf persons would also be a useful research area. These are only a few of the necessary areas for research. We see such research as an integral part of any therapeutic or preventive effort, for, unless we know more about the vicissitudes and developmental crises of the deaf, we cannot hope to work effectively for the primary prevention of mental health problems.

COMMUNITY ORGANIZATION

The mental health community that can be organized for a comprehensive program of community psychiatry for the deaf includes the deaf individual, his family members, professionals specializing in deafness, and professionals specializing in mental health. Unfortunately, deaf individuals themselves have often been overlooked in past efforts at organization. Generally, the most effective programs are those that show the greatest rapprochement among professionals representing different disciplines. Our own efforts in this direction include an attempt to involve pediatric residents in caring for young deaf children so as to augment their knowledge about deafness. Also, attempts have been made to promote the formation of a mental health association of and for the deaf, and collaboration among professionals involved with deafness at different stages of the life span of the deaf individual.

DISSEMINATION OF INFORMATION TO THE PUBLIC

Lack of understanding of and information about deafness in the general community can contribute to an environment inimical to mental health in the deaf community. Thus, education of the general public is seen as a major task for a comprehensive program of community psychiatry which includes as one of its goals the primary prevention of mental disorders. Included in the "general public" are employers, medical and paramedical personnel, and those employed in communications media.

In our work to date, we have found the use of videotape to be especially effective in presenting problems related to mental health and deafness to the community at large. Visual presentations generally, of course, can be much more effective than either written papers or verbal lectures. However, the general public has so little contact with deaf individuals, especially with deaf children, that it is even more important to be able to communicate some of the flavor of behavioral patterns. The use of manual communication (or total communication) by parents and by teachers can be demonstrated much more effectively than it can be described.

Videotape is a more convenient means of capturing visual data than is film. Where resources and personnel are limited for this purpose, it is especially useful. Our staff have put together two composite tapes that have been helpful in illustrating our work. The possibilities in this area are unlimited (see Cottrell, 1971).

ADMINISTRATION OF A PROGRAM OF COMMUNITY PSYCHIATRY FOR THE DEAF

Administration of a comprehensive program involves the development of an understanding of the legal sanctions for its operation; sources of funding for staff and services; development of institutional liaisons; and planning for the expansion of demand in response to a new program. One characteristic of the deaf population that makes administration more difficult is the wide geographic distribution of those who may need mental health services. Thus, the 215 families served by our project staff to date came from twenty-one different California counties. We have found that administrative details involve a larger proportion of staff time than would a comparable program for a hearing population which has a smaller geographic base.

IN-SERVICE TRAINING OF STAFF

The final ingredient of a comprehensive program of community psychiatry is the ongoing training of staff members involved in the work. As for any staff, lectures by resident and visiting authorities in the same or related field, films, reviews of current literature are all important. We have scheduled such meetings regularly. Another important area for development among our staff members has been continuing classes in the use of sign language and fingerspelling.

SUMMARY

Thus, a model program of community psychiatry for a deaf population should include clinical services, collaboration with other agencies, mental health consultation, research, community organization, public education, as well as administration and staff development. Staff members working in such a program need special training in order to understand the language and the special needs of the deaf community. Professionals working with deaf individuals need to acquaint themselves with the manual sign language of the deaf, with the cultural factors, the conflicts, and the developmental stresses to which deaf individuals are subjected. They need also to understand, and be ready to try to reduce, the stigma attached to deafness by persons with normal hearing. Through such knowledge, training, and understanding, more cohesive, less fragmented services can be developed with the aim of reducing noxious conflicts and promoting optimal development for each deaf individual. Sound and sign need not conflict in the world of deaf children and adults.

Appendix A

SUPPLEMENTARY TABLES FOR CHAPTER 5

TABLE 1
Intercorrelation of Mother and Child Scenario Ratings Which are Significant at the .01 Level*
($N = 40$)

Ratings of Mothers	*Ratings of Child*	*r*
Permissive	Enjoys interaction	.476
Permissive	Proud in accomplishments	.434
Effective	Compliant	.765
Effective	Attentive	.533
Effective	Relaxed	.422
Effective	Enjoys interaction	.724
Effective	Happy	.533
Effective	Proud in accomplishments	.477
Nonintrusive	Enjoys interaction	.566
Nonintrusive	Proud in accomplishments	.494
Nondidactic	Enjoys interaction	.559
Nondidactic	Happy	.489
Nondidactic	Proud in accomplishments	.446
Creative	Compliant	.468
Creative	Attentive	.408
Creative	Relaxed	.423
Creative	Enjoys interaction	.676
Creative	Happy	.554
Creative	Proud in accomplishments	.424
Relaxed	Compliant	.403
Relaxed	Attentive	.469
Relaxed	Enjoys interaction	.673
Relaxed	Happy	.434
Relaxed	Proud in accomplishments	.464
Flexible	Compliant	.611
Flexible	Attentive	.444
Flexible	Enjoys interaction	.559

TABLE 1 (cont.)

Ratings of Mothers	*Ratings of Child*	*r*
Flexible	Happy	.447
Uses gestures	Compliant	.473
Uses gestures	Relaxed	.406
Uses gestures	Enjoys interaction	.630
Uses gestures	Happy	.540
Enjoys interaction	Compliant	.526
Enjoys interaction	Relaxed	.513
Enjoys interaction	Enjoys interaction	.751
Enjoys interaction	Happy	.643
Enjoys interaction	Proud in accomplishments	.538
Encouraging	Compliant	.585
Encouraging	Enjoys interaction	.510
Encouraging	Happy	.420
Encouraging	Proud in accomplishments	.458

* Correlations of .502 or above are significant at the .001 level.

TABLE 2

Intercorrelation of Maternal Ratings from Scenario Rating Scales
($N = 40$)

	Permis-sive	*Effec-tive*	*Non-intrusive*	*Non-didactic*	*Crea-tive*	*Re-laxed*	*Flex-ible*	*Use of gestures*	*Enjoyment of interaction*	*Encour-aging*
Permissive	1.000									
Effective	.509*	1.000								
Nonintrusive	.919*	.555*	1.000							
Nondidactic	.757*	.531*	.731*	1.000						
Creative	.459	.545*	.547*	.691*	1.000					
Relaxed	.684*	.587*	.757*	.726*	.839*	1.000				
Flexible	.799*	.611*	.765*	.705*	.568*	.656*	1.000			
Use of gestures	.382	.560*	.485	.586*	.829*	.735*	.502*	1.000		
Enjoyment of interaction	.390	.613*	.467	.537*	.678*	.632*	.485	.677*	1.000	
Encouraging	.446	.478	.488	.528*	.480	.459	.585*	.421	.794*	1.000

* $p < .001$.

TABLE 3

Intercorrelation of Child Ratings from Scenario Rating Scales

($N = 40$)

	Compliant	Independent	Attentive	Curious	Use of Gestures	Creative	Relaxed	Enjoyment of Interaction	Happy	Proud
Compliant	1.000									
Independent	.022	1.000								
Attentive	.446	−.333	1.000							
Curious	.141	.533*	−.045	1.000						
Use of gestures	.172	.525*	.300	.419	1.000					
Creative	.301	.667*	.136	.412	.470	1.000				
Relaxed	.334	.586*	.102	.641*	.620*	.533*	1.000			
Enjoyment of interaction	.522*	.212	.433	.479	.367	.522*	.706*	1.000		
Happy	.309	.435	.280	.564*	.628*	.446	.753*	.767*	1.000	
Proud	.311	.468	.269	.359	.461	.665*	.666*	.742*	.603*	1.000

* $p < .001$.

Appendix B

SUPPLEMENTARY TABLES FOR CHAPTER 6

TABLE 1
Characteristics of Deaf Children in Three Research Groups

	Group 1 Residential: Deaf Parents		*Group 2 Residential: Hearing Parents*		*Group 3 Day School: Hearing Parents*	
1. Sex	%	(*N*)	%	(*N*)	%	(*N*)
Girls	41	(24)	41	(24)	50	(37)
Boys	59	(34)	59	(34)	50	(37)
Total	100%	(58)	100%	(58)	100%	(74)
	$X^2 = 1.33$; n.s.					
2. Age	%	(*N*)	%	(*N*)	%	(*N*)
−13 years	62	(36)	57	(33)	73	(54)
13+ years	38	(22)	43	(25)	27	(20)
Total	100%	(58)	100%	(58)	100%	(74)
	$X^2 = 3.89$; $p < .10$					
3. IQ score[a]	%	(*N*)	%	(*N*)	%	(*N*)
−100	17	(10)	16	(9)	23	(11)
100–109	28	(16)	38	(22)	21	(10)
110–119	24	(14)	29	(17)	29	(14)
120–129	26	(15)	14	(8)	21	(10)
130+	5	(3)	3	(2)	6	(3)
Total	100%	(58)	100%	(58)	100%	(48)
Mean IQ	111.53		108.84		110.98	
	Kruskal-Wallis $H = 1.28$; n.s.					
4. Residual hearing[b]	%	(*N*)	%	(*N*)	%	(*N*)
60–70	5	(3)	5	(3)	8	(6)
71–80	17	(10)	19	(11)	19	(14)
81–90	22	(13)	36	(21)	24	(18)
91+	55	(32)	40	(23)	49	(36)
Total	99%	(58)	100%	(58)	100%	(74)
	Kruskal-Wallis $H = .55$; n.s.					

[a] From school records. Usual measure was performance portion of WISC.
[b] Average decibel loss at 500–1000–2000 cps.

TABLE 2

Mean School Achievement Test Scores, Grade Level, Reading, and Arithmetic (Groups 1 and 3)

Achievement Test	Group 1 (Residential—Deaf Parents) Mean*	S.D.	(N)	Group 3 (Day School) Mean*	S.D.	(N)	t	p
Grade level	56.23	23.83	(26)	51.95	19.55	(21)	.66	n.s.
Reading	57.38	28.13	(26)	52.85	13.76	(26)	.74	n.s.
Arithmetic	67.23	30.00	(26)	65.14	16.20	(22)	.29	n.s.

* In months.

TABLE 3

Mean School Achievement Test Scores, Grade Level Reading, and Arithmetic (Groups 2 and 3)

Achievement Test	Group 2 (Residential—Hearing Parents) Mean*	S.D.	(N)	Group 3 (Day School) Mean*	S.D.	(N)	t	p
Grade level	47.19	19.45	(26)	51.95	19.55	(21)	−.83	n.s.
Reading	45.88	21.95	(26)	52.85	13.76	(26)	−1.37	n.s.
Arithmetic	55.96	25.19	(26)	65.14	16.20	(22)	−1.47	n.s.

* In months.

TABLE 4

Mean School Achievement Test Scores by Age Level (Groups 1 and 3)

Achievement Test	Group 1 (Residential: Deaf Parents) Mean*	S.D.	(N)	Group 3 (Day School) Mean*	S.D.	(N)	t	p
Younger (−159 months)								
Grade level	42.73	14.32	(11)	50.18	7.41	(11)	−1.53	n.s.
Reading	39.91	12.29	(11)	48.38	10.63	(13)	−1.81	<.10
Arithmetic	45.91	17.18	(11)	58.92	17.72	(13)	−1.82	<.10
Older (159+ months)								
Grade level	66.13	24.89	(15)	53.90	27.93	(10)	1.15	n.s.
Reading	70.20	29.82	(15)	57.31	15.44	(13)	1.40	n.s.
Arithmetic	82.87	27.88	(15)	74.11	8.07	(9)	.91	n.s.

* In months.

TABLE 5
Mean School Achievement Test Scores by Age Level (Groups 2 and 3)

Achievement Test	Group 2 (Residential: Hearing Parents)			Group 3 (Day School)				
	*Mean**	*S.D.*	*(N)*	*Mean**	*S.D.*	*(N)*	*t*	*p*
Younger (−159 months)								
Grade level	34.10	8.94	(10)	50.18	7.41	(11)	−4.50	<.01
Reading	32.80	6.48	(10)	48.38	10.63	(13)	−4.08	<.01
Arithmetic	36.90	15.32	(10)	58.92	17.72	(13)	−3.13	<.01
Older (159+ months)								
Grade level	55.38	19.92	(16)	53.90	27.93	(10)	.16	n.s.
Reading	54.06	24.33	(16)	57.31	15.44	(13)	−.42	n.s.
Arithmetic	67.88	22.88	(16)	74.11	8.07	(9)	−.78	n.s.

* In months.

TABLE 6
Mean School Achievement Test Scores: Younger Day School Children (Group 3a without manual facility and Group 3b with some manual facility)

Achievement Test	Group 3a Day: Hearing Parents No Manual Skills			Group 3b Day: Hearing Parents Some Manual Skills				
	Mean	*S.D.*	*(N)*	*Mean*	*S.D.*	*(N)*	*t**	*p*
Grade level	45.60	2.79	(5)	54.00	7.28	(6)	2.37	<.05
Reading	43.14	9.76	(7)	52.83	6.74	(6)	2.27	<.05
Arithmetic	63.57	19.66	(7)	53.50	11.05	(6)	1.07	<.10

* *t*-test values are corrected for inequality of variance. (See Hays, 1963:322.)

Appendix C

RATING SCALE

I. Personal style and characteristics:

a. has strong sense of moral values—always honest and trustworthy.	lacks understanding or moral values—may cheat or lie when convenient.
b. generous—will almost always share what he has with others.	very selfish—refuses to share toys, books, other personal belongings.
c. almost always happy and cheerful: a "sunny disposition."	sad, morose, unhappy.
d. has extreme, almost "uncanny" ability to sense what others are thinking or feeling.	insensitive to the feelings of others; lacks empathy.
e. always responds to a situation with appropriate emotion: laughs, cries, smiles, frowns, etc., at times when occasion demands.	responds to situations in a highly inappropriate manner: always laughs, cries, smiles, frowns, etc., at the wrong times.
f. calm and placid; almost never has temper outbursts.	has frequent and uncontrolled outbursts of anger, temper tantrums.
g. almost always kind and considerate of others, both adults and peers; acts to make others feel better.	somewhat ruthless in hurting others, kicks, hits, teases; enjoys making others suffer.
h. has self-confidence; stands up for ideas and rights without fear.	fearful of others, gives in immediately when challenged, hesitates to assert self.

i. has good grasp of socially accepted behavior: good manners, personal habits.	either doesn't know or doesn't care about manners and habits: often rude or crude; socially unacceptable behavior.
j. has a strong feeling of personal worth and importance.	feels inferior; no feeling of being a worthwhile person.
k. exhibits appropriate sex-role characteristics: if a boy, is very masculine; if a girl, very feminine.	shows some sex-role confusion, i.e., if a boy, may have many "feminine" traits or interests; if a girl, many "masculine" traits or interests.

II. Communication skills and adjustment to deafness:

a. extremely good ability to communicate in writing (for age).	ability to communicate in writing rated far below that of peers (i.e., deaf children of about the same age).
b. has unusually good ability in speechreading (cf. age group).	almost completely lacking in speechreading skills.
c. unusually good oral abilities—shows promise of speaking very well.	has almost no intelligible speech; no aptitude; probably will never speak understandably.
d. uses fingerspelling with great facility; ahead of others in age group.	very poor at fingerspelling, either too slow or inaccurate.
e. can understand the fingerspelling of others very readily.	unable to get very much when other people fingerspell.
f. knows and understands a large vocabulary of signs; communicates well.	doesn't know many signs; unable to communicate in this manner.
g. never seems to be bothered by lack of ability to communicate.	is often frustrated by inability to make self understood.
h. is willing to try to communicate with hearing strangers; not bothered by shyness, fear, or sensitivity.	too shy or scared to try to communicate with hearing strangers.
i. has made very positive, realistic adjustment to deafness.	resents fact of deafness—bitter; doesn't accept.

III. Social relationships:

a. is gregarious, friendly, outgoing, likes to be with other people; sociable.	makes no effort to be with other people; withdrawn, shy, solitary.
b. is popular with classmates, sought as a friend.	unpopular with classmates; ignored or rejected.
c. is popular with adults.	unpopular with adults.

d. looks forward to new experiences; enjoys meeting new people.	fearful of meeting new people; afraid of new experiences.
e. is a good sport; can be a good loser.	a bad sport; poor loser.
f. almost always obeys the rules; follows instructions or demands of teachers and counselors.	disobedient; doesn't get along with people in authority; deliberately breaks rules.

IV. Intelligence and work performance:

a. appears to have extremely *high intellectual ability*.	quite dull; has *little intellectual ability*.
b. Makes highly *efficient use* of natural intelligence.	performs *far below* apparent ability.
c. *works very hard* on any task assigned; strives hard to do a good job.	refuses to put forth any effort; *lazy;* takes no pride in a job well done.
d. shows extremely *responsible* attitude; can be depended upon.	very *irresponsible;* can't be counted on to take any responsibility.
e. compared to peers, is quite *mature*—acts more grown up than they do.	compared to others in class or dorm group, is very *immature* for his age—acts much younger than peers.
f. quite independent; can think and act for himself; self-reliant.	demands attention and help constantly; dependent on others; makes unnecessary requests for assistance.

V. Physical health and appearance:

a. never seems to be ill; rarely misses school because of sickness.	often sick; has frequent colds, some more serious illnesses; misses school often for this reason.
b. almost never has accidents resulting in personal injury.	accident prone; often sent to nurse for first aid.
c. never complains about aches and pains—doesn't ask for unwarranted attention on health grounds.	complains constantly of lack of physical well-being; has many intangible ailments (headaches, stomach aches, etc.).
d. has unusually attractive physical appearance; is very pretty or handsome.	natural physical looks or appearance quite unattractive or unappealing.

e. always neat, well groomed, clothing, hands, nails, teeth, are clean.	messy, unkempt, slovenly; never neat and well groomed.
f. seems to feel pride and some vanity in appearance.	seems to be ashamed of own appearance.

VI. Family relationships and home environment:

a. family situation is stable: infrequent changes in home address.	family extremely unstable; moves frequently.
b. family situation is stable: parents, relatives, roomers don't move in and out of home.	parents or relatives or roomers frequently move in and out of home.
c. father warm, loving, accepting; displays affection often.	father appears to be unloving, rejecting; never shows overt affection.
d. mother appears to be warm, loving, accepting; displays affection often.	mother seems unloving, rejecting; never shows overt affection.
e. family always promptly provides for supplies, money, etc., for school needs.	family neglects to provide necessary supplies, clothing, money, or letters.
f. family encourages independence; expects child to help himself.	parents "over-protect" child; unwilling to encourage independence.
g. parents have good understanding of limitations and possibilities for deaf child.	parental expectations for child are unrealistic in terms of deafness: too much achievement is expected.
h. parents make an effort to sign or fingerspell at home; don't discourage manual communication.	parents refuse to attempt manual communication; discourage it.
i. general home atmosphere is warm, loving, calm.	general atmosphere of home is disagreeable, quarrelsome, unpleasant.
j. child enjoys his family; looks forward to home visits.	child dreads vacations and weekends; prefers school to home.

VII. Rater's judgment:

a. How well do you feel that you know this student?
b. Do you know the student's family?

Appendix D

SUPPLEMENTARY TABLE FOR CHAPTER 8

Distribution of Case Load by APA*
Diagnostic Categories and Condition
(numbers and percentages)

Diagnostic Categories	*APA*	*N*	%
Psychoses			
Schizophrenia			
Paranoid	295.3	6	
Latent	295.5	1	
Schizo-affective	295.7	1	
Childhood	295.8	14	
Paranoia	297.0	3	
Psychotic depressive	298.0	1	
Total		26	19%
Neuroses			
Depressive	300.4	5	4%
Personality Disorders			
Schizoid	301.2	7	
Obsessive-compulsive	301.4	1	
Antisocial	301.7	2	
Passive-aggressive	301.81	1	
Inadequate	301.82	9	
Total		20	15%
Special Symptoms			
Specific learning disorder	306.1	1	
Disorders of sleep	306.4	1	
Other	306.9	1	
Total		3	2%

(cont.)

Distribution of Case Load by APA*
Diagnostic Categories and Condition
(numbers and percentages)

Diagnostic Categories	*APA*	*N*	*%*
Transient situational			
Adjustment reaction of childhood	307.1	10	
Adjustment reaction of adolescence	307.2	11	
Total		21	16%
Behavior disorders of childhood and adolescence			
Hyperkinetic	308.0	2	
Withdrawal	308.1	14	
Overanxious	308.2	3	
Runaway	308.3	1	
Unsocialized-aggressive	308.4	13	
Group delinquency	308.5	3	
Other reaction	308.9	1	
Total		37	27%
Social maladjustments			
Social maladjustment	316.1	1	
Dyssocial behavior	316.3	1	
Other	316.9	3	
Total		5	4%
Mental retardation			
MR due to prenatal influence	769.0	3	
MR associated with psychotic disorder	784.0	5	
MR with functional reaction manifest	789.0	2	
Total		10	7%
Diagnosis Deferred	319.0	8	6%
Total		135	100%

* American Psychiatric Association.

Bibliography

Altshuler, K. Z. "Personality Traits and Depressive Symptoms in the Deaf." In *Recent Advances in Biological Psychiatry,* vol. VI, edited by J. Wortis. New York: Plenum Press, 1964.

Anthony, D. A. "Signing Essential English: A Suggested English Language Medium for the Deaf." Unpublished paper, 1966.

Arieti, S. *The Intrapsychic Self: Feeling, Cognition, and Creativity in Health and Mental Illness.* New York: Basic Books, 1967.

Avery. C. "The Social Competence of Pre-School Acoustically Handicapped Children." *Journal of Exceptional Children* 15 (1948):71–73.

Babbidge, H. *Education of the Deaf in the United States.* The Report of the Advisory Committee on Education of the Deaf, Washington, D.C.: U.S. Government Printing Office, 1965.

Barker, R., in collaboration with B. A. Wright, L. Meyerson, and M. R. Gonick. *Adjustment to Physical Handicap and Illness: A Survey of the Social Psychology of Physique and Disability.* New York: Social Science Research Bulletin 55 (Rev.), 1953.

Barrabee, P., and O. Von Mering. "Ethnic Variations in Mental Stress in Families with Psychotic Children." In *Mental Health and Mental Disorder,* edited by A. Rose. New York: Norton, 1955, pp. 161–167.

Barry, H., III, and H. Barry, Jr. "Birth Order, Family Size, and Schizophrenia." *Archives of General Psychiatry* 17(1967):435–440.

Bateson, G., D. Jackson, J. Haley, and J. Weakland. "Toward a Theory of Schizophrenia." *Behavioral Science* 1(1956):251–264.

Bell, R. Q. "The Effect on the Family of a Limitation in Coping Ability in the Child: A Research Approach and a Finding." *Merrill-Palmer Quarterly* 10(1964):129–142.

Bellugi, U. *The Emergence of Inflections and Negation Systems in the Speech of Two Children.* Paper presented at New England Psychological Association, 1964.

———. "The Acquisition of Negation." Unpublished doctoral dissertation, Graduate School of Education, Harvard University, 1967.

Berko, J. "The Child's Learning of English Morphology." *Word* 14(1958)150–177.

Berlin, I. N. "Preventive Aspects of Mental Health Consultation to Schools." *Mental Hygiene* 51(1967):34–40.

Bernstein, B. "Social Class and Linguistic Development: A Theory of Social Learning." In *Education, Economy and Society,* edited by A. H. Halsey et al. New York: Free Press of Glencoe, 1961.

Best, H. *Deafness and the Deaf in the United States.* New York: Macmillan, 1943.

Bettelheim, B. *The Empty Fortress.* New York: Free Press, 1967.

Biber, B. "Integration of Mental Health Principles in the School Setting." In *Prevention of Mental Disorders in Children,* edited by G. Caplan. New York: Basic Books, 1961, pp. 323–352.

Bloom, L. "Language Development: Form and Function in Emerging Grammars." Unpublished doctoral dissertation, Columbia University, 1969.

Bowen, M. "A Family Concept of Schizophrenia." In *The Etiology of Schizophrenia,* edited by D. D. Jackson. New York: Basic Books, 1959.

Bower, E. M. "A Process for Early Identification of Emotionally Disturbed Children." *Bulletin of the California State Department of Education* 27(1958).

———. "Primary Prevention of Mental and Emotional Disorders: A Conceptual Framework and Action Possibilities." *American Journal of Orthopsychiatry* 33(1963):832–848.

Bowerman, M. "The Pivot-Open Class Distinction." Unpublished paper, Harvard University, 1969.

Bowlby, J. *Attachment and Loss,* vol. 1. New York: Basic Books, 1969.

Braine, M. D. S. "The Ontogeny of English Phrase Structure: The First Phase." *Language* 39(1963):1–13.

Brill, R. G. "A Study in Adjustment of Three Groups of Deaf Children." *Exceptional Children* 26(1960):464–466.

———. "The Superior I.Q.'s of Deaf Children of Deaf Parents." *The California Palms,* 1969, pp. 1–4.

Brown, R. *A First Language.* Cambridge: Harvard University Press, in press.

Brown, R., and C. Fraser. "The Acquisition of Syntax." In *The Acquisition of Language,* edited by U. Bellugi and R. Brown. Society for Research in Child Development, Monograph 29 (1964):43–78.

Brown, R., C. Cazden, and U. Bellugi. "The Child's Grammar from I to III." In *Minnesota Symposium on Child Psychology,* edited by J. P. Hill. Minneapolis: University of Minnesota Press, 1968.

Bruner, J. S., R. Olver, and P. M. Greenfield and others. *Studies in Cognitive Growth.* New York: Wiley, 1966.

Brunschwig, L. *A Study of Some Personality Aspects of Deaf Children.* Contributions of Education No. 687. New York: Teachers College, Columbia University, 1936.

Bullowa, M., L. G. Jones and A. R. Duckert. "The Acquisition of a Word." *Language and Speech* 7(1964):107–111.

Burchard, E. M. L., and H. R. Myklebust. "A Comparison of Congenital and Adventitious Deafness with Respect to its Effect on Intelligence, Personality, and Social Maturity." *American Annals of the Deaf* 87(1942): 140–154, 241–251, 342–360.

Burlingham, D. "Developmental Considerations in the Occupations of the Blind." *Psychoanalytic Study of the Child,* vol. XXII. International Universities Press, 1967.

Butt, D. S., and F. M. Chreist. "A Speechreading Test for Young Children." *Volta Review* 70(1968):225–235.

Caldwell, B. M. "What is the Optimal Learning Environment for the Young Child?" *American Journal of Orthopsychiatry* 37 (1967):8–21.

Caplan, G. *Principles of Preventive Psychiatry.* New York: Basic Books, 1964.

———. *The Theory and Practice of Mental Health Consultation.* New York: Basic Books, 1970.

Cawthorne, T. "Children with Defective Hearing." In *Deafness in Childhood,* edited by F. McConnell and P. Ward. Nashville: Vanderbilt University Press, 1967, pp. 3–21.

Cazden, C. "Environmental Assistance to the Child's Acquisition of Grammar." Unpublished doctoral thesis, School of Education, Harvard University, 1965.

———. "Subcultural Differences in Child Language: An Interdisciplinary Review." In *Disadvantaged Child,* edited by J. Hellmuth. New York: Brunner/Mazel, 1968.

Clausen, J. A. "Family Structure, Socialization and Personality." In *Review of Child Development Research,* vol. 2, edited by M. Hoffman and L. Hoffman. New York: Russell Sage Foundation, 1966, pp. 1–53.

———. "Perspectives on Childhood Socialization." In *Socialization and Society,* edited by J. A. Clausen. Boston: Little, Brown, 1968, pp. 130–181.

Coles, R. *Children of Crisis: A Study of Courage and Fear.* Boston: Little, Brown, 1964.

Cooley, C. H. *Human Nature and the Social Order.* New York: Charles Scribner's Sons, 1922.

Cottrell, A. "Some Implications of the Use of Videotape at Mental

Health Services for the Deaf." *Journal of Rehabilitation of the Deaf* 5(1971):15–20.

Craig, W. N. "Effects of Preschool Training on the Development of Reading and Lipreading Skills of Deaf Children." *American Annals of the Deaf* 109(1964):280–296.

Crammatte, A. B. *Deaf Persons in Professional Employment.* Springfield, Ill. Charles C. Thomas, 1968.

Daniel, W. G. "Some Essential Ingredients in Educational Programs for the Socially Disadvantaged." In *Disadvantaged Child,* vol. 1, edited by J. Hellmuth. New York: Brunner/Mazel, 1967.

Davis, F. *Passage Through Crisis, Polio Victims and Their Families.* Indianapolis: Bobbs-Merrill, 1963.

Despert, L. *Schizophrenia in Children.* Robert Brunner, 1968.

Deutsch, M. "The Disadvantaged Child and the Learning Process." In *Education in Depressed Areas,* edited by A. Passow. New York: Teacher's College, Columbia University, 1963, pp. 163–179.

———. "Facilitating Development in the Pre-School Child: Social and Psychological Perspectives." *Merrill-Palmer Quarterly* 10 (1964):249:263.

Diaz-Guerrero, R. "Neurosis and Mexican Family Structure." *American Journal of Psychiatry* 112(1955):411–417.

Diebold, A. R., Jr. "The Consequences of Early Bilingualism in Cognitive Development and Personality Formation." Paper prepared for the symposium, The Study of Personality: An Interdisciplinary Appraisal. Rice University, Houston, Texas, 1966 (mimeographed).

Downs, M. P. "Identification and Training of the Deaf Child—Birth to One Year." *Volta Review* 70(1968):154–158.

Elliott, H. *Speechreading in Relation to Educational and Personal Characteristics of Deaf Children.* Unpublished master's thesis, Sacramento State College, Sacramento, Calif., July 1970.

Entwisle, D. R. "Developmental Sociolinguistics: Inner-City Children." In *Annual Progress in Child Psychiatry and Child Development,* edited by S. Chess and A. Thomas. New York: Brunner/Mazel, 1969, pp. 202–216.

Erikson, E. H. *Identity and the Life Cycle.* New York: International Universities Press, 1959.

———. *Childhood and Society.* New York: Norton, 1963.

———. *Insight and Responsibility.* New York: Norton, 1964.

———. *Identity, Youth and Crisis.* New York: Norton, 1968.

Ervin, S. "Imitation and Structural Change in Children's Language," In *New Directions in the Study of Language,* edited by E. H. Lenneberg. Cambridge: M.I.T. Press, 1964.

Ervin-Tripp, S. "Language Development." In *Review of Child Development Research,* vol. II, edited by M. L. Hoffman and L. W. Hoffman. New York: Russell Sage Foundation, 1966, pp. 55–105.

Eysenck, H. J. "The Effects of Psychotherapy." *International Journal of Psychiatry* 1(1965):99–142.

Farber, B. *Mental Retardation: Its Social Context and Social Consequences.* Boston: Houghton Mifflin, 1968.

Fellendorf, G. W. and I. Harrow. "Parent Counseling 1961–1968." *Volta Review* 72, 1(1970):51–57.

Fiedler, M. F. "Developmental Studies of Deaf Children." *Journal of Speech and Hearing Disorders,* Monograph No. 13, 1969.

Filippi, R., and C. L. Rousey. "Delay in Onset of Talking—A Symptom of Interpersonal Disturbance." *Journal of the American Academy of Child Phychiatry* 7(1968):316–328.

Fraser, C., U. Bellugi, and R. Brown. "Control of Grammar in Imitation, Comprehension, and Production." *Journal of Verbal Learning and Verbal Behavior* 2(1963):121–135.

Fromm, E. *Escape from Freedom.* New York: Rinehart, 1941.

———. *Man for Himself.* New York: Rinehart, 1947.

Furth, H. G. *Thinking Without Language: Psychological Implications of Deafness.* New York: Free Press, 1966.

———. "A Review and Perspective on the Thinking of Deaf People." In *Cognitive Studies,* edited by J. Hellmuth. New York: Brunner/Mazel, 1970.

Garrett, J. F., and E. S. Levine. *Psychological Practices with the Physically Disabled.* New York: Columbia University Press, 1962.

Glazer, N., and D. P. Moynihan. *Beyond the Melting Pot.* Cambridge: M.I.T. Press, 1963.

Goffman, E. *Stigma, Notes on the Management of Spoiled Identity.* Englewood Cliffs, N. J.: Prentice-Hall, 1963.

Goldfarb, W., L. Sibulkin, M. Behrens, and H. Jahoda. "The Concept of Maternal Perplexity." In *Parenthood, Its Psychology and Psychopathology,* edited by E. J. Anthony and T. Benedik. Boston: Little, Brown, 1970, pp. 411–420.

Goodman, M. E. *Race Awareness in Young Children.* New York: Collier Books, 1964.

Gough, H. G. *California Psychological Inventory.* Palo Alto: Consulting Psychologists Press, 1957.

Gozali, J. "Teacher Expectations and the Performance of the Mentally Retarded." *Focus on Exceptional Children* 1(1969).

Greenberg, J. *In This Sign.* Canada: Holt, Rinehart and Winston, 1970.

Haley, J. "Whither Family Therapy?" *Family Process* 1(1962):69–100.

Hardy, W. G., and J. E. Bordley. "The Child with Impaired Hearing." In *Management of the Handicapped Child,* edited by H. Smith-Michal. New York: Grune and Stratton, 1957.

Hays, W. L. *Statistics for Psychologists.* New York: Holt, Rinehart, and Winston, 1963.

Hess, R. D., and V. C. Shipman. "Maternal Influences upon Early Learning: The Cognitive Environment of Urban Pre-School Children." In *Early Education,* edited by R. Hess and R. Bear. Chicago: Aldine, 1968.

Hollingshead, A., and F. C. Redlich. *Social Class and Mental Disease.* New York: Wiley, 1958.

Hollis, F. *Casework: A Psychosocial Therapy.* New York: Random House, 1964.

Hume, P. B. "General Principles of Community Psychiatry." In *American Handbook of Psychiatry,* vol. 3, edited by S. Arieti. New York: Basic Books, 1966, pp. 515–541.

Hunt, J. M. *Intelligence and Experience.* New York: Ronald Press, 1961.

———. "How Children Develop Intellectually." *Children,* Children's Bureau, United States Department of Health, Education and Welfare, 11 (1964).

Hunt, J. M., and L. S. Kogan. *Measuring Results in Social Casework: A Manual of Judging Movement.* New York: Family Service Association of America, 1950.

Irwin, O. C., and H. P. Chen. "Development of Speech During Infancy: Curve of Phonemic Types." *Journal of Experimental Psychology* 36(1946):431–436.

Jaco, E. G. *The Social Epidemiology of Mental Disorders.* New York: Russell Sage Foundation, 1960.

Johnson, L. J., and J. H. Reed. "Hope for Three out of Four." *Survey Mid-Monthly* 83(1947):271–273.

Joint Commission on Mental Health of Children. *Crisis in Child Mental Health: Challenge for the 1970's.* New York: Harper and Row, 1970.

Katan, A. "Some Thoughts About the Role of Verbalization in Early Childhood." *Psychoanalytic Study of the Child* 16(1961): 184–188.

Kessler, J. W. "Contributions of the Mentally Retarded Toward a Theory of Cognitive Development." In *Cognitive Studies,* edited by J. Hellmuth. New York: Brunner/Mazel, 1970.

Klima, E. S., and U. Bellugi. "Syntactic Regularities in the Speech of Children." In *Psycholinguistics Papers: The Proceedings of the 1966 Edinburgh Conference,* edited by J. Lyons and R. J. Wales. Edinburgh: Edinburgh University Press, 1966, pp. 183–208.

Kogan, K., and H. Wimberger. "An Approach to Defining Mother-

Child Interaction Styles." *Perceptual and Motor Skills* 23(1966): 1171–1177.

Kohl, H. R. *Language and Education of the Deaf.* New York: Center for Urban Education, 1966.

Kohn, M. L., and J. A. Clausen. "Social Isolation and Schizophrenia." *American Sociological Review* 20(1955):265–273.

Labov, W. "Stages in the Acquisition of Standard English." In *Social Dialects and Language Learning,* edited by R. Shuy. N.C.T.E. Report, 1964.

Lach, R., D. Ling, A. Ling, and N. Ship. "Early Speech Development in Deaf Infants." *American Annals of the Deaf* 115(1970): 522–526.

Lamb, H. R., D. Heath, and J. J. Downing. *Handbook of Community Mental Health Practice.* San Francisco: Jossey-Bass, 1969.

Lambert, W. E., and E. Peal. "The Relation of Bilingualism to Intelligence." *Psychological Monograph* 76(1962).

Langner, T. S. "Psychophysiological Symptoms and the Status of Women in Two Mexican Communities." In *Approaches to Cross-Cultural Psychiatry,* edited by J. M. Murphy and A. H. Leighton. Ithaca: Cornell University Press, 1965, pp. 360–392.

Lenneberg, E. H. "The Natural History of Language." In *The Genesis of Language: A Psycholinguistic Approach,* edited by F. Smith and G. A. Miller. Cambridge: M.I.T. Press, 1966.

———. *Biological Foundations of Language.* New York: Wiley, 1967, pp. 128–130.

Lenneberg, E. H., F. G. Rebelsky, and I. A. Nichols. "The Vocalizations of Infants Born to Deaf and to Hearing Parents." *Vita Humana* 8(1965):23–37.

Lenski, G. *The Religious Factor, A Sociological Study of Religion's Impact on Politics, Economics, and Family Life.* Garden City: Doubleday, Anchor Books, 1963.

Levine E. S. "Historical Review." In *Family and Mental Health Problems in a Deaf Population,* edited by J. D. Rainer et al. New York: New York State Psychiatric Institute, Columbia University Press, 1963.

———. *Youth in a Soundless World, a Search for Personality.* Washington Square, N. Y.: New York University Press, 1956.

Levy, D. M. "Oppositional Syndrome and Oppositional Behavior." In *Psychopathology of Childhood,* edited by P. Hoch. New York: Grune and Stratton, 1955.

Lidz, T. *The Family and Human Adaptation.* New York: International University Press, 1963.

Lillywhite, H. "Doctor's Manual of Speech Disorders." *Journal of the American Medical Association* 167(1958):850–858.

Lunde, A. S., and S. K. Bigman. *Occupational Conditions Among the Deaf.* A Report on a National Survey Conducted by Gallaudet College and the National Association of the Deaf, Washington, D.C.: Gallaudet College, 1959.

Malzberg, B. "Mental Disease Among Negroes in New York State." *Mental Hygiene* 37(1953):450–477.

McCall, E. "A Generative Grammar of Signs." Unpublished master's thesis, University of Iowa, 1965.

McCandless, B. R. *Children and Adolescents.* New York: Holt, Rinehart, and Winston, 1961.

McNeill, D. "The Capacity for Language Acquisition." In *Research on Behavioral Aspects of Deafness.* Proceedings of a National Research Conference on Behavioral Aspects of Deafness, New Orleans, 1965, pp. 11–28.

———. "Developmental Psycholinguistics." In *The Genesis of Language: A Psycholinguistic Approach,* edited by F. Smith and G. A. Miller. Cambridge: M.I.T. Press, 1966.

———. "The Development of Language." In *Carmichael's Manual of Child Psychology,* vol. 1, edited by P. Mussen. 3rd edition, New York: Wiley, 1970*a,* pp. 1061–1162.

———. *The Acquisition of Language: The Study of Developmental Psycholinguistics.* New York: Harper and Row, 1970*b.*

Mead, G. H. *Mind, Self, and Society.* Chicago: University of Chicago Press, 1934.

Meadow, A., and D. Stoker. "Symptomatic Behavior of Hospitalized Patients." *Archives of General Psychiatry* 12(1965):267–277.

Meadow, K. P. "The Effect of Early Manual Communication and Family Climate on the Deaf Child's Development." Unpublished Ph.D. dissertation, University of California, Berkeley, 1967.

———. "Early Manual Communication in Relation to the Deaf Child's Intellectual, Social, and Communicative Functioning." *American Annals of the Deaf* 113(1968*a*):29–41.

———. "Parental Responses to the Medical Ambiguities of Deafness." *Journal of Health and Social Behavior* 9(1968*b*):299–309.

———. "Toward a Developmental Understanding of Deafness." *Journal of Rehabilitation of the Deaf* 2(1968*c*):1–18.

———. "Self-Image, Family Climate, and Deafness." *Social Forces* 47(1969):428–438.

Meadow, K. P., and L. Meadow. "Changing Role Perceptions for Parents of Handicapped Children." *Exceptional Children* 38 (1971):21–27.

Mecham, M. J. *Verbal Language Development Scale.* Circle Pines, Minn.: American Guidance Service, 1958.

Mechanic, D. "Some Factors in Identifying and Defining Mental Illness." *Mental Hygiene* 46(1962):66–74.

Meltzoff, J., and M. Kornreich. *Research in Psychotherapy.* New York: Atherton Press, 1970.

Menyuk, P. "A Preliminary Evaluation of Grammatical Capacity in Children." *Journal of Verbal Learning and Verbal Behavior* 2(1963):429–439.

Mindel, E. D., and M. Vernon. *They Grow in Silence—the Deaf Child and his Family.* Maryland: National Association of the Deaf, 1971.

Moores, D. "Psycholinguistics and Deafness." *American Annals of the Deaf* 15(1970):37–48.

Myklebust, H. R. *The Psychology of Deafness: Sensory Deprivation, Learning, and Adjustment.* New York: Grune and Stratton, 1960.

Myklebust, H. R., and E. M. L. Burchard. "A Study of the Effects of Congenital and Adventitious Deafness on Intelligence, Personality, and Social Maturity of School Children." *Journal of Educational Psychology* 34(1945):321.

Neyhus, A. I. "The Social and Emotional Adjustment of Deaf Adults." *Volta Review* 66(1964):319–325.

Nida, E. A. "Analysis of Meaning and Dictionary Making." *International Journal of American Linguistics* 24(1958):279–292.

Opler, M. K. "Cultural Differences in Mental Disorders: An Italian And Irish Contrast in the Schizophrenias–U.S.A." In *Culture and Mental Health,* edited by M. K. Opler. New York: Macmillan, 1959, pp. 425–442.

Orr, W. F., and S. C. Cappannari. "The Emergence of Language." In *The Psychology of Language, Thought and Instruction,* edited by J. P. DeCecco. New York: Holt, Rinehart and Winston, 1967.

Osofsky, J. D. "The Shaping of Mother's Behavior by Children." *Journal of Marriage and the Family* 32(1970):400–405.

Parker, B. "Some Observations on Psychiatric Consultation with Nursery School Teachers." *Mental Hygiene* 46(1962):559–566.

Parker, S., and R. J. Kleiner. *Mental Illness in the Urban Negro Community.* New York: Free Press, 1965.

Pearson, L. *The Use of Written Communication in Psychotherapy.* Springfield, Ill.: Charles C. Thomas, 1965.

Penfield, W., and T. Rasmussen. *The Cerebral Cortex of Man: A Clinical Study of Localization of Function.* New York: Macmillan, 1950.

Penfield, W., and L. Roberts. *Speech and Brain-Mechanisms.* Princeton: Princeton University Press, 1959.

Pettigrew, T. F. *A Profile of the Negro American.* Princeton: Van Nostrand Company, 1964.

Pintner, R., and J. F. Reamer. "A Mental and Educational Survey of Schools for the Deaf." *American Annals of the Deaf* 65 (1920):451.

Quigley, S. P. *The Influence of Fingerspelling on the Development of Language, Communication, and Educational Achievement in Deaf Children.* Institute for Research on Exceptional Children, University of Illinois, 1968.

Quigley, S. P., and R. Frisina. *Institutionalization and Psycho-Educational Development of Deaf Children.* Council for Exceptional Children Research Monograph, Series A, Number 3, 1961.

Rainer, J. D., and K. Z. Altshuler. *Comprehensive Mental Health Services for the Deaf.* New York State Psychiatric Institute, Columbia University, 1966.

———. *Psychiatry and the Deaf.* U.S. Department of Health, Education, and Welfare, Social and Rehabilitation Service, 1968.

———. *Expanded Mental Health Care for the Deaf: Rehabilitation and Prevention.* New York: New York State Psychiatric Institute, 1970.

Rainer, J. D., K. Z. Altshuler, and F. J. Kallman, eds. *Family and Mental Health Problems in a Deaf Population.* New York: New York State Psychiatric Institute, Columbia University Press, 1963.

Ransom, S. S., and S. O. Clark. *The Anatomy of the Nervous System.* Philadelphia: Saunders, 1959.

Riesman, D. "Some Clinical and Cultural Aspects of Aging." *American Journal of Sociology* 29(1954):379–383.

Riessman, F. *The Culturally Deprived Child.* New York: Harper and Row, 1962.

Rioux, J. W. "The Disadvantaged Child in School." In *The Disadvantaged Child,* vol. 1, edited by J. Hellmuth. New York: Brunner/Mazel, 1967, pp. 77–120.

Rogers, C. R., and R. F. Dymond. *Psychotherapy and Personality Change.* Chicago: University of Chicago Press, 1954.

Rosenberg, M. *Society and the Adolescent Self-Image.* Princeton: Princeton University Press, 1965.

Rosenstein, J. "Current Studies of Language Acquisition of Deaf People." In *Research on Behavioral Aspects of Deafness,* Proceedings of a National Research Conference on Behavioral Aspects of Deafness, New Orleans, 1965, Vocational Rehabilitation Administration, pp. 29–33.

Rosenthal, R., and L. Jacobson. *Pygmalion in the Classroom.* New York: Holt, Rinehart, and Winston, 1968.

Ross, A. O. *The Exceptional Child in the Family.* New York: Grune and Stratton, 1964.

Ruesch, J. "General Theory of Communication in Psychiatry." In *American Handbook of Psychiatry,* vol. 2, edited by S. Arieti. New York: Basic Books, 1959.

Sarason, S. B., K. S. Davidson, F. F. Lighthall, R. R. Waite, and

B. K. Ruebush. *Anxiety in Elementary School Children.* New York: Wiley, 1960.

Schaefer, E. S., and R. Q. Bell. "Development of a Parental Attitude Research Instrument." *Child Development* 29(1958):339–361.

Schlesinger, H. S. "Headstart in Deafness—Early Home Environment." In *Report of the Proceedings of the Forty-Fourth Meeting of the Convention of American Instructors of the Deaf.* U.S. Government Printing Office, 1970*a*.

———. "Deaf Children and Their Parents in Wonderland." *Report of the Proceedings of the Forty-Fourth Meeting of the Convention of American Instructors of the Deaf.* U.S. Government Printing Office, March 1970, pp. 10–12.

Siegel, S. *Nonparametric Statistics for the Behavioral Sciences.* New York: McGraw-Hill, 1956.

Slobin, D. I. "Early Grammatical Development in Several Languages, with Special Attention to Soviet Research." In *The Structure and Psychology of Language,* edited by T. G. Bever and W. Weksel. New York: Holt, Rinehart and Winston, in press.

Slobin, D. I., ed. *A Field Manual for Cross-Cultural Study of the Acquisition of Communicative Competence.* Berkeley: University of California, 1967.

Spitz, R. A. "Hospitalism: An Inquiry into the Genesis of Psychiatric Conditions in Early Childhood." *Psychoanalytic Study of the Child* 1(1945):53–75.

Stanton, A., and M. Schwartz. *The Mental Hospital: A Study of Institutional Participation in Psychiatric Illness and Treatment.* New York: Basic Books, 1954.

State of California, *Mental Health Survey of Los Angeles County.* Sacramento: Department of Mental Hygiene, 1960.

Stevenson, E. A. "A Study of the Educational Achievement of Deaf Children of Deaf Parents." *California News* 80(1964):1–3.

Stokoe, W. C., Jr. *The Study of Sign Language.* Educational Resources Information Center, Clearinghouse for Linguistics, Center for Applied Linguistics, Office of Education, Department of Health, Education and Welfare, Washington, D.C., 1970*a*.

———. "Sign Language Diglossia." *Studies in Linguistics* 21 (1970*b*):27–41.

———. *Semiotics and Human Sign Language: Approaches to Semiotics, ws. Awvwok.* The Hague: Mouton, in press.

Stokoe, W. C., Jr., D. C. Casterline, and C. G. Croneberg. *A Dictionary of American Sign Language on Linguistic Principles.* Washington, D.C.: Gallaudet College Press, 1965.

Streng, A., and S. A. Kirk. "The Social Competence of Deaf and

Hard-of-Hearing Children in a Public Day School." *American Annals of the Deaf* 83(1938):244–254.

Stuckless, E. R., and J. W. Birch. "The Influence of Early Manual Communication on the Linguistic Development of Deaf Children." *American Annals of the Deaf* 111(1966):452–460; 499–504.

Sullivan, H. S. *Conceptions of Modern Psychiatry*. Washington, D.C.: William Alanson White Psychiatric Foundation, 1947.

———. *The Interpersonal Theory of Psychiatry*. New York: W. W. Norton, 1953.

Tervoort, B. T. "Linguistics in Language Learning for Deaf People." *International Research Seminar on the Vocational Rehabilitation of Deaf Persons,* 1968.

Thomas, A., S. Chess, and H. Birch. *Temperament and Behavior Disorders in Children*. New York: New York University Press, 1968.

Tilgher, A. "Work Through the Ages." In *Man, Work and Society,* edited by S. Nosow and W. Form. New York: Basic Books, 1962.

Upshall, C. C. *Day Schools vs. Institutions for the Deaf*. Teachers College, Columbia University, Contributions to Education, No. 389. New York: Bureau of Publications, Teachers' College, Columbia University, 1929.

Vernon, M., and S. D. Koh. "Early Manual Communication and Deaf Children's Achievement." *American Annals of the Deaf* 115(1970):527–536.

———. "Effects of Oral Preschool Compared to Early Manual Communication on Education and Communication in Deaf Children." Typed manuscript, 1971.

Vetter, H. J. *Language Behavior and Psychopathology*. Chicago: Rand McNally, 1970.

Visotsky, H. M. "Primary Prevention." In *Comprehensive Textbook of Psychiatry,* edited by A. Freedman and H. Kaplan. Baltimore: Williams and Wilkins, 1967, pp. 1537–1546.

Werner, H., and B. Kaplan. *Symbol Formation: An Organismic-Developmental Approach to Language and the Expression of Thought*. New York: Wiley, 1963.

Williams, C. E. "Some Psychiatric Observations on a Group of Maladjusted Deaf Children." *Journal of Child Psychology and Psychiatry* 11(1970):1–18.

Wolfenstein, M. "Trends in Infant Care." *American Journal of Orthopsychiatry* 23(1953):120–130.

Wright, B. A. *Physical Disability—A Psychological Approach*. New York: Harper and Row, 1960.

Wrightstone, J. W., M. S. Aronow, and S. Moskowitz. "Developing

Reading Test Norms for Deaf Children." *Test Service Bulletin,* No. 98. New York: Harcourt, Brace and World, 1962.

Wyatt, G. L. *Language Learning and Communication Disorders in Children.* New York: Free Press, 1969.

Wynne, L., I. Ryckoff, J. Day, and S. Hirsch. "Pseudo-mutuality in the Family Relations of Schizophrenics." *Psychiatry* 21(1958): 205–220.

Yamamoto, K. "Bilingualism: A Brief Review." *Mental Hygiene* 48(1964):468–477.

Zuk, G. H. "The Religious Factor and the Role of Guilt in Parental Acceptance of the Retarded Child." *American Journal of Mental Deficiency* 64(1959):139–147.

Index of Subjects

Index of Authors